I Wanna Do It Myself

ALSO BY WILLIAM SAMMONS, M.D.

The Self-Calmed Baby

I Wanna Do It MYSELF

From
Baby to Toddler—
a Radical Three-tiered
Approach to Helping
Your Child Achieve
Independence

William Sammons, M.D.

HYPERION

New York

Book design by Richard Oriolo

Library of Congress Cataloging-in-Publication Data

Sammons, William A. H.
    I wanna do it myself : from baby to toddler—a radical three-tiered approach to helping your child achieve independence / William Sammons.—1st ed.
        p.   cm.
    Includes index.
    ISBN 1–56282–972–6 : $10.95 ($13.95 Can.)
    1. Toddlers. 2. Child-rearing. 3. Autonomy in children.
4. Self-control in children. I. Title.
HQ774.5.S25 1992
649'.1—dc20   92–3555
                                           CIP

FIRST EDITION

10 9 8 7 6 5 4 3 2 1

To Carol, Red, and the boys
and
my parents who did their
best to help me
do it myself

AUTHOR'S NOTE

There are many people I want to thank:

As you read this book it is clear that the most indispensable people are the parents and patients in my practice and those from around the world who have called me at Red Tae—without the opportunity to listen to their questions and to find ways to help them I never could have put this book together.

Of course the book itself would never have happened without my agent Tory Pryor, the excellent advice of Beth Rashbaum, and the efforts of Bob Miller and Judith Riven at Hyperion.

And as always Kathy DiPilato, my secretary, gets done what has to be done despite the odds.

Finally I can't forget the mentor of the monitor and expert on word processing: Albert J. Cat. He's always there lending a paw of assistance at any hour of the day and night.

It is customary, but I think it is a mistake to speak of happy childhood. Man ought to be man and master of his fate; but children are at the mercy of those around them.

—Sir John Lubbock, 1st Baron Avebury
The Pleasure of Life

Respect the child. Be not too much his parent. Trespass not on his solitude.

—Ralph Waldo Emerson

Who is mature enough for offspring before the offspring themselves arrive? The value of parenting is not that adults produce children but that children produce adults.

—Peter DeVries

Contents

■ ■ ■ ■ ■ ■ ■ ■ ■ ■ ■ ■ ■

Introduction

■ ■ ■ ■ ■ ■ ■ ■ ■ ■ ■ ■ ■ ■

Writing a book, before I'd done it, always seemed like such a solitary achievement. And it's true that the hours I was able to steal for my writing activities, which tended to be late at night after spending the evening with my wife and son, or early in the morning, before going off to my full-time job as a pediatric physician, were lonely ones. Formulating and refining the ideas that appear in this book, however, were not something I accomplished entirely on my own. Like every author, "I wanna do it myself," and like every child who dauntlessly pursues that goal, I try, but ultimately I've benefited from a number of instructors and instigators. What they have said or done is very much a part of what you will read in the following chapters.

Many of the adults who have heard me speak about self-calming, the subject of my last book, and about its corollaries, self-control and the ability to self-entertain, which are explored in this book, remark on how obvious these ideas seem once they've heard them described. "Why, that's nothing but common sense," they exclaim in surprise. And they're right. But it's not the common sense, or indeed the consensus, of most child-care experts; it's the common sense of those who are most affected—the children themselves. Listening to the one-, two-, three-, and four-year-old patients in my practice has been my ultimate education. Their parents may have clarified or amplified what they said, but it is the children who were the ultimate source of most of what I now know, their words the inspiration for my most dramatic breakthroughs in understanding. Maybe that is what makes so many of these ideas sound now like such basic common sense.

I know of nowhere besides a primary-care pediatric practice that could have given me this opportunity to learn and to test out new ideas. Unlike pure research, which is done in carefully controlled circumstances involving a preselected group of subjects, a practice includes a random assortment of families living in widely varied circumstances—single parents, divorced parents, several generations under one roof, one, two, or no careers, different ethnic groups, cultures, income levels, and so forth. They teach you that advice has to be workable in the real world.

Of course in order for me to give good advice, I needed first to learn to listen. Many people, adults and children alike, had patience while I improved that skill. Before I ever started, however, there was one short conversation that really got me to take the "wax out of my ears." When I started my fellowship with Dr. T. Berry Brazelton in 1977, one of the first things he said to me was: "Forget everything you learned about child development." In other words, question everything in the books and test it against reality—which in my case turned out to mean the experiences of the people in the practice I began in 1979. That advice was invaluable, not just because it was correct, and not just because it indirectly encouraged me to give three-year-olds the credibility they deserve, but because it was so relevant to the time, an era that saw much of the received wisdom of the past crumbling before the discoveries made possible by the technology of the present.

For instance, while I was in residency, researchers using sophisticated new cameras and electronic tracking devices startled pediatricians and parents by documenting how much babies could see. Previously it had been believed that newborns saw only fuzzy shadows. New EEG (electroencephalograph) equipment and more sensitive monitors provided a clearer definition of different awake behaviors like crying or fussing, and in conjunction with infrared photography enabled psychologists to discover that night waking was a universal infant activity—in other words, no infant ever "sleeps through." Though commonplace now, twenty years ago the VCR was a wondrous new electronic toy making possible stopframe analysis of parent-infant play, which hastened the realization that babies as young as a few days of age are not simply passive reactors to their parents, limited to mere reflex actions like sucking, but have both the motor and social skills to be able to initiate exchanges with the adults around them.

These discoveries certainly undermined our long-held beliefs in the total helplessness and utter dependency of infants. If infants could really make such decisions, if they were active social participants, not the animate but passive dolls they'd long been considered to be, if they were capable of choosing what they wanted and figuring out how to get it, then, as Dr. Brazelton said, it really was time to start over, to question everything. Unfortunately until I was in practice I didn't fully comprehend all that that would entail.

Within a few weeks, however, it became clear that I had to come up with some practical advice to offer in place of the old ideas I was discarding—and I had to do it fast. I saw reality dislodging theory on a daily basis. Behavioral traits I'd been taught to look for as markers of specific developmental stages seemed inaccurate, and the stages themselves were too rigidly defined to be helpful as guides. Certain "normal behaviors" expected of parents seemed downright incompatible with adult existence—the emotions they were expected to feel in no way reflecting the realities of family life. What I thought would be the comfortable, reassuring core of my practice, taking care of "normal infants," in "normal" families, was anything but comfortable.

When faced with tough but typical problems like colic, discipline that didn't work, or endless sleep disturbances, for example, I found to my horror that the answers I'd been taught to give weren't effective. Parents came back for the next appointment or called on the phone—the problem still not resolved. Often they felt that if only they had tried harder, then the advice would have worked, so they now had not only the unresolved problem to contend with, but also guilt due to feelings of incompetence. Sometimes they were angry with me, which I resented, as I felt that I was not only giving them the best that modern pediatrics and training at Harvard could provide, but giving generously of myself as well by talking with them at all hours of the day and night. Since it was the advice itself that was flawed, however, not the doctor-patient relationship, it didn't help that I was willing to spend extra time with people or to explain the same things over and over again. And it also didn't help for them to apply it diligently, although in my frustration I did sometimes think that maybe it was the parents who were at fault. Eventually it dawned on me that all the recent changes in our factual knowledge about vision, hearing, reflexes, sleep, and especially infants' social interactions were going to require corresponding changes in our ideas about parenting. What had been discovered in the laboratory was going to have to be imported into our practical, everyday experiences. *How* to do this was the question, but I didn't know the answer.

This was an exciting but deeply disturbing time. I felt that I couldn't help many families, yet I wasn't going to lie to them or dismiss my ignorance by saying that their child would "outgrow" problem behaviors. The common wisdom was that separation crises, discipline battles, sleep disturbances, and such dreaded phenomena as the "terrible twos" were inevitable and self-resolving over time. I wasn't convinced of either. In fact I began to wonder whether the belief in the inevitability of these developmental crises had become a self-fulfilling prophecy. And I had a feeling that since self-assertion struggles were at the heart of so many of these problems, there had to be ways of dealing with them that respected the child's feelings, without either endangering the child or making life impossible for the parents.

I might never have been able to follow through on these ideas without the help of Catherine Morrison, a social worker at Beth Israel Hospital in Boston. Working with her, I began to understand how "I wanna do it myself" was a profoundly accurate statement of the underlying desires of all human beings, even the youngest. For instance, the "terrible two" takes no inherent delight in confrontation; in fact, all the energy of his negativism and rebellion is really for purposes of telling us a rather poignant message: Show me that you believe in me. Be my ally, not a well-intentioned adversary who, by trying to do too much for me, gives me the message that I'm incompetent and thwarts me in my attempts to do things my own way.

One morning I awoke at four o'clock, my head buzzing with excitement from the realization that this message, if heeded, could transform the relationship between parent and child, lay the groundwork for a solution to the common problems of colic, sleep disturbance, separation anxiety, discipline, and sibling rivalry as well as many other obstacles to a happy family life. Moreover, and still more energizing, was the further perception that parents acting on this message could give children a sense of personal self-assurance they would carry with them for the rest of their lives. If we could find practical ways of helping children achieve their autonomy, I felt that preventing all these "inevitable" problems would become a realistic goal. That is the kind of challenge I love. I could hardly wait to get to the office to start putting these ideas into practice.

My initial efforts were directed toward helping parents understand self-calming. As a resident I had noticed that critically ill infants could help to stabilize themselves physiologically by sucking or rhythmically grasping a finger or a piece of intravenous tube or whatever else was handy. During the fellowship I had become familiar with the term "self-calming," but it wasn't until I was in practice that I understood how powerful this skill can be and how it offers the child one of the first, if not *the* first opportunity to experience a feeling of self-control. I discovered this after many futile approaches to that pediatric bugaboo: colic. Baby-carrying packs, altered diets for nursing mothers, hydrolyzed formulas, constant holding and rocking— none of them worked. Self-calming, which I originally suggested as a last-ditch, desperation measure, did. As first ten, then fifty, then hundreds of parents learned to help their infants to self-calm, not only did colic become a thing of the past in my office, but suddenly I began hearing stories about how happy these children were, how much easier life was for everybody. This response made me open to other possibilities that were equally anathema to the standard wisdom about children. For instance, if a six-week-old could self-calm when given the opportunity and encouragement to do so, perhaps he could go to sleep on his own as well. Rather than the usual scenario in which a parent decides when the child should sleep and then employs a variety of sleep-inducing techniques, soothing as well as coercive, which are in any case destined to fail unless the child is ready for sleep, I've found with hundreds of families that it's more harmonious, and much quicker, to let the child make the decision. With the help of his self-calming skills, he'll be able to rest quietly until his body tells him the time is right, and then go to sleep on his own.

Parents were jubilant when they tried this new approach, and so was I. As the parents did fewer bedtime and middle-of-the-night interventions, their babies fussed less and slept better, so everyone's life improved. The enthusiasm was contagious. Parents and I asked each other questions in a spirit of willingness to help children assume the control that they clearly wanted over other aspects of their lives as well. Why couldn't the ten-month-old be encouraged to manage by himself for a while, so that he wouldn't be reduced to screaming for mom whenever she left the room? Why couldn't the fifteen-month-old choose what she wanted for dinner and feed herself? And didn't it seem possible that the two-year-old who spent so much energy trying to assert himself against a wall of parental no's could rechannel that energy in a constructive manner if given the chance to make many of his own decisions?

As one positive answer after another was confirmed, each day I felt a combination of dread and anticipation as a fascinating world of new possibilities opened before me. I wondered if parents could really accept that a toddler was happy making choices (with appropriate parental supervision) rather than having all his choices made for him, but fortunately they didn't have to be convinced. They could remember their own childhoods and the feelings aroused by their struggles for independence. Furthermore, they too were excited by the possibilities. They could see the advantages of self-calming for the infant and the older child, so they were eager to work with me on ways to enhance self-control and the ability to self-entertain, a natural progression from the pivotal skill of self-calming. The parents readily understood how this approach might enable a child to reach the longed-for "wanna do it myself" goal and why this was in everyone's best interest. Confirmation came from the kids as well: I knew that I was on track since they were smiling and talking more during office visits. Indeed, many didn't want to leave even after hour-long discussions of their behavior between me and their parents—the type of conversation most children try to put an end to as quickly as possible.

What was already a flourishing practice suddenly took off,

while at the same time becoming much more fun for me. I now got to hear families describe how their lives had improved, and eventually had the pleasure of listening to seven-, eight-, and nine-year-olds, those children who had benefited from several years of exposure to this new approach, tell me how much better prepared they were to deal with school and changing relationships.

I do not mean to imply that all of these individuals were now straight-A students bound for exclusive colleges and professional careers. That's not the kind of success I was looking for. Some of the families who benefited most were those whose children had a learning deficit or a problem with attention span or motor coordination, because my new emphasis on building self-esteem through increased self-calming and self-control enabled such children to get maximum satisfaction and enjoyment out of their lives despite the limitations they faced.

Things were going so well I was amazed—except for one stumbling block. No matter how good my reputation for understanding children's behavior became, and no matter how self-confident I was about the validity of my advice, there was always one escape route available to parents who were uncomfortable with a suggested change: "Well, you don't know how hard that will be because you aren't a parent." Frequently I tried to comfort myself by recalling the comments of a very experienced pediatrician whom I respected immensely. He had told me I could be helpful to many families precisely because I didn't have children, and therefore didn't have a vested interest in getting parents to do the same things I'd done in raising my own. "Once you've made a personal commitment it's much harder to be a dispassionate, objective listener," he said. Nevertheless, I still regretted the times when parents didn't follow through on advice because they had that convenient excuse, and I still had moments of doubt because in my heart of hearts I knew they had a point—that no one can really understand the trials and tribulations of parenthood without being a parent.

That all changed on May 14, 1987, when my wife Carol

gave birth to our son Red. Not that ideas about child-rearing were running through my mind at that time. I was totally caught up in the excitement of becoming a parent and thankful that they had both survived a complicated delivery. But I did notice that when I went back to work a month after Red's birth, I never heard that excuse again. The last five years, however, have clarified why many resort to it so often. It is certainly true that the experience has been trying, but it is even more true that I have found parenthood to be one of life's truly remarkable pleasures. Looking back, now that Red has passed his fifth birthday, I can see that some of the parents were right to think that I didn't fully appreciate the awesome sense of responsibility that comes with parenthood. But conversely, I never had any idea what the great joys were either. It is an experience that has been worth all the other compromises: decisions to limit my career goals, an inability to write as often or as much as I wanted, new family relationships, and the wrinkles that having a child places in any marriage. The rewards are great, but the investment of time and energy and self, if you want to be a primary parent, is substantial.

As a result of the adjustments that Carol and I made to accommodate the conflicting demands of parenthood and career, often in the last five years I've been the one to stay at home with Red. Now that I have lived through it, not just listening to other parents or my wife tell me how much effort and attention parenting requires, I understand these conflicts. I seem never to have enough time to do all the things I wish I could with my son. I live in ceaseless anxiety about whether those of-necessity spur-of-the-moment decisions are the right ones, and I wonder whether I'm expecting too much of Red or am inhibiting him by my own fear and ambivalences. I've had days when I'm so tired, emotionally needy, or upset that I'm tempted not to follow some of my own advice on discipline or sleep—and occasionally I don't. So I know not just the temptation but the price you pay for giving in to it. I myself have paid that price at times, just as parents tell me they have. I know how easy it is to compromise a bedtime routine, or do something you regret in order to go back to sleep in the middle of the night. I've inadvertently done things that built certain dependencies in my son, and while I know the undoing is painful, I also know that the consequences of maintaining those dependencies are much worse. The decisions are tough, and following through is even more difficult, because the longer you're a parent the more often you have to acknowledge that you're not automatically right, that you don't always know what's best because your self-interest and the child's are not identical. That's part of what parents talk about.

But all these insights were merely practical corroborations of what I already knew intellectually. The real revelation of parenthood—for me—was the tremendous need to be needed. Though I had talked often to parents who were fearful of the emotional cost of losing that form of gratification, I had no idea until I became a parent myself what those feelings of loss were really like.

Today's parents are generally the products of a culture that viewed children as totally helpless creatures, completely dependent on a mommy and daddy (mainly mommy of course) who were the benevolent rulers of their universe. Even if we still feel surges of the old rebellion and anger at the way our instincts toward self-assertion were frustrated in childhood, we are our parents' children, their view of the world having imprinted itself on us, whether we like it or not. Remembering our past we may have vowed to set our own children free, but it turns out not to be so easy. As soon as we begin to acknowledge the innate competence of our children we face losing all the rewards of being the loving guarantor, protector, provider, and center of another human being's universe. And that is what I'm asking you to do when I tell you to heed the very real message in the "I wanna do it myself" credo.

Now finally I understand the cost I was asking parents to

pay, because I'm paying it myself. (Or trying to, not always successfully.) The demands I made on parents in the past have, I hope, been tempered by a new understanding that parents also have legitimate needs and expectations of the parent-child relationship. Though I don't believe in covering these needs up with a facade of self-sacrifice, or tricking yourself into believing that what you're doing is for the child's benefit, not your own, I do now understand that these needs must be acknowledged. In short, I have to be able to follow my own advice.

I'm not going to pretend that encouraging your child to gain the self-sufficiency he or she craves won't sometimes be scary and other times downright painful, but I am going to tell you that I think it's vital to her—and good for you as well. The more usual approach these days, which holds up as the ideal the mother (or father) who is at all times available, no longer seems creditable to me. It's unrealistic to expect a parent to be always available to her child, or even to put this commitment in words, telling the child that she'll always be there for her. Worse, it's damaging. Any child, even a one-month-old, let alone a two-year-old, knows from experience that this is a deceit. So the trust between parent and child is threatened, and the mother usually feels a heavy burden of guilt at being unable to live up to this expectation. On the more immediate, practical front, I'm not going to advise you to ignore temper tantrums, since I know this requires a talent for acting that would easily garner an Academy Award. Nor am I going to suggest that you *make* your child go to sleep at the proper time. Because the contestants each feel convinced of the justice of their cause, this is doomed to be a losing battle, with emotional scars on both sides. Or you may be wondering if I'm going to tell you that saying no firmly and with authority is an effective form of discipline. Hardly. Like every parent, I've heard that same no echoing with equal force and authority—not to mention greater volume—from the mouth of my child. Children don't acknowledge no unless it is backed up with some kind of action. The best such action, in my experience, is time-out, the method of discipline I describe in this book. Used appropriately, time-out encourages self-control, thereby becoming yet another way of facilitating the child's longing for autonomy, while ensuring that she acknowledges appropriate limits.

After many years of listening to parents and children, and now with several years of personal experience under my belt, I'm convinced that the greatest joy of parenthood is hearing a child say, "I wanna do it myself," and then watching her succeed—with your encouragement. At times, that can take patience: you need to get to a business appointment and the thirty-month-old is struggling to get her shoe on. Frustrated, she says, "I can't." It's hard to take the time to say, "You can"—harder than simply doing it for her. But the next day, certainly next week, you won't remember whether you got to the meeting on time, and neither will the other participants. What you will remember is the look on your child's face when she got that shoe on by herself.

You'll also find that the successes your child experiences on her early forays into self-sufficiency will make her more confident socially, as her feelings of competence carry over into her relations with the people around her. This is a great advantage in a society like our own, which is only reluctantly exchanging the ideal of a cozy two-parent nuclear family, with a full-time mom at home, for the realities of modern life.

I think it's not just doable but downright exciting to expose a child to the much wider social universe that this way of life requires. If you'll take the opportunity to create an extended family for your child by encouraging your friends, neighbors, relatives, and professional child-care people to become an intimate part of her world, you'll find that all the worries you probably have about separation anxiety and fear of strangers are unnecessary. In families where an exclusive attachment between mother and child has been the goal, these *are* often serious problems, and you may even have believed that the screams of a child being left in day care were a sign of the health of that relationship. But I think they're sad—and unnecessary. Children who have the kind of self-mastery skills that are the subject of this book can thrive in much more diversified situations than the nuclear family could ever offer. They do not suffer terrible feelings of abandonment when their parents leave them at day care, they deal well with babysitters, they even survive their parents' vacations away from them with a minimum of pain—and often with actual enjoyment.

Similarly, when the fantasy of exclusivity is no longer the ideal, and the child enjoys relationships with people outside the family, the birth of a new sibling does not threaten the parent-child relationship. And of course the parents themselves thrive. The pain which all of us feel when our need to be needed meets up with the reality of a child's joy in independence is more than compensated for by that joy. The tears that no longer get shed at separation are not missed when there are so many smiles at reunion.

The ideas in this book go beyond practical advice, beyond my recommendations for more effective parenting, beyond my belief in a child's right to have his or her yearnings for self-realization nourished by parents who will help with self-calming, self-control, and self-entertainment. Like all parents everywhere, my ultimate concern is the affection between parent and child, the glue that makes family life enjoyable. I see in the faces of parents in my practice the mutual trust and affection that result from using these ideas. I hear it in the thunder of little feet running to greet me when I go home to my own son, I experience it in the bright smiles and exuberant enthusiasm of children happy with their lives. As we all know, there's nothing like the joy of feeling our own love for our children reflected in their feelings toward us. To walk into a room and see a child's eyes light up when they meet ours is a thrill as electric, as memorable, as momentous as any of the big moments in life, but in some ways even better, because it can be ours day after day. As a parent it still astounds me to realize the thrill never wears off.

We all want love; no parent-child relationship could endure without it. And ultimately that's what it's all about. I haven't developed my ideas about self-calming, self-control, and self-entertainment because I think they will mold superchildren. And I certainly don't see my ideas as a way out of the hard work of parenting. Just because you're encouraging your child in her desire to do-it-herself doesn't mean you're not on the premises playing a crucial role while she tries. To stay on the sidelines and learn to offer just the right amount of encouragement, support, and, when necessary, help is every bit as demanding as hovering over her.

What I see as the most important outcome of any approach to child-rearing is the love that develops between parent and child when respect between them is mutual. Every child says, "I wanna do it myself." The best way of achieving your child's enduring love and affection is to help her realize that goal.

I Wanna Do It
Myself

"**I** Wanna Do It Myself"—a great title for a book you may think, but certainly not a realistic goal for a young child. Most parents are convinced that their child can't do whatever it is that she thinks she can do. In an effort to help and protect, many will try to do the task for her, but doing it for the child never lets her reach her goal—which is well and truly expressed in that oft-repeated (and generally ignored) phrase: "I wanna do it myself."

The fact is, she can and eventually will achieve *her* goal, though it may be at the price of great conflict between you, and leave a residue of bitter resentment at having been thwarted; while conversely, you can never achieve *your* goal—to spare your child the pain of failing by always stepping in to help. You can't change the world; you can't prevent every heartbreak, every frustration, every temporary setback, that life holds for your child. What you can do is to make sure that she knows you support her in her desire to do what she wants to do as well as she is capable of doing it. If that idea doesn't make you smile and tingle with excitement, you've got the wrong book.

Survival Skills: Self-Calming, Self-Control, Self-Entertainment

Starting in the first few days of life, when the child has to learn an effective way to communicate with the world, and going right through her struggles to move, walk, and talk, to succeed at school, choose a career, sustain a marriage, raise a family, and eventually cope with old age and dying, each member of the human race confronts an endless number of demands and challenges. In every case the baby, child, or adult will feel anxious, scared, pressured, and threatened, depending on the situation. Rather than incapacitating her, these emotions can be a stimulus to do her best. The best way of preparing a child for challenge is by giving her a deep-rooted sense of personal competence from her earliest days, not by trying to shield her from life's minor hurdles, or even the major mountain climbs when she's ready to tackle them. Since life's initial challenges do in fact come with all but built-in guarantees—children who do not have serious physical or mental deficiencies will all eventually learn to crawl and walk and talk, etc.—you have a wonderful opportunity to facilitate a series of successes. The key is to enable the child to feel that they are *her* successes—achieved on her own terms, at her own pace, to her own satisfaction and standards—not those of her parents or the world at large. To accomplish this in each of the many demanding situations she will face after the first few months of life, the child needs to be able to do the following:

Self-calm. This enables her not to be overwhelmed by physical needs like hunger and sleep, and gives her a start on dealing with emotions like anxiety and fear. Infants and toddlers usually manifest one or two physical actions which serve as self-calming mechanisms, such as sucking, rocking, head rolling, hair twirling, or staring at some object they find visually attractive, but many older children and adults have equally apparent techniques, such as deep breathing, humming, and other rhythmic, repetitive activities. At any age the physiological result is that heart rate and respiration stabilize and body tone generally relaxes.

Achieve self-control. This is more of a mental than a bodily process, with no obvious physical correlates by which it can be identified. Once physiologic readiness has been achieved through self-calming, the child's ability to get her emotions under control is what allows her to take effective action to meet the challenge or avoid the danger she faces. Since each situation demands a different response—sometimes instant action, other times a slowing down; sometimes assertiveness, other times the ability to stage a quick retreat, and so forth—the only consistent sign of self-control is the child's adaptability and resiliency, her ability to use her mental and physical resources as well as her temperamental characteristics to get through a variety of situations successfully. Since all self-control has a basis in self-calming, however, the child who has achieved self-control will usually exhibit some of the physical mechanisms typical of self-calming.

Self-entertain. Once the child is physiologically stable, and emotionally prepared, she must be able to devise some activity that will make the situation more bearable. For infants and young children, this frequently means entertaining themselves until an adult can come play and offer social attention or be available to change a diaper or provide food. The more they discover about what they can do to amuse or divert themselves, the more they broaden their choices of action in any given situation, stressful or not, and the more ability they have to maintain self-control, since they are much less likely to be overwhelmed by fear or anxiety if they can divert their attention outward.

The ability to self-entertain also enhances self-esteem by giving children a sense of their own powers of invention and creativity. These are resources they'll be able to draw upon for the rest of their lives, as they face the inevitable frustration that comes with any effort to master new skills. Self-entertainment will be invaluable as they struggle to crawl, walk, draw, or find the right word, and will be just as important in the early school years, throughout adolescence and adulthood.

Self-calming, self-control, and the ability to self-entertain are what I call survival skills—actually, a parent initially applied that label. At the social level, from childhood on, they make everyone more fun to be around, and better able to have fun themselves. At the most profound, existential level they are powerful antidotes to humankind's most incapacitating fear: being alone.

There is no particular age when these skills are developed—self-calming appears to begin in the womb, but can be fostered at any age, as we shall discuss later—and they continue to be used and, it is hoped, improved throughout life. They are not magic capable of preventing the stresses of life, but they will give a child the ability to deal with such stresses as adeptly and proficiently as possible. It's that kind of success, not the experience of being rescued and protected by a parent, that builds feelings of security and self-esteem. So your responsibility is to create opportunities for your child to develop and enhance these basic survival skills. To do this you must have enough self-control of your own to be able to step aside when necessary, and enough humility to accept this new role as facilitator of your child's longing for autonomy.

Though many parents like the sound of these ideas, they often lack the courage to see them through, out of fear that too much is being asked of the child. I hope the many examples I've given throughout the book will counteract that fear, but I must also warn that the alternative to encouraging self-mastery seems to me to be far worse than any of the possible dangers. Even so noted a world figure as Dr. T. Berry Brazelton has stated that he sees more and more children, as young as nine months of age, who have a clear expectation of failure. To me this indicates that the "you-*can't*-do-it-yourself" message is getting across often, early, and with great impact.

This doesn't happen because parents don't love their children enough. To their chagrin many parents have learned that bonding at birth, unconditional love and affection, and constant availability are not sufficient to create a happy family relationship and a well-adjusted child. Their two-year-old says no to everything, and the "terrible twos" just don't seem to end. Their three-year-old, despite all parental efforts, is sad, withdrawn, and lacking in self-esteem or, alternately, angry, hyperactive, and vacillating between overcompliance and adamant self-assertion. Their primary-school-age child lacks enthusiasm for learning and expresses zest for little in life other than Nintendo. Their adolescent is worse than rebellious, willfully experimenting with drugs or other life-threatening behaviors, while lacking any sense of direction or self-motivation. Such outcomes are occurring with alarming frequency in our society while multiple scapegoats are blamed: television, the schools, lack of religion, the excesses of affluence, permissive parenting, peer pressure, single parents, working mothers, overly ambitious fathers, and so on.

Though I do not belittle the significance of many of these forces in various individual situations, two decades of pediatrics have convinced me that the child is *not* just a passive entity, a blank slate on which her parents and various other outside influences inscribe her destiny. She's an actor in her own drama.

One of the special things about being a pediatrician—and a parent—is the opportunity to watch the innumerable ways children of all ages find to achieve their goals. But on days when my neuroses are out of their cage, and I see a child, especially my own son, make a choice that I know can't possibly work out well, I long to intervene, to shortcut the road to achievement. I wonder if I should do the task for him or lessen the difficulty. But my son Red, like every other child, quickly says "No," or "Me do it" or "I want to" whenever he senses that I may intrude. Almost without exception, he and his peers are right; their way works no matter how dubious I or the other adults may be beforehand. After ten years of seeing the light as a pediatrician, and five years as a parent, I still slip up, but the kids never do. Their commitment to the "I wanna do it myself" credo has reinforced my determination to nurture the skills that will make that goal a reality.

What any child needs most is not the never-never land of parent-guaranteed successes, but the courage and self-confidence to bounce back from her mistakes. That's what self-calming, self-control, and the ability to self-entertain do for a child, which is why many parents view them as literal survival skills, not just for the child, but for the whole family. To see them in action, let's watch ten-month-old Nell as she learns to walk, and her mother, who's trying to activate these survival skills, learns to let her. We'll pick up in midaction:

For the tenth time Nell has gone from crawling to balancing on her feet with one hand on the floor. Face contorted with concentration and effort, she stands upright, wobbling, her arms spread to maintain her balance. One step forward, but then her head (the heaviest part of her body by far) juts a little too far out beyond her body and causes her to fall. Nell's mother, Linda, is reminded of similar scenes three years ago with her son, Noah, who would do the same thing and then cry. Usually his reaction was to gesture her away if she even went near him, so determined was he to get up again and walk. Some days she'd pick him up anyway and he'd cling, sobbing, which made her wonder whether it was a good thing to have intervened. Other times, consumed with rage and frustration, he'd thrash around and make it impossible for her to pick him up or console him. Nell has given no signs of wanting help, so Linda, having learned from experience, is holding herself back from offering it. Of course she realizes now that Noah rarely asked for help either, but in those days she thought she should give it anyway.

Meanwhile, Nell is trying again. Same moves. Same result. As she falls she almost hits her head on the wall and Linda ponders the advisability of at least moving her away from the corner. Just as she's about to go to her, however, Nell tries something new—she puts her head up against the wall for added balance. But as soon as she gets two steps away from the wall she falls again. Clearly frustrated, teeth clenched, she cries for about ten seconds and then gets herself back in control without hysterics by doing some brief head-rolling, followed by two deep sighs. She looks at Linda. Is this an invitation? If so, Linda doesn't want to miss it, having been so careful up to now about not intruding.

Linda offers her hand. "Maybe I can help." Nell looks skeptical, as if Linda didn't know how to walk herself. But she takes the hand, tries a few steps, and then sits down and pulls her hand away—which makes Linda question if she should have just waited. The whole process reminds her of training wheels on a bike—you never know when to take them off. So she walks away and watches four more of Nell's attempts, and four more falls. Each time Nell takes a little longer to calm down—the last time she even sucked on her hand briefly, a strategy she hasn't used for months. For ten minutes she takes a break, playing with her hand in front of her face (a calming strategy she's used for the last five months) and then exploring the cracks between the floorboards with her fingertips. Linda pushes a toy toward her, figuring that she's probably had enough by now, but Nell ignores it.

She's up again! Four more tries, no luck. She grabs a pillow and stares very fixedly out the window, rolls over, pulling the pillow over her head, and falls asleep.

What a change from the events of three years ago. At this juncture Noah would have quit in tears or forced himself to try over and over again, despite being so tired from his previous efforts as to be hopelessly uncoordinated and usually quite distraught, even hysterical. Linda had felt trapped between a rock and a hard place. Either she ignored his crying and felt like a monster, or went to pick him up, which would cause him to collapse and look hopeless. Scenes like that are the beginnings of the sense of failure that Dr. Brazelton talks about. Linda has made sure that her daughter has more emotional resources and resilience. Because of her ability to calm herself with techniques like head-rolling, hand-sucking, and vision, to control herself by taking whatever time she needs to rebound from her unsuccessful efforts, and to entertain herself during those interludes with whatever is at hand, even if it's only the spaces between the floor boards, Nell is able to stay in control for longer periods of time and to avoid being overwhelmed by the frustration involved in mastering a new skill. And she's not about to give up, either. She paces herself. A nap lets her recharge. How often Linda had wished that Noah would sleep rather than getting himself and her caught up in a frenzy.

When Nell wakes up, Noah has just returned from nursery school, and you can see her watching his every move as he comes walking into the room. "Why can he do it but not me?" is clearly written all over her face. "Not forever" glistens in her eyes.

The learning-to-walk drama continues another twelve days. When Nell is really frustrated she goes to sleep, but that is now happening less often. Most of the time she distracts herself by crawling over to a toy or a picture book for a while, rarely getting to the point where she needs to tune out completely. Linda is increasingly able to sit back and enjoy Nell's learning process, because it doesn't involve her in the kind of dilemmas she created for herself with Noah, besides which it's obvious that Nell is accomplishing much more than just learning to walk. The effort continues. On day twelve, half an hour before Noah gets home from nursery school, while Linda is busy getting lunch ready, she hears a sudden squeal, then a laugh—sounds of pure joy and unmitigated delight. She turns to find Nell standing in the middle of the floor, perhaps not walking so much as tottering without support. The expression in her eyes tells all, from "I'm so proud of myself" to "When does Noah get home?" The next thirty minutes may be the slowest half hour of Nell's life.

As a parent reading this story you may ask, "Where do I come in? I want to participate in my child's development, but Linda just sat on the sidelines." Nothing could be further from the truth. Linda was intensely involved in Nell's progress. Through many months of trial-and-error attempts to help Nell develop the self-calming, self-control, and self-entertainment skills she put to such good use in learning to walk, Linda has become more and more adept at learning when to intervene and when to step aside, taking into account considerations of both physical safety and emotional well-being. She knows that Nell will eventually learn to walk, regardless of the amount of adult intervention she receives, and that the optimum quantity is whatever helps Nell feel capable of doing for herself but able to call upon the love and support of her parents when she needs them. Each child is different, however, and you must learn to read your child's cues, just as Linda learned Nell's. If your child, unlike Nell, is eager for you to give him your hand, then you should, while also encouraging him to use the extra support just as a starter, for the first few steps. Once he gets moving reduce the support or let go so he learns to balance and walk by himself. On the other hand, if you go over to him and he pushes you away, back off, no matter how much you long to be at his side. After all, he may accept your hand if you really insist, but the big smile comes only when he walks on his own.

The Competent Child

If you have any doubt that children are full-fledged individuals with the ability to make their own decisions about the kind and quantity of interaction they want with adults, it will interest you to know there is a mounting body of research to suggest that they are already playing a very active role in shaping such interactions when they are no more than two or three weeks of age. No, that's not a typo—*two or three weeks of age!* Since I was taught in medical school that young infants were for all intents and purposes blind and deaf, I was astonished to learn that they are not simply passive reactors to the actions of those around them, and I'm certainly sympathetic to the parents who find it hard to believe that their one-month-old can hear, or that she cries for reasons other than food, or, heaven forbid, that smiling is caused by more than gas pains. In fact after reading all this fascinating research one has to wonder if many of the baby's mental processes aren't just as sophisticated as the parents'. (That statement may make some of you sleep less well at night, but read on; it really is easier to take care of a competent child than a totally helpless, dependent baby. The child's competence, if acknowledged, ultimately means that you will *all* sleep better.)

Studies using videotapes of what are called "face-to-face interactions" indicate that by the second month of life, the child is well embarked on the process of deciding when and how to interact with his parents. What the tapes show is that the baby registers changes that are very rapid and sometimes quite subtle, and can use his skills to shape the course of the interaction. The communication between the participants is generally cyclical in nature, with parent and infant vocalizing and looking at each other for several seconds until the interaction reaches what is for the baby a peak of intensity, after which he looks away, often neutralizes his facial expression, decreases the motions of his hands and arms, and uses thumb-sucking as a way to calm himself. If the parent respects his need to calm and gain self-control (which may take the form of looking out the window or at another object for as long as twenty or thirty seconds), then the baby will turn back and re-engage the parent with a smile or a coo, and the whole sequence begins all over again, reaching another peak that requires another break. This pattern is exactly parallel to the way that adults break eye contact and change facial expression during a conversation to modulate the intensity of an interaction.

Though much of the research has focused on the parent's being able to read the child's cues, equally important is the child's ability to self-calm and his ability to maintain control. In fact, recent analyses of the data show that as often as not it is the child who initiates the interaction, not the parent. And the child will continue to try to control it, even in the face of interference. If, for example, the parent tries to induce the baby to increase the level of interaction before he's ready, by talking loudly or moving into his line of vision, the child makes further efforts to stay in control by shutting his eyes, sucking harder on his fist, or even attempting to push the parent's face away. If nothing else works, the baby starts to cry in a final effort to convince the adult to back off. All of these are the child's way of trying to keep the interaction manageable for himself so that it can be resumed. If the child has no ability to self-calm, however, he cannot participate in these cycles and the whole process immediately disintegrates. Such a child is much harder to play with, which of course makes for a less fulfilling parent-child relationship. On the other hand, the child who can self-calm can sustain a high-intensity, pleasurable interaction for a relatively long period of time, rarely crying unless the parent repeatedly ignores all his signals.

Self-calming

This brief research review shows how important self-calming and self-control are for establishing the overall quality of the parent-child relationship. Unfortunately, our traditional mode of parenting makes it difficult for the baby to master these skills, because the whole idea of self-calming seems so far beyond what most parents expect a baby to do. But, like the sense of touch, the capacity to self-calm is essential to survival. And like sight, hearing, or touch it is an ability that the baby has already begun to acquire while in the womb, as I discussed in my earlier book, *The Self-Calmed Baby* (St. Martin's Press, 1991). Let me now summarize some of the points I made in that book, first by using an experience my wife, Carol, and I had with our son, Red, to illustrate what self-calming is, and how parents can facilitate it in their child if they learn to read the child's cues; then by giving an in-depth portrait of a family getting to know each other during the baby's first few weeks of life.

The experience with Red was interesting because he quite unexpectedly switched his preferred mode of self-calming when he was six weeks old, leaving Carol and me momentarily confused. Like Red, the vast majority of babies use sucking as their primary self-calming mechanism in the first few months of life, although they can also use vision, body position, and body motion in addition to, or even to the exclusion of, sucking. It's rare to see any baby be entirely dependent on just one mechanism, and some children, as Red was to teach me, switch suddenly. Red was very adept at sucking, and since we did all we could to facilitate his use of that mechanism for self-calming, we were thrown into turmoil when he lost his former equilibrium and started to fuss and cry a lot. When we turned him onto his stomach as we were accustomed to doing, since he found it easier to get his hand to his mouth from that position, it no longer seemed to calm him but appeared to provoke a great deal of frantic head-bobbing and body-twisting. Since he had never been a baby who liked sustained body contact, carrying him around or putting him in a Snugli only made him all the more frantic—and did nothing to calm his increasingly anxious and concerned parents.

Gradually it dawned on me that, like many babies who use vision for self-calming, Red would stop crying when I first picked him up, but then start crying again soon after I had him nestled against my shoulder. The motion causes the child to open his eyes and focus on something in order to regain his orientation, and for the child who uses vision to self-calm, the momentary glimpse of a white ceiling, a dim lamp, or any other low-intensity, monotone object he sees once he's been picked up can be soothing—*if* he is able to maintain the visual contact. But all too often, as happened with Carol and me, the contact is interrupted when the adult then positions him so that he's turned toward the adult's neck, unable to find a new target on which to focus. That's when the baby starts to cry again. I realized that many of the moves we were making to try to assist him were in fact no longer helpful since they worked against his attempts to use his new self-calming technique. Lying on his stomach, for example, limited his visual field, as did holding him against my chest or shoulder. We now had to retrain ourselves to match our strategies to his.

We saw a dramatic decrease in fussing and crying once we put him on his back and made it easier for him to see what we discovered to be favorite targets such as the lamp shade in his bedroom or a particular pillow in the kitchen. We also made a number of other changes, like carrying him around on the hip facing outward, not chest to chest, so he could see better. As he's grown older, he's learned to use vision not just for self-calming, but to explore and assess new environments and new people, which allows him to feel in control of situations as he ventures beyond the familiar. And his visual imagination, which enables him to see animal shapes in clouds and to delight in what seem to me like perfectly ordinary phenomena, has provided him with a wonderful means of self-entertainment, especially on long car rides.

The end result of the change that Red made was important both for him and for us. Like many parents who have told me their own stories of becoming more adept at enabling their child to self-calm, we had the gratification of knowing that we had played a vital role in furthering his skills. And Red benefited because he now had more experiences of successful coping to reinforce his burgeoning self-confidence, as well as a reinforced belief in his ability to communicate his needs to his parents, and a stronger trust in our ability to understand him.

Each child is unique in his self-calming preferences. The parents' obligation is to learn them by studying his behavioral cues and to create a nurturing environment that honors them and promotes his sense of personal efficacy in the world.

What follows is a detailed description of a baby and her parents during her first weeks. The baby's main job at this stage of life is to achieve enough of an equilibrium via her self-calming skills so that her own life and that of her parents can be pleasant; the parents' task is to learn how and when to intervene to make her goal achievable.

Paul pulled into his driveway one Wednesday night with mixed emotions. He used to look forward to coming home at night, but that had changed since the birth of his daughter three weeks before. As he closed the garage door, he ruefully admitted to himself that what he now looked forward to was making himself a large martini—or two. As he reached for the door he could already hear the sounds of crying. Taking a deep breath, he paused before entering the house and starting on the most grueling part of his day. Alison of course would cry for most of the evening, then keep her parents awake all night long. And no telling what shape Lindsay, his wife, would be in since Alison had already reached a hysterical pitch by noon, when he had called to check on them. He certainly had a new appreciation for work, since it meant he could escape from the house every day. He couldn't imagine how Lindsay was going to live through this.

"How's my favorite mother?" he asked as he walked into the kitchen, expecting Lindsay to collapse sobbing into his arms. But her answer was a surprise: "I probably feel a little better than I look. I realize there's a lot of crying now, but this has been a better day than any so far. When you were away in Tucson on Monday, I took Alison to the doctor again because I couldn't believe she wasn't sick, and Dr. Jean told me about a book describing how babies can calm themselves down. I went directly from her office to the bookstore, stayed up all of Monday night to read it, and have been trying to use the techniques it recommends for the last two days. I think we're making progress."

"Really? I can't hear it." Paul reached in the refrigerator for the olive jar. "Sure you don't want one of these?"

"No, really! Even though she sounds terrible now, she was quiet for almost three hours this afternoon until just before you walked in. I'm beginning to understand what we've been doing wrong. Apparently a lot of her crying is because we're not helping her do what she wants to do—which is to calm herself down long enough to be able to stop crying."

Paul gagged on his first sip. How could some book dare to suggest that they were preventing their child from ceasing to cry? Had Lindsay lost her mind? Raising his glass and his right eyebrow, he tried to sound lighthearted: "You must have beaten me to this and had the businesswoman's three-martini lunch. We've read God knows how many books, practically worn out the carpet walking around with her day and night, bought two different backpack/Snugli contraptions trying to find one to make her comfortable, we're both exhausted, you're driving yourself to distraction and me to drink wondering if something is wrong with your milk, whether you can eat anything that we like to eat without somehow, in some very undefined way screwing up your milk supply . . ." Paul paused to come up for air and to try to recapture what he hoped was a bantering tone—only to be stunned by the total silence that had descended on the house while he'd been giving his speech.

"What's that?" he asked.

"What do you mean?"

"There's no sound coming from Alison's room," he said

as he ran to the stairs. "I'm going to go check to make sure she didn't suffocate."

"I'll bet she's sucking her hand," Lindsay called after him as he sprinted up the stairs two at a time, genuine concern on his face. She waited for a minute, then two, fighting off her own rising panic. Maybe there was something wrong. Why didn't Paul say anything? She started to call out to him, but then remembered that part of the reason she and Alison had had a better day was that she'd taken the book's advice and lowered the noise level in the house by turning off the radio and the TV and turning down the volume on the telephone ringer. Alison had immediately looked less jittery and started smiling more. Lindsay could see Paul standing stock-still in Alison's doorway when she got to the top of the stairs. "What's she doing?" she whispered.

"Sleeping."

"That's impossible this time of day. She never falls asleep now, no matter what we do. Are you sure she's still breathing?"

"She'll be okay if she doesn't swallow her hand. You were right. She was obviously sucking on her hand."

"Let's see how long it lasts. Maybe through dinner."

"And what delicious concoction awaits us tonight?" Paul asked sarcastically, resigned to yet another bland frozen meal, which was all that they ever seemed to have anymore now that Lindsay had no time to cook and had eliminated all seasonings from her diet to make her milk agree better with Alison's digestion.

"No need to be such a pessimist," Lindsay replied. "I actually got Alison to nap this afternoon. Correction: she napped; I didn't make it happen. So I made that veal dish we love so much."

"I didn't think that you could eat all those spices."

"This book says maybe I can—that once we've helped her to stop crying, by doing things like making the house quieter and darker and getting her hand to her mouth so she can suck it and calm herself down, then the rest is mainly out of our hands. It's probably not my breast milk or anything else to do with me that's causing the problem, so I should stop thinking I can cure it. And here I've been starving myself to death and making you eat frozen mush—all for nothing!"

Paul forgot the martini as they talked for the next two hours, until Alison awoke hungry. He started to read *The Self-Calmed Baby* while watching Lindsay nurse. Tonight for the first time Alison seemed to be enjoying it, not fighting the experience. Lindsay said this was because she was holding her in a different position and not looking at her constantly or talking to her, which the book said was often too much stimulation for a new baby.

Silence. Boy, did he appreciate it. While both Alison and Lindsay slept on the sofa, he read on. They had bought the whole standard program, believing that Alison was a helpless blob who would respond to their unconditional love and bond to them automatically, especially since Lindsay was breast-feeding her. It sure hadn't worked out that way, and now he was beginning to understand why. If this book was right, Alison was already a person, not just a blob, and she was giving them signals about her needs which they could learn to read. But up to now it hadn't occurred to them that her movements and sounds were as purposeful as their own. When she pushed his face away, he had thought it just a random movement; when he then moved in closer and she shut her eyes or looked away, he thought that he needed to stimulate her more to get her to pay attention. No wonder she went berserk when he held her up close to his face and bounced her around even after she'd said "enough" in her own way. And no wonder nursing had been such a hassle. They'd ignored every signal Alison gave them, never dreaming that she could possibly mean anything by them. Like that cry that really zinged his nerves—maybe that was a "put me down" not a "pick me up" or "hold me longer" cry. A couple of times when he *had* put her down, because he couldn't stand walking around with this wailing monster one minute longer, he'd noticed that she stopped crying almost immediately. But he hadn't realized why. Actually, he'd been so upset with her that he'd been irrational on the subject and decided she was just perverse—an ungrateful wretch who didn't appreciate the fact that he'd gotten up at two A.M. to walk her for the better part of an hour. In less distraught moments he'd interpreted the fact that she'd stopped crying once he put her down as a tribute to his sense of timing—he'd walked her until the exact moment when she was ready to settle down.

Now that he thought about it, he realized that she really didn't seem nearly as helpless and passive as most people think babies are. How many times had he marveled at her strength when he'd tried to pull her hand out of her mouth in anticipation of saving her from the orthodontist? And how many times had he had to convince himself that she couldn't possibly be trying to communicate with them, no matter how much it looked as though she was? It pleased him to think that his instincts were right, and the experts were wrong. Alison *did* have something to say, and it would be fascinating to try to decipher it.

He cringed when he thought about how difficult they'd made Alison's life up to now. It wasn't just the way they'd held her and talked to her and nursed her, either. Since he and Lindsay were both media freaks, there were televisions and radios all over the place, always on. Neither of them had ever given a thought as to whether this might be upsetting to Alison. And then there were all those days they'd put her in the sun room because his mother had told them it would help her eyes get accustomed to light and be good for her. What must Alison have felt when, no matter how many faces she made or how much crying she did, they ignored the fact that she kept her eyes closed all the time and left her in the sun room for hours? The only time she kept her eyes open in the sun was when they put that little hat with the visor on her, but of course they hadn't thought to do that when she was indoors. Sometimes they'd tried to calm her down when she was in the sun room by putting a music box in her bassinet. The tune drove him nuts, and now he realized it was probably driving her nuts too. Poor kid—she must have felt every bit as frustrated with them as they did with her. Paul vowed he'd make it his business to learn to understand the signals his daughter was giving him.

Three days later, Saturday, is his first chance to take care of Alison on his own. He and Lindsay both feel they've learned a lot this past week, but his stomach is in knots now that he's been left alone with his daughter. What if he can't figure out what to do and sabotages all the progress Lindsay has made?

At least Alison is off to a good start today, not fussy or grouchy. She'd been up at four A.M. as usual, but this time they'd let her cry by herself, since the cry sounded different from what they were beginning to recognize as her hunger cry— which made sense, given that Lindsay had nursed her at two o'clock. Listening to her crying had been anguishing for them, but they'd held out, and soon they could hear her sucking on her hand, the sound of her lip-smacking echoing down the hall and alternating with her crying. Cry, suck, cry, suck—then, after fifteen minutes, silence. Practice—that's what the book called it. Hard to live with, but she had gone back to sleep on her own. That was a miracle in itself.

While Alison lay quietly in her playpen nearby, Paul made sure he had a packet of frozen breast milk defrosted and ready. Soon she was fussing, and he started to go to her, but then stopped in his tracks and asked himself: "What's the message? What's that cry mean?" He glanced at the clock. Nine-thirty. Almost time to eat, probably, but the cry didn't sound right. He looked over at her. She was turning her head back and forth, looking and sounding irritated. Why? Suddenly it came to him—the sun. She had been in the shade but the sun was now streaming in through the window directly onto her face. He pulled the playpen back about three feet. Alison opened her eyes, grinned, and made some pleasant noises. This was getting easier!

A half hour later Paul said to himself, "I know that cry"—
and went to give her a bottle, making sure to talk softly and
not look directly at her while she nursed. As she did at every
feeding now, she smiled up at him, until after eight ounces
she started to fuss and he wondered if it was time for her to go
to sleep. Though he now understood that feeding doesn't always
lead to sleeping, she did seem to be exhibiting a number of
the signs—subtle though some of them may be—that indicate
tiredness. She was showing some tremor, looking past his ear,
not at him, and sneezing in response to his whispered attempts
to communicate with her. He decided to get her into position
for sleeping, remembering what they'd learned about her preferences. He carefully placed her on her side, rather than the face-
down position they'd been putting her in, because she could
get to her hand more easily from there. Standing by her crib,
he watched her become frustrated as she hit herself in the eye
each time she tried to maneuver her hand into her mouth, until
finally she grabbed her right wrist in her left hand and got it
into her mouth. Bingo. Paul tiptoed to the other room. What
a difference in three days.

His feeling of triumph lasts for about fifteen minutes. He's
not even finished with the sports section when Alison starts to
wail. Uh oh. He waits a few seconds, which seems like an
eternity, but she's clearly getting more hysterical, not less. He
climbs the stairs, thinking more negative thoughts with every
step. He stops at the door. Somehow she's gotten over on her
back. He starts to pick her up and then stops, thinking: "Don't
fall into the same pattern. What can you do to help her get
back together? Ah—her hand: That's probably what she needs."
Without talking he gently rolls her back onto her side. She
quickly starts to settle, doing less windmilling of her arms,
and stretching her legs out from that knee-to-chest position
that made everyone think she had colic. But her fists are still
scrunched up and she seems to need some help getting to her
hand. Paul reaches over her shoulder from behind her head.

He doesn't talk and he doesn't get in her line of vision. Her mouth closes on his finger like a vise and starts sucking. "Okay," he reminds himself, "what's the rhythm? What's the message from the sucking pattern?" In the last several days of working on this new relationship with Alison, he and Lindsay have learned that babies suck in different ways depending on whether they're tired or hungry or distressed, and he's beginning to be able to decipher his daughter's own patterns. When she's hungry, for example, she sucks four times in rapid succession, then pauses. Right now she's not doing that (she just ate), but is in what he calls her "I need to sleep" pattern: two to six sucking motions, then a push accompanied by a little tongue flutter. This is different from the continuous hand-sucking she does when she's upset, or the completely random, arrhythmic sucking when she's totally fatigued. And he used to think that she couldn't communicate with them!

He stands there for almost a minute. Since her sucking is slowing down, the tongue flutter is gone, the mouth pressure is more consistent, he knows that she's getting calmer. He sees her hands relax, and then she uses them to grab onto the finger that she's been sucking. "Amazing to think that that's intentional." Now the real trick, which they've been working on for two days—getting her to transfer from his finger to her own hand. The first time, he pulls his fingers away too fast, and she begins to cry but won't immediately take his finger back. Meanwhile his own throat is tightening and he's beginning to sweat. Two more times he tries, but doesn't make the transfer successfully. Thoughts of having to stand there for hours float through his head until he realizes that he needs to pay attention to her hand position as well as the sucking rhythm and the pressure. Like most one-month-old infants, she really likes to suck on the base of her thumb, at the back of her hand. When he was pulling his finger away, Paul had inadvertently positioned her hand so that her thumb rather than the back of her hand was in her mouth. On the fourth try he places her wrist up against her mouth, and after some head-bobbing and fussing she is able to get her hand into her mouth and suck on it long enough to go back to sleep.

She stays asleep for almost another forty minutes and then starts to fuss. Later that night Paul would tell Lindsay that he reacted too fast at that point. Thinking she woke up because her diaper was wet, he went in and started to change her. She had been groggy, but all the handling made her wake up, and she was fussing more after the change than before. It probably would have been better to wait and see if she went back to sleep, since he's known her to sleep even when she was soaked through. What then ensued was twenty minutes of walking and talking—and continued crying and fussing—before she got herself back to sleep.

Another half hour went by before she started to cry again. Ninety-nine percent sure that what he was hearing was a hunger cry, he checked it out by giving her his finger, and she confirmed his hunch: four sucks and stop, four sucks and stop, nice even pressure, good coordination—Alison's hunger pattern.

While warming another packet of milk he tried to help her suck on her hand until it was ready. He was rewarded with a giggling episode of several minutes' duration and then he gave her the bottle. Since he found it hard not to interact with her while feeding her, he sat with her in front of the TV and watched a game with the sound off. He could feel her gazing up at him, but if he looked down more than briefly, she started to lose her sucking rhythm, so he continued to stare at the silent TV while she stared at him—for a few minutes at least. But after that Paul doesn't remember anything until Lindsay got home a little later than planned, bustling in, all apologetic, to find them both asleep on the sofa.

After this there was another week of what sometimes seemed like three steps forward and two steps backward while Paul, Lindsay, and Alison got to know each other better, but by the following Saturday, when Paul again was on duty, he was feeling much more self-confident. Everything went smoothly that morning. When he gave Alison a bottle she gazed raptly at him and smiled between sucks, but he was careful to let her initiate most of the interactions between them and to speak softly. He noticed that while lying in her crib she was staring at the black-and-white photograph of trees and snow that Lindsay had put nearby, and that when he put her down on the living room rug she seemed transfixed by the dim light of one of the wall sconces, so he made a mental note to be sure to position her so that she would be able to further develop her use of vision as a calming mechanism.

After lunch, in a burst of enthusiasm over the transformation in their lives, he decided to take Alison on a quick run to the grocery store. That turned out to be too much, however, and he soon realized that if he was going to do it at all, he should have done it in the morning when Alison had more energy. The store was too noisy, the lights were too bright, and too many people were coming up to Alison and sticking their faces in hers to goo at her. Exasperated by one particularly aggressive woman in the checkout line, he found himself nose to nose with her, asking her how *she* liked being moved in on that way! She was astonished by the question, and he was equally astonished—at the change in himself after just one week. He now viewed Alison not as a passive crying and feeding machine, but as a little person with the right to be treated with respect.

I can't condense every idea and every technique in *The Self-Calmed Baby* into one anecdote, but I hope that Paul and Lindsay's experience will show you how active a role the baby plays, and how important it is for parents to learn to recognize their baby's behavioral cues so that they can make appropriate decisions about when and how to intervene. As Paul and Lindsay discovered, often it's the times when you don't intervene that are the most rewarding, since that's when your child makes the biggest strides forward.

Of course some people react to Alison's story as if the change in her behavior was a fluke, something that would have happened of its own accord over time. It wasn't. Once her parents stopped doing the things that inadvertently got in the way of her using sucking, and subsequently vision, as calming mechanisms, and did instead what they could to make self-calming easier for her, she was able to get herself under control.

Self-calming depends not just on the two-month-old's capacity to learn to do it himself, but on the parents' ability to learn the meaning of specific cry messages and body motions. Establishing this communication system is a necessary prelude not just to self-calming but to the other survival skills that give your child a feeling of competence and success. Self-control and the ability to self-entertain, which I will describe in the following pages, are the next steps in the child's developmental agenda.

Reminders About Self-Calming

▪ Try to learn your child's communication system. Most children have eight to twelve different cries with very specific messages. The tone and cadence of the cry, not the act of crying itself, tell you what you need to do next.

▪ All children also give behavioral cues that will tell you much of what you need to know about how to help them remain calm, well rested, and happy.

▪ If the cry message or the nonverbal communication does not indicate a physical need (to be fed or changed or moved to a warmer place, for example) or any kind of illness or other problem, then do only what is necessary to get the baby sufficiently reorganized to be able to calm himself down. The point of intervening is not to do it for him, but to give him the sense that he can do it himself. If for instance he's fussing but you can see him making continued attempts to calm himself, then let him keep working at it. Your willingness to let him practice, and your ability to know when it is appropriate to intervene, are what enable him to succeed at self-calming.

▪ Babies tend to use sucking, vision, body motion, and body position as ways to self-calm. You should learn your baby's preferences, since you can play a valuable role in facilitating his preferred techniques. As the child gets older, he will develop additional means of self-calming, such as singing, rocking, hair-twirling, and other rhythmic body activities like running around the table in a brief burst of manic energy, which will need much less facilitation from adults.

▪ For babies the optimal environment is likely to be one which is relatively low key—darker and quieter than you're accustomed to, with as few intrusions as possible. So don't wake the baby to feed him, or overwhelm him with social contacts or outings; the fewer the better at an early age. For older infants, careful management of the number and timing of transitions, making sure that most outings are completed earlier in the day when they have more energy, will be helpful.

Self-Control

There is more to self-control than the gradual evolution of self-calming mechanisms. Nor is self-control limited to simply being able to resist acting on impulse or acting out. Faced with a demand to perform, a threat, or any other kind of challenge, the self-controlled child marshals inner resources that go far beyond a mere ability to control physiologic *and emotional* forms of arousal. His self-control involves everything from his personality traits—for example, whether he's persistent and rigid or distractable and adaptable, slow and steady or fast and erratic—to his capacity to make valid judgments about the social acceptability of his actions. The degree to which his self-control is developed will determine whether he's an initiator of action or a passive reactor to circumstances, whether he's easily overwhelmed by difficulties and looks to his parents to rescue him or can use his skills to resolve them successfully himself.

Over time, self-control becomes not just a skill but a state of mind, since each challenge successfully handled builds self-confidence and self-esteem. *Both* parent and child gain a sense of security in the child's inner grit and competence, and this develops early on, as opposed to what happens in most families where it is achieved only after years of struggle for independence and innumerable separation crises. Impossible for most children? Not at all. In fact, you may realize as you read on that various children you know—perhaps even your own—already possess this wonderful quality.

Self-control is a mental process. Though self-calming provides an excellent foundation for it, and it can certainly be enhanced by the ability to self-entertain, it has no obvious physical correlates like sucking or hair-twirling, and it need not be expressed in any particular activities which serve as self-entertainment like reading, working on puzzles, or exploring the cabinets. You can't actually see it at work. You will, however, recognize the end result: the child who is self-confident, adaptable, and resilient enough to meet whatever challenges and adversities life throws in his path. Self-control is what allows the six-month-old to harness the determination to make his thirty-fourth attempt to crawl today; the one-year-old to demonstrate the patience to try to aim the spoon into his mouth; the fifteen-month-old to persist in searching for the right word; the two-year-old to show the self-mastery not to stage a temper tantrum when you refuse to buy a third package of cookies at the grocery store; the three-year-old to exercise the restraint to go to his room without arguing when told it's bedtime; or the four-year-old to display the composure to talk to his nursery school class about what he did last weekend. In these and hundreds of other demanding situations that occur every day, the child will undergo both a physiologic response to the challenge, involving some combination of increased heart rate and altered respiration, slight hand tremor, sweating, flushing, butterflies in the stomach, and so forth, and an initial emotional response, consisting of some combination of anger, fear (of rejection, of failure, of physical harm), envy, jealousy, pride, excitement, etc., but he will be able to harness these responses rather than letting them run away with him. The child with self-control will choose actions that make good use of his motor and/or cognitive skills while staying within the boundaries of acceptable behavior.

How do you know when your child is gaining self-control? It's when you don't end up feeling that you have to rescue him two dozen times a day, although of course you'll be available to offer guidance and help. He whines less, and makes decisions that, while they may not be the ones you'd make in a given situation, don't create conflicts and don't result in actions requiring additional discipline. In general he's fun to be around. Let me cite some of the behaviors you may see as a child develops self-control.

- The two-month-old uses hand motions, yawns, facial expressions, changes in eye contact, or physical position to maintain an active social exchange without having to tune out or cry.

- The three-month-old switches off between sucking and vision as self-calming mechanisms. He sucks his hand at night, since he can't use vision in a dark room, stares at the picture in the corner when he's trying to settle down for a nap in the daytime, and is flexible enough to be able to alternate between the two if necessary.

- The seven-month-old just learning to crawl takes a break from her efforts every so often and naps or tunes out for a brief period—thus giving herself enough time to reorganize and regroup so that she doesn't disintegrate into helpless crying.

■ The one-year-old wakes in the middle of the night and, instead of crying or calling out to you for attention or a feeding, chooses head-rolling or rocking as a way to get back to sleep.

■ The eighteen-month-old voluntarily goes to take a nap when she's tired.

■ The twenty-eight-month-old "helps" unload the moving van but manages to stay out of everyone's way.

■ The three-year-old insists he *has* to have the latest Ninja Turtle accessory but doesn't have a prolonged tantrum when he doesn't *get* it.

All of these are normal behaviors, but they aren't typical. For instance, the one- or two-year-old who decides to take a nap is a rare bird—and yet voluntary nap-taking is an expectable milestone for the children in my practice, because they have self-calming as a basis on which to build. But what if your child is already toddler age or older and doesn't yet have much in the way of self-calming skills? Throughout the book I will try as often as possible to talk about how to enhance self-calming in older children. I've worked with many preschool and even adolescent children who were able to gain self-calming, hence self-control skills at relatively advanced ages. Achieving self-control is always possible; it's just that it requires a much greater expense of energy to the child if he doesn't have the stable physiologic base that self-calming can provide.

Parents: Allies or Adversaries in the Battle for Self-Control

Parents need to understand that self-control has innumerable benefits for the child—this isn't just something that parents try to impose for their own benefit. And one can see children struggling to attain it from an amazingly early age, precisely because it does have so much to offer them. Perhaps its earliest use is, as already discussed, for purposes of enhancing social interactions. The six- or eight-week-old who has the rudiments of self-calming in her repertoire can use them not just to settle down physiologically, but to act in such a way as to get more out of the human environment around her. Using self-calming as a buffer lets her take control. Rather than having to escape into sleep, withdraw into a cocoon, or disintegrate into crying, she gets some of her first feelings of being able to impact the world—a wonderfully exciting discovery—and she may then start to explore the possibilities of play even further. She'll learn what actions are in her repertoire, what strategies of action meet her needs—for example, if she wants to play, smiles and coos work better than frantic crying, but if she wants playtime to end, that, too, is within her control and need not involve crying, for she can look away, cease to respond to social overtures, or even push her play partner's face away. Already she's starting to learn the social rules—not just what actions she can take, but what will provide the kind of attention she needs. But all of this is dependent on the active encouragement of the adults around her. If you don't respond to her signals, she'll have no choice but to escape into either crying or sleep.

Your child relies on you to be an ally, someone who will enable her to discover what options really work, given her abilities, her temperament, and the expectations of society. The sooner you help her out the better. But remember: she does want to do it herself, and your job as ally is to make that goal a reality, not to do things for her. As a person with much greater experience of life than your child, you provide guidance about what is possible, limits to mark off what is impossible (especially when it may involve physical danger to her), and good judgment about what is socially acceptable. Your ultimate goal is the phasing out of your role so that your child can make her own choices.

Does that mean that the child is ignored and unattended?

That your involvement is minimal? Exactly the opposite. To be an effective ally, you must be highly attentive. You must notice each increment of progress in your child's abilities so that you can make adjustments in anticipation of her new accomplishments. There will be many difficult decisions about when and how to intervene so that frustration, anger, and impatience don't become destructive of self-esteem, on the one hand, but the child still feels in control on the other. You yourself have to have enough self-control to be able to allow your child to make her own mistakes. And finally you must learn how to use discipline to establish safe and secure boundaries within which your child can act freely. This is the very opposite of neglect. It's an exquisitely subtle, demanding form of attention.

The whole point of encouraging self-control is to help the child make sound choices about her own course of action. You'll find that the result of being this kind of ally to your child is that you can say yes to her more often than no, while watching her grow and succeed in remarkable ways. This is what she will most thank you for—in both the short and the long run.

The Art of Discipline

Discipline involves setting limits and enforcing them appropriately. Some limits prevent actions that are physically harmful, others define what's socially acceptable. The goal is to set as few limits as possible, but to enforce them firmly and consistently. The method of enforcement I advocate is time-out, in which the child who goes beyond established limits is isolated from the rest of the household and, in the absence of any kind of social contact or other distracting activity, allowed to calm down. There is no physical punishment, no repetition of warnings, no argument—in short, none of the opportunities for rising hysteria that other methods of discipline create. Instead there is an opportunity for the child to regroup emotionally—very similar to what self-calming offers. Time-out works as punishment because it speaks to both of the child's primary motivations for any behavior: the desire to gain and perfect new skills, which he can't do in the stripped-down environment of time-out, and the thirst for social attention. It also helps the child build self-control, because he will much more readily internalize lessons that are not reinforced by emotional coercion or physical threat.

The in-depth discussion of the time-out method of discipline is in Chapter Four, but for a look at how it works and in particular how it relates to self-control, the following story will be illuminating. It shows how the mother of a toddler used time-out to help her as the child struggled to master a new skill.

Along the way to being able to assemble Legos, Anna learned important lessons of self-mastery which will be useful to her long after she's lost interest in building blocks. Her mother was an effective ally in enabling her to do what she wanted to do—by herself! At nineteen months, Anna had good motor coordination, but whenever she got into Peter's Legos she would fall apart. Nothing seemed to get her goat faster than to watch her five-year-old brother build marvelous buildings and airplanes out of those little plastic components, while she was unable to put even two of them together. Such situations were a constant challenge to Anna's mother, Jenny, as she tried to encourage Anna's attempts to master Lego construction and yet to deal with the conflict of frustration and determination that arose during these efforts.

Although it was only nine-fifteen A.M., Jenny announced, "Anna, I think I'm just going to prohibit you from trying to use Peter's Legos." Drumming her fists, and kicking her feet, Anna was the very picture of misery as she lay amidst a scatter of red, blue, and green Legos that she had hurled about. Fearful of losing the opportunity to keep working on them, however, Anna soon managed to calm herself down by modulating her beating of the floor to a sort of metronomic tapping.

Next she began to whine, until a brief reprimand from

Jenny reminded her that whining wasn't allowed. Anna then grabbed two Legos and brought them over to her mother—a direct request for help, so Jenny complied immediately. "This takes a lot of concentration, it's even hard for me," she explained sympathetically, demonstrating how to fit the pegs into the little holes as she gave words of encouragement to her daughter. "It takes a couple of tries. But if you are patient enough to keep trying, eventually you'll do it."

The demonstration didn't help much, and soon Anna was screaming out her frustration. "Any more tantrums and you go to your room. Why don't you give yourself a break from Legos and go play with your doll?" Jenny suggested. But Anna wasn't interested in being diverted, and soon she was pounding her fists on the floor again, furious that she could not make the Legos do what she wanted. "Off to your room, young lady" put an end to that scene, and to any more experiments with Legos for that day.

A few days later, the playroom scenario looked a little different. Anna had brought her doll in for backup. Watching from the kitchen, Jenny saw Anna hand the pieces to the doll and then admonish her with much shaking of the head and a few well-chosen words like "No" and "Don't get mad." Although neither Anna nor her doll succeeded that day, there were no tantrums either. Anna had effectively internalized her mother's instructions to her by directing them at the doll—a very neat trick! Eventually Jenny walked over to observe their progress. "Still at work on this? I admire your persistence. Keep practicing—soon you'll be able to surprise Peter with what you can do. I'm also very glad that you didn't have a tantrum today. You're doing a much better job of not letting your frustration get the better of you."

Of course Jenny had other occasions to give Anna the same message—when Anna was throwing a ball, trying to color inside the lines, learning to eat with a fork, and facing all of life's other daily challenges—and Anna was getting better at modulating her perfectionist tendencies by switching from one activity to another if she became too frustrated. She had also stopped whining, after having been sent to her room several times.

The big stickler remained the Legos. She kept working at them relentlessly, and on the occasions when she exploded from the frustration of not being successful, she went to time-out. Then one afternoon, Anna came running down the hall, yelling, "Mommy, Mommy," and flashing something bright red which for one horrified moment Jenny thought was blood. Anna skidded into her legs, breathlessly holding up two red Legos stuck together. "Oh, Anna, you did it. You attached the Legos to each other all by yourself. That's a big achievement. Hooray, Hooray!" It's amazing the joy such an accomplishment brings to the parent of a twenty-one-month-old, to say nothing of what it does for the child herself. "I know how hard you had to work on this, and how frustrating it was. I'm so proud of you. You accomplished much more than just putting those two pieces together."

Anna grinned like the proverbial cat, held up the Legos, and said, "More." Not one to stop when she was ahead, Anna collected all the red pieces into a pile she then spread around herself on the floor. Perhaps color was the secret to success, Jenny could almost hear Anna thinking. Methodically, Anna next turned her attention to the two pieces she had joined, carefully searching her construction for any other mysteries that might block her from repeating her achievement. But none of her subsequent attempts to imitate it with the other red pieces worked. So she got up and walked around the room—a recent method of trying to stay in control learned by imitating her father. Then she sat down and tried again. Jenny noticed a lot of hair twirling and muttering, both alternatives to whining, which Anna had now given up. But soon she was getting upset again. When Jenny saw her throwing Legos at the floor, she reminded her that throwing things in the house wasn't allowed— a rule enforced very firmly after a ball had destroyed a treasured heirloom crystal bowl.

"Perhaps you need to try something different for now," she suggested, but this brought a defiant no, and Jenny was once again reminded that telling Anna what to do rarely succeeded. Well, the choice was hers, since within certain guidelines she was allowed to make her own decisions.

Soon, however, she was starting to lose control again. Performing further investigations on her two-piece module, she tried to attach a third Lego to the initial two, and as happens to everyone, the first two came apart. This was too much for her. She screamed at the top of her lungs—again and again. "Anna, get it back together. That's disappointing, but it's not the end of the world. If you don't stop now you'll have to go to your room." Anna gulped for air, then threw a Lego onto the floor. "Anna, I'm sorry you're so upset, but throwing isn't allowed. Now go to your room and cool out."

Later that night Jenny talked to Anna about her day, and praised her accomplishment again before telling her, "Everybody gets mad, everybody gets frustrated sometimes. But it's not good to push yourself to the point where you explode. Screaming, whining, and throwing things are not allowed, no matter how good your reasons."

Jenny had to say this more than once over the next few days, although Anna was starting to have more and more successes with the Legos, which allowed her to spend a lot more time with Peter, from whom she was more willing to accept help than from her mother—perhaps because with him it seemed more like play than a teaching exercise. One day when the two of them had been in the playroom for a while, Peter suddenly started screaming, "Stop her, stop her" (evidence of his own developing self-control, since until recently he had hit her whenever she provoked him). As Jenny came around the corner to check what was happening, Peter looked as if he was about to defect from the pacifist camp. Jenny surveyed the havoc Anna had wreaked and sent her to her room. "Thanks for not clobbering

her, Peter. I'm sorry she wrecked your airport building." A
three-afternoon effort was a shambles. From Peter she found
out that Anna had started her own building, couldn't get a
square Lego to fit on one of the curved ones (geometrically difficult
as well as motorically demanding), and became so upset she
laid waste to Peter's airport.

This wasn't the last such episode. But the next time Anna
started to get overwhelmed by her frustration she made a real
change. All three of them were working on the Legos, and
Anna had four small structures built, when one broke apart as
she tried to attach it to a second. She stood up, stomped her
foot, and announced, "I hate this. Can we play with the trains?"

"Do you want help with your Legos?" Jenny countered.

"No. I built those." This was a big advance. She was acknowledging her own success—something she had never done
before, no matter how much reinforcement Jenny had tried to
give her.

"Let's help Peter finish his here, and then we can all play
with the trains."

"I drive," Anna announced. Jenny was thrilled.

In another child the transfer of attention to another activity
might not be such a positive development—persistence does
after all have its virtues—but in Anna it was a welcome sign
because of her compulsive, perfectionist tendencies. No one is
going to change her basic style, and who would want to? Determination, focus, and energy are all necessary attributes to have in
the twenty-first century. On the other hand, by learning to
accept her own limits, and not be defeated by them, Anna has
begun to master many of the emotional impulses that were standing in her way. Tantrums are less frequent, she is less destructive,
even sibling altercations are decreasing—all this because of the
self-control her mother has helped her to acquire, through a
careful balance of discipline and praise. Jenny was also very
adept at knowing when to intervene, when to step back.

The Art of Intervention

Decisions about when to let a child follow through on his intention to do it himself are always a challenge. You have to be familiar with the child's abilities so that you'll know whether he *can* do what he wants to do, and you then have to have enough courage, patience, and self-control of your own to step back—sometimes quite literally—and let him try. Or conversely, you need to be able to say no to a request that is unreasonable. In the story below, I was tempted to say no, but agreed to give my son a chance, and then was repeatedly tempted to intervene "for his own good" (actually because of my own nervousness), but managed to hold myself back. I was almost as proud of my own self-control as I was of his; the combination resulted in Red's enjoying a great triumph.

At fourteen months, having conquered walking to his satisfaction, Red announced that he was now ready for the stairs. Since he still occasionally tripped and fell when he was walking, with sometimes painful results because he didn't watch what he was doing, I had made the stairs off limits. He'd chafed at the restriction, but I felt all the more justified because it was a three-flight staircase, and from top to bottom was a long way down (even longer in my imagination). One morning, however, Mr. Stubborn was not to be denied. He sat on the floor, about two feet from the stairwell, effectively blocking anyone else from it, and shouted, "Down, down."

In such situations, if I feel that close supervision can ensure the safety of the child, I try to go by the rule that Red—or any of my patients—is allowed one attempt. If he can't do it, and shows no sign of learning a new technique or being able to recover on his own, I then feel on firm ground saying no. So reluctantly I told Red he could try, and went to take my place four or five steps below him. As he stood at the top of the stairs, radiating confidence, I couldn't resist what I thought was a legitimate "Don't look at me, look at the stairs, it will be much easier."

Despite my anxiety, he gave no signal that he wanted any help, or for that matter any more advice, as he wrapped his arm around the newel post and quickly got down one step. I smiled, impressed, and said, "Nice job." No anxious tremor, no tripping; perhaps I had been overly concerned. Then I realized that without the newel post to grab onto, he was hesitating a little bit, eyes darting back and forth. With both feet on the second step he grabbed the baluster with his right hand, pursed his lips, and closed his eyes in a partial squint, studying his next move. Noticing his white knuckles I leaned forward, hands open, offering to pick him up. The withering look I got made me pull back, so I let him decide what to do next.

Bottom lip stuck out, facing me, he was so intent on seeing to it that I kept a proper distance that, as I realized too late, he wasn't watching what he was doing. As he swung his left foot down toward the next step, all of a sudden he yelped, started to lose his balance, and then pivoted on his right foot, while grabbing the baluster with both hands. It all happened so fast I couldn't do much to prevent it. He whimpered a second, stared very intently at the baluster, and got regrouped, planting both feet firmly at the stair's edge. Vision had for some time been his major self-calming mechanism, and I could see the staring relax him, to the point that I figured his heart rate was probably back down below mine. As I wiped my damp palms on my pants, I congratulated him once again on his balance as well as his courage, hoping that he'd think he had accomplished enough for the day—without saying so, of course. Obviously the near fall had been scary to him. Since it had taken its toll on me, too, I couldn't resist at least making the offer: "Want a free ride downstairs?"

One deliberate shake of the head no was followed by about thirty seconds during which nothing happened. I was about to pick him up, thinking he was too embarrassed to ask for help, when I noticed that he wasn't just standing there, he was carefully looking at his hands and feet. Unlike his behavior a minute before, when he had stared at the baluster to calm down, he was now using vision to figure out a new strategy for descending the stairs.

For Red, vision has turned into an amazing system of being able to assess new people and/or situations—one which I'm frankly jealous of, since I'm so deficient in that respect. However, since I myself don't use vision that way, and also have an inordinate fear of falling, I was dubious about his ability to get himself out of his current predicament, and therefore once again bent toward him to offer help. This was entirely uncalled for, since he hadn't asked for help, which he was quite capable of doing. Like all offers of rescue, it implied a belief in the necessity of rescue, which he rightly resented. As I moved closer, he gripped the baluster even harder, the look on his face one of determination, not fear. Heeding his message, I said, "Okay, do it your way, but we can't stay like this all morning. You are determined, so I'm sure you'll pull it off."

He checked his feet, checked his hands, and I realized that he had devised a new strategy: He was going down sideways, having figured out that the face-forward method he had been trying wasn't going to work. He slowly extended his left foot halfway down to the third step, and then quickly transferred his left hand from a baluster on the second step to one on the third step. The furrowed brow eased a little. Next moves: let the left foot come down flat onto the third stair, bring the right foot down to join its mate, and then transfer hands to the next baluster down respectively.

By now I could relax a little—and even allow myself to enjoy Red's wonderful accomplishment. Despite his fear, despite the near fall, using the resources of his own unique temperament, he'd been able to figure out how to make this crablike descent actually work. I was impressed, so was he! "That's great. You figured out how to go down sideways. A grand idea." Big grin.

I thought he might be tired out enough by the effort to ask for a free ride, but no, he kept going. How many more steps before he'd quit the field? Red looked up and grinned. Proud of himself, he showed no signs of wearying. And then he started on the next stair, fully conscious of his own achievement and eager to demonstrate it. "Down"—clearly a command for me to get out of his way. It's a steep stairway, three flights, with two landings per flight, eighteen stairs per flight. He negotiated every single one of them. It took a long time to get down, but he went all the way to the bottom of the staircase that day.

Needless to say it was quite a while before I let him do the stairs without supervision, but he had certainly proved his point. He knew that he had the physical abilities, but more important, when he didn't get it quite right on the first trial and nearly fell, he had the self-calming and self-control skills to be able to regain both his emotional and physical equilibrium and then to figure out a new approach. I don't think anyone in New England was more proud that morning than Red—with the possible exception of his father.

Many parents have confided that in trying to put these ideas about self-calming and self-control to work in the lives of their children, they have moments of feeling that they lack such skills themselves, so they experience embarrassment, even jealousy. I've felt like that too, as the story about Red's triumph on the staircase certainly reveals. Although I wish that my own skills in these areas were more developed, I do think, as the Peter DeVries quote at the beginning of the book suggests, that parenting can be a growing-up process for the adult that is every bit as profound as childhood and adolescence are for the child. Self-calming and self-control build over a lifetime— therefore parents at twenty or thirty or forty or fifty shouldn't feel so defensive about not having perfected them. Similarly, they should not despair if their child has yet to master the rudiments of these skills.

Achieving self-control is a particularly gradual—and personal—process. Unlike self-calming, which can for example yield dramatic behavioral results within twenty-four hours in a colicky child, the results for the child who is learning self-control tend to come in unpredictable fits and starts. They *do* come eventually, but there will be days when you'll wonder whether it's really worth the effort. I certainly do. On the other hand I know that it's even more difficult—and less rewarding for both Red and me—if I try to control all of his choices for him. That mode of parenting is based on the erroneous assumption that the child isn't competent to make decisions. Inevitably this results in one developmental crisis after another as the child seeks to have some say in his own life. These stabs at autonomy are difficult for many parents to accept, for they themselves have probably been raised to believe that the child does what the parent says "because I say so, that is why." That style of parenting, however, removes the "self" from self-control. By following the principles I advocate, the kids don't run the family, but they don't salute and click their heels either. The parent establishes the boundaries, reinforcing them with discipline, and within those boundaries the child is free to act. The end result is what I call socially acceptable behavior. Thus the parent has the security of knowing the child will make a choice she can live with, and the child has the security of knowing that his competence has been acknowledged. This leads to greater feelings of love and respect for each other on both sides. In short, everyone is much happier.

Reminders About Self-Control

- Self-control is what enables a child to explore her environment effectively and enjoyably, and to make good decisions on the basis of those explorations. Parents can help this process by establishing clear limits, which define physical safety and social acceptability, within which those explorations and choices can proceed.

▪ Self-control is a measure of competence, and it enhances competence. The parent's role is to convey to the child that he believes in her competence, which he does by acting as her ally when she declares "I wanna do it myself."

▪ The parent's belief in the child's competence is conveyed not just with verbal messages, but by a careful balance of intervening and stepping back. Rescue statements and actions, when the child has not asked for help, always say to the child that the adult doesn't think she's capable.

▪ Once safety limits have been set, the child should be allowed to try what she wants to do—with supervision. If she fails, with no signs of learning from the experience, then you're justified in saying no to further efforts at that time. If she asks for help, then a parent should do only what's necessary to enable the child to meet her goal, but avoid doing it for her.

▪ Reinforcing self-control demands a lot of parents. They may have to accept that their child uses techniques which are quite different from the ones that work for themselves.

▪ The process of acquiring self-control enhances the young child's self-esteem. The result is fewer developmental crises and less emotional trauma. Family life is happier and more stable, its ties more enduring.

Self-Entertainment

Even the most responsive parent can't be on call all of the time. So what happens when social attention, one of a child's prime motivators, is unavailable? Ideally, after the initial protest (probably some crying or yelling), the child turns quickly to self-entertainment. When you're in the middle of setting up your three-year-old with his finger paints, for example, and your eleven-month-old wakes from her nap hungry and in want of company, she first calms herself down and stops crying after you call out to her that you'll come get her as soon as you can, for she surely understands the verbal reassurance if not the words themselves. And then, while waiting the additional eight minutes it takes you to finish with her brother, she figures out a way to keep herself occupied. Perhaps she'll play with a crib toy or a stuffed animal, but it's equally likely she'll practice standing and walking in her crib, because the acquisition of new skills can be just as entertaining to a child as any of the expensive "educational" toys.

Red, for example, was as excited and absorbed by the process of learning to walk those stairs as he would have been by any game he could have played. Of course, self-entertainment in those circumstances does involve the parents, since no child can learn skills like stair-walking without careful adult supervision. Many forms of self-entertainment, however, including the acquisition of various skills, can be done completely autonomously (though they all depend on the child's having gotten plenty of feedback and support on occasions when she needed it).

Self-entertainment tends to follow self-calming and self-control, but not in a true progression, since the child doesn't complete the mastery of one and then go on to the next. All of them are skills that she will spend a lifetime expanding and perfecting. Though there is no strict time sequence to their development, self-calming is always the first to be undertaken, and self-entertainment usually becomes possible only when the child has the rudiments of self-calming and self-control. Nonetheless, I've seen a child as young as seven weeks old entertain herself, and also had the pleasure of watching the same child—Sarah—continue to develop her skills in all three areas over several years. At three, Sarah is able to find entertainment in many situations—at her day-care group, with her friends, her parents, even her baby brother.

Recently I paid a visit to her home and saw her wander out of her room after waking from her nap, just as her mother started to nurse her six-week-old brother. Sarah wanted attention. Under these circumstances some mothers might try to read or otherwise engage the three-year-old while nursing the baby, but Sarah's mom knows that such a disruption would mean that she wouldn't be able to keep her mind on either the nursing or the reading, with the result that both the baby and Sarah would be unhappy. She tells Sarah that she has to feed Matthew now but that she will come play with her for a little while afterward. Fortunately Sarah has good self-entertainment skills and she also remembers that yesterday her mother had finished playing blocks with her and made the baby wait when he woke up from *his* nap (intentionally giving him a chance to exercise his self-calming ability), so she goes back to her room, where fifteen minutes later her mother finds her talking animatedly into her plastic telephone with her imaginary friend Booboo.

As we'll see many times over in the course of the book, self-entertainment is extremely important to the child. It's invaluable if he likes to stay up late or wake up early, and particularly if he's trying to adjust to the competition for your attention caused by the arrival of a new sibling. Practically speaking, being able to self-entertain results in behaviors like the following:

- The six-month-old, frustrated with his inability to crawl, diverts himself by grabbing a toy and playing with it, or investigating the pattern printed on his blanket, or finding some other new activity to keep himself busy during the ten-minute break he takes from his crawling efforts.

- The one-year-old, unwilling to go to sleep when you decide it's bedtime, sits in his crib chattering to himself for over an hour before deciding it's sleep time. When he does finally lie down, there's little or no fussing or crying.

■ The eighteen-month-old rides in the back of the car in his car seat for three hours, looking out the window, talking to you, pointing out cloud formations, eating bananas and graham crackers, while you're able to spend much of your time having a conversation with your husband.

■ The two-year-old who's been told you need to spend the next two hours working on a project of your own looks at picture books or rearranges his wooden train track until you're finished.

■ The twenty-six-month-old flying from Chicago to San Francisco goes to sit with the three-year-old across the aisle when the little girl's mother invites him. Rather than being frightened and unsure of strangers, he's happy to make a new acquaintance, so long as you say it's okay.

■ The thirty-month-old who by accident knocks a glass off the table with his ball (it nearly breaks) puts the glass back on the table and gets down on his hands and knees, saying, "I roll the ball on the floor," thus creating a new activity for himself instead of doing something destructive to get your attention.

All these examples illustrate both self-control and self-entertainment, since they all require that the child have enough emotional equilibrium to look within himself for the way to deal with a potentially upsetting, frustrating, boring, frightening, or lonely situation.

Situations like these arise dozens of times a day in every family. The child whose upbringing is based on the assumption that he is totally helpless and that his parents must therefore supply his every need will feel constant insecurity each time he's left on his own. Because his parents accept the current dogma that a one- or two-year-old cannot entertain himself, they are unlikely to provide opportunities which allow him to create his own diversions and games to fill the time. All he'll know is how to turn on the TV/VCR or play with expensive toys that open, whir, or percolate when the switch is thrown—usually by an adult. But the child whose parents have encouraged him to self-entertain is able to sit down with a big paper bag from the grocery store and make a cave out of it, engage in conversation with a stuffed animal, or invent other simple games with whatever is at hand—and then to feel proud of himself for what he's done, rather than unhappy about having to play by himself.

You will of course want to make sure that your house has been made childproof so that he won't do himself any harm if left on his own for periods of time. Among the many things you should do are install gates at stairways and grates at any open windows he can get to, remove breakables from tabletops and other surfaces within reach, place guards over electrical outlets, store carefully any poisonous substances or dangerous objects like knives or hammers or other tools. You want to feel confident that you have protected your child.

Don't mistake leaving the child on his own for ignoring him. This is not a question of parking a kid in front of a TV, which is what the overburdened parents of completely dependent children often resort to doing. Instead you must spend considerable time cultivating his inner resourcefulness and creativity, so that during those inevitable periods when you can't spend time with him, he'll know how to be an active participant in his own enjoyment—not just a passive recipient of whatever is on the tube. Your willingness to be actively engaged with him during the hours you do spend together is crucial.

This means that rather than just flipping the switch, you become enthusiastically engaged in his world. If he's done a series of twelve crayon drawings while you were reading the last of the papers you had to grade today, then take the time to look at them carefully when you've finished your work. Don't just tell him they're all pretty. Get involved. Talk about why you like some better than others, go into details about the colors and shapes, or better yet ask him which ones he really likes and why. If he's just built a tower of blocks, ask him why he made it so tall (or short, or straight, or crooked). Remark on how happy he's made the cat by petting her and talking softly to her instead of pulling her tail and yelling in her ear. Tell him how much you admire him for being able to play on his own and being so inventive.

What you don't have to do is spend a lot of money. Every fall I talk with parents about the type of gifts that might be appropriate during the holiday season. And every January I hear stories which confirm that it's the simple toys, the ones that allow the child to supply the imagination and make things happen, that are the best. Children want to be the actors, not the reactors. They want to create something they can show off to others, since it affords another opportunity for social contact while giving a boost to their self-esteem. Simple toys, like blocks, paper, crayons, old pots and pans, dolls, even a blanket which can become a tent or a cardboard box that's suddenly a store, a train station, or a hotel, are what make the holiday season and every other day so much fun.

If you hear yourself saying about your child, "She can't be by herself at all; I have to give her something new to do every ten minutes," then you should rethink your approach. Have you ever watched a cat play with an old wool sock, instead of whatever they're pushing at the pet shop this week? Why not give your child credit for possessing as much imagination as the average cat? Your child, like every child, does have the ability to entertain herself, if only you will believe in it and foster it. The following observations may help you do this.

Reminders about Self-Entertainment

- The ability to self-entertain is one of the most important capabilities a child can acquire. It is the foundation for a lifetime of protection against loneliness, boredom, and low self-esteem.

▪ Parents facilitate the ability to self-entertain by being intensely involved with their child when time is available, not by ignoring her or saying "That's nice" whenever they can put her off no longer. That means giving lots of feedback and showing genuine interest in her activities.

▪ Self-entertainment does not require expensive or elaborate toys. It requires a safe environment in which the child can wander at will, and plenty of simple raw materials on which the imagination can act—blocks, crayons, paper, pots and pans, wooden spoons, whatever else is at hand that is safe and potentially interesting to a child. Don't underestimate the potential of either the person or the object.

▪ Self-entertainment depends on the creativity which is present in all children. Don't thwart it by making your child feel that she's dependent for her enjoyment on you, the television, or a fancy toy.

The main deterrent to encouraging the skills of self-calming, self-control, and self-entertainment is the parent's belief that the child is a helpless, dependent creature. I hope I have convinced you that this is false.

Remember: more than anything else it's the capacity for self-regulation that determines what happens to a person in life, not unconditional parental love, socioeconomic status, or any of the other currently popular candidates. Encouraging this capacity in our children is the greatest gift we can give them. To do this, however, we must be clear about our goals as parents—which is the subject of the next chapter. Only then will we be able to throw our energies into making "I wanna do it myself" a reality—to the great joy of our children, and, ultimately, ourselves as well.

Parenting:
What's Your Goal?

What's your goal as a parent? That may strike you as an odd question. Most would simply answer, "I try to do what's best for my child—whatever will help him enjoy a happy, successful life." But what that translates into each day depends on your view of childhood.

If you, like most adults, characterize a six-month-old, even a one- or two-year-old, in terms of his dependencies, then you will probably see parenthood as requiring nothing less than a total dedication to this endlessly needy child whom you have brought into the world. This means that you have an awesome responsibility—in fact, too awesome for anyone to live up to, which makes failure certain.

Alternatively, if you are able to look beyond the conventional view of children to see their many competencies, to focus on what they can do rather than what they can't, then your goals, hence your whole way of parenting, change accordingly. You will view yourself as the facilitator, not the cause, of your child's progress through life. Acknowledging the limits of your role—a very difficult thing for a parent to do—also spells relief from an unnecessary burden of responsibility.

I don't endorse the idea of sacrificing oneself for one's child, because in the long run it never pays off for anybody. There's too much resentment on the parent's part, guilt on the child's. I don't want relations with my child in later life to be based on feelings of obligation and indebtedness—on either side. Only when the self-sacrifice model of parenting is abandoned in favor of what I call the mutual-gain model can the family as a whole, and everyone in it, thrive despite the other pressures and demands of modern life.

"Mutual gain." Sounds too good to be true, doesn't it? I admit that many days I have to overcome my own neuroses to believe in it, let alone make it work, but it can be done.

I actually first heard the phrase in McAllen, Texas, where I had gone to give a talk on self-calming and self-esteem. Some thirty or so concerned and committed parents had come to a seminar after the general presentation. As I was answering questions, a sudden hush fell over the crowd at the approach of an elderly woman who came forward and introduced herself. At eighty-three she was still working part-time as a psychologist, but this was not the authority she invoked for the message she wanted to give me: "Young man, over the last sixty years I've watched five children, fourteen grandchildren, and now even some of my great-grandchildren grow up, and I've listened to what all the greats have to say about child rearing—Jung, Skinner, Gesell, Spock, Brazelton, Leach, White, Gordon, and Dreikurs. But you're the only one who understands children *and parents* [her emphasis] well enough to make any sense. If parents follow your advice, then no one's self-interest is sacrificed, no one feels beholden, and there are no long-term debts in the family, which is what keeps psychologists like me busy. What you've constructed is a way to create a family life which is based on mutual gain."

She then turned and walked away, using two canes for support, and leaving a momentary silence in her wake.

It was only hours later, as I was traveling alone on an airplane, that I realized how important this concept really is, and how I'd been undermining it by the way I presented my ideas. In my eagerness to tell parents what I myself was only just beginning to understand about the incredible abilities of even newborn infants, I'd been using phrases like "children's rights." I did and still do sincerely believe that we owe our children help in enhancing their innate self-sufficiency through skills such as self-calming, self-control, and the ability to self-entertain. It does seem to me like one of their fundamental rights, as important as food, clothing, or a good education, and something which every parent, and every society, is obligated to provide. Nor do I see this in terms of the totally independent individual who does everything on her own. This is a process that is a joint achievement of parent and child. Children can ask for assistance, and when they do they should get it.

But to talk to parents about children's rights makes it sound as if parent and child are in an adversary relationship, which is not at all what I mean. Suddenly I was beginning to understand the ambivalent reaction of some of my listeners. Not only did the children they'd brought into the world have rights, but these rights seemed to be in direct conflict with the emotional satisfactions they had expected from their role as parents. While almost all parents acknowledged that my ideas were in the best interest of the child, they were worried about what it would mean for their own lives if they changed the way they were parenting. What was their role, if not as the ultimate authority, control, and safeguard in the life of their child?

Part of the security and attraction of being a parent for many people is that it does give them such an important position. Questions about their worth and identity that have not been satisfactorily answered in other areas of life—career, relations

with friends, family, spouse, and religion—may seem to be resolved once a child arrives. Parenthood looks like a kind of
personal safety net, guaranteeing one's stature as the most important figure in the world to at least one other person—one's
child. The next step in this kind of thinking is to believe that
a parent's entire life must be dedicated to helping this child.
Unfortunately, justifying every decision that is made on the
basis that it's for the good of the child is often a way of rationalizing
what's good for the parent. The parent's safety net is the child's
trap.

Parents who attempt to do everything for their offspring
are likely to come up against a defiant, rebellious person, and
to become angry and estranged themselves when they hear the
"I wanna do it myself" refrain once too often. They may feel
rejected by their child's need to be self-sufficient—and their
perception is accurate: they *are* being rejected, because they are
blocking the realization of one of the child's most fundamental
needs.

There is nothing inevitable about this conflict, although
it is currently accepted as part of normal development. In my
view we can no longer ignore the role played by parents in
producing the negativism of the two-year-old, the revolt of the
adolescent, and, ultimately, the ingratitude of the grown child
who somehow never repays the parents with the kind of financial
and emotional support to which they feel themselves entitled
after so many years of sacrifice.

Parents who become their child's allies in making the desire
for autonomy a reality, however, are much more likely to receive
the love and attention we all want from our children. The two-
year-old, for example, is not inherently terrible. He can be very
loving and affectionate, but he will best love those people who
help him to do things on his own, not those who do things for
him. He wants a catalyst, a facilitator, not an all-powerful parent
who is constantly blocking the path to self-sufficiency.

To redefine the goal in parenting as catalyst of change and

accomplishment, rather than cause, is a very formidable task. I've seen how much others have had to struggle to do it, and I know what a struggle it's been for me as well. After all, the catalyst is important in the life of his or her child, but not indispensable or irreplaceable. Even to write that hits me in the gut, hard. Now that I've faced these conflicts as a parent myself, I understand firsthand the feelings of loss and confusion parents had when I presented them with what I thought were the "magic answers" to such problems as separation anxiety, the terrible twos, the transition to adolescence, and so forth— especially because I always described my philosophy of child rearing in terms of children's rights.

What about parents? Don't we have any rights? And if so, isn't it a violation of those rights to have to give our children the kind of autonomy I am describing? The underlying answer is that it is not ours to give; if not acknowledged, it will simply be seized, sooner or later, and at however great a cost of pain, anger, resentment and long-term damage to the relationship. That was how I tended to answer my critics in the early years. But my friend in McAllen, Texas, gave me a new way to think about family life and what it can mean for parents. "Mutual gain," she said, and the more I thought about it, the more I could see how right she was, and how helpful her idea could be for today's parents.

Regardless of whether we still believe in previous generations' models of child rearing, parenting in this country is changing because, socially and economically, our circumstances are changing. Today's parents are open to new models of parenting. They have to be. What does this mean in practical terms? Well, fifteen years ago I never expected to see fathers coming in to the intensive care nursery at five A.M. to feed a baby, as many of them do now on a daily basis. Fifteen years ago if you'd told me that I myself would be home in 1990 with a two-year-old while my wife was on a two-week business trip to the Far East, I would have been willing to place a sizable wager against it. If you had suggested that that would happen when my son was five months old, I would have confidently told you to get a new crystal ball. But I would have been one hundred percent wrong.

Breaking out of the restrictive and discriminatory models of being a mother or a father has parallels with other changes that have taken place in society during the last forty years. Life is different from what I remember as a child in North Carolina. Blacks don't have to sit in the back of the bus, women aren't limited to being housewives and mothers, and men aren't relegated to the position of breadwinner—and second-class parent. But the average two-year-old still faces as much prejudice and skepticism about her abilities as she ever did. Perhaps this is because we still cling to the old stereotypes of family life, so that at the same time that our practical approach to parenting has changed, out of necessity, our notions of children as totally helpless and dependent on their parents live on—thus preventing family life from being as rewarding as it could be. If we could acknowledge that there was nothing inevitable or even normal about the parenting models of the generations just preceding ours, then I think we might be able to live more comfortably with our own ways of doing things. It would be helpful, as a first step, if we recalled that it was only in the affluent years following World War II that large numbers of women were encouraged to remain in their homes and devote themselves exclusively to their families. For many women who had done whatever they had to to supplement the family earnings during the Depression, or had worked at "men's jobs" Rosie-the-Riveter style to help the war effort, the opportunity to stay at home full time must have looked good. Unlike previous generations of women who played multiple roles in a more agrarian, less urban and suburbanized society, however, they were expected to stay in those homes, mopping floors till they glowed, baking cookies, turning out babies, and tending to them.

Caring for these babies was their job in life, and a whole

mythology about the irreplaceability of the mother in the emotional life of the child supported this approach to parenting. In retrospect, it's now possible to understand that we mistakenly extrapolated from the physical dependence of the infant to a belief in his helplessness on all fronts. From there it was an easy leap to the belief that only a mother who was available to her child twenty-four hours of the day could satisfy the child's emotional needs. Reciprocally, only complete helplessness on the part of the child could validate the kind of total commitment that was expected of the mother. So there was a certain symmetry, even symbiosis, in these views. Having been denied the self-esteem one gains through playing any other valuable role in society, women as much as anyone else needed to believe in their children's absolute dependence on them.

Unfortunately the scientific/technological approach to the field of child development that prevailed during the 1960s reinforced this view. A cataloguing held sway over the supposedly universal stages of maturation through which every child marched, complete with descriptions of how crucial the mother's role was at each of these plateaus. Little attention was paid to the role of the father (or other family members), or to what children wanted and could legitimately be expected to do for themselves.

During the last two decades we have learned, and only because economic necessity has forced change upon us, how limiting this primary-parent role was. Mothers wanted more out of life than motherhood, and fathers wanted to be more than breadwinners. But perhaps the real victims were children. Ultimately the belief in their helplessness was most stifling to them.

Now both parents typically work outside the house, single-parent families are more and more the norm, and there's even the occasional role switch whereby the man stays home with the children while his wife works in another location. With these changes has come the opportunity to reexamine many of our old ideas about parenthood. And lo and behold, they're not as graven in stone as we'd thought.

On the one hand this reexamination has been exciting; on the other it's been scary. Change of this magnitude brings so much uncertainty. As the father of a five-year-old and husband of a woman whose job has less potential for flexibility than my own we have decided that I should generally be the one to stay home with our son when he's sick or on vacation from school. A typical day begins with my editor calling to ask where the next chapter is (she's understandably not interested in hearing how difficult it is to get even one page written on a rainy, chilly day when Red can't go out to play), and ends with my lying awake, staring at the ceiling, wondering how well I did as a father during the preceding sixteen hours. So I know how real the challenges of this new freedom are. Working out your own variations on how you choose to play your roles as parents, while balancing those roles with career goals and the economic realities of putting food on the table tomorrow and sending children to college a decade or two from tomorrow—these are challenges that do not guarantee a sound sleep every night. But they are liberating. For everybody.

That's not to say that there wasn't a certain allure to the exclusive mother-child relationship. It was the power and privilege of this relationship that induced many women to stay home and accept the stifling gender roles of the 1950s. If it had turned out that their presence there was not absolutely necessary, and yet there were no satisfying alternatives for them in the outside world, what role would they have had in life? Similarly, it was the purported special quality of this relationship that made so many men resist the changes that have occurred in family life, the workplace, and society as a whole during the last twenty years. Having failed to develop any special place in the lives of their children during the critical early years, they weren't about to give up being king of the household and lord of the office, no matter how emotionally hollow these roles might have been. After all, what else was there for them? No wonder it's taken so long to realize the benefits to both parents of rethinking the parent-child relationship.

Finally, perhaps the most upsetting emotional barrier to men and women revising their personal definition of what it means to be a parent has been the fear engendered by numerous writers' declarations that the infant learns to trust because the mother is always available. As any parent knows, however, the practical realities of life make the ideal of perpetual availability totally impossible. Nevertheless, mothers struggle mightily to realize it, making nervous, guilty wrecks of themselves and doing their children no favor either. In fact, rather than creating trust and security, this type of upbringing often burdens the children just as much as it does the mothers. Any child who's become accustomed to the more or less constant presence of mom will protest violently when she's not there. If she so much as leaves the room, much less leaves for the night or—worse yet—goes on vacation, the child who many psychologists call "securely attached" will scream, protest, often refuse to eat, and no doubt sleep poorly. Ironically, the constant togetherness of mother and child results in the very separation anxiety that it's supposed to alleviate, or even prevent. But children aren't born that needy— they're made needy.

The child whose innate competence is not acknowledged, who is constantly hovered over and denied any opportunity of doing things on her own, hence any feeling of achievement, will eventually become convinced of her dependence on others. "I can't cope," she internalizes. It's no wonder that she cries when her mother leaves the room; that heartrending cry which is so paralyzing, so accusing, is an expression of the gut-wrenching anxiety she feels at being left alone. It's also a quite legitimate expression of feelings of betrayal. Again, it seems to me to be a situation in which what parents see as the solution is in fact a part of the problem. If nothing else, my experience in pediatrics has taught me that neither feelings of trust nor feelings of security will be promoted by the constant-availability school of parenting.

When a baby is born, it's an alien and in many ways alarming new world for both her and her parents. There is no evidence that trust is established by anything that happens during pregnancy, delivery (including such praised practices as natural child-birth), or the first few days of life, breast-feeding, or the bonding which ethologists have noted as "imprinting" in parts of the animal world. The baby is not a gosling. She is, however, a stranger—both to the world and to you, her parents.

From my observations, it seems to me that children learn trust when they get the sense that their parents will respond to them in a predictable fashion. And the converse is true for parents as well. Trust begins to develop with the expectation that the other person will recognize and react appropriately to verbal and nonverbal signals. Security, too, is enhanced by the baby's growing realization that things she does will elicit a consistent, predictable response from those around her—and your own realization that you are an accurate interpreter of your baby's signals. But consistency is in fact undermined by a style of parenting in which the mother must eventually wean her child from the constant availability she had tried to offer in the early months or even years. Changing from "I'll always be here to take care of you" to "You're a big girl now and you have to learn to do things yourself" creates anxiety, not trust. Such a shift is inevitable if you start out by offering guarantees of availability that become increasingly impossible and inappropriate as the years pass. While trust can eventually be reestablished, it requires forgetting old precedents and establishing new ones, an emotionally exhausting process.

Consistency *is* possible with the style of parenting I recommend, which doesn't depend so much on uniformity of behavior through the years. Obviously, thousands of behaviors must change as the child grows and matures, but an unchanging commitment to helping your child master the survival skills will give her a sense of self-mastery. This begins with the self-calming that is possible in her earliest days.

Helping your child with self-calming requires learning to read her cues, which probably is the best training you could have in learning to communicate effectively with her. Listening to her cries to become familiar with which one means "I'm hungry" and which one "I'm tired" or "I'm cold" or "I'm wet," observing her visual response to people and objects so that you know how much distance is comfortable for her in face-to-face interactions and which things are soothing for her to look at, becoming sensitive to the body signals that she gives so that you get her into bed before she becomes too disorganized and exhausted to be able to self-calm—all these are wonderful aspects of learning to communicate with your child. "Maternal instinct" is much overrated. Why operate on instinct when, by careful observation of your child, you can get her to *tell* you what she wants rather than having to guess at it? This ability to read cues makes things easier on both parent and child, and being able to communicate with each other so effectively also helps you to trust each other, since you know what to expect, and to be secure in your feelings about yourselves, since you each have a wonderful feeling of competence.

It's true that not all infants have uniformly readable behavior cues or the same range of identifiable cry messages (as I discussed in *The Self-Calmed Baby*). Some babies are much harder to get to know than others. But again, maternal instinct is not the best way to compensate for this indecipherable behavior. Patient observation is better than random guesswork, and this often involves a willingness not to intervene too quickly. Every week I hear distressing tales of parents who are up all night with fussy infants. A much better way to help their children would be learning to wait until the baby either self-calms or gives them a recognizable cry that tells them what intervention is necessary. Hard as it may be to believe, it is possible to increase a child's predictability by simply waiting for further cues about what it is she really wants.

Unfortunately, the protector role most parents have been encouraged to assume doesn't allow for this kind of restraint. If you leap up and run to your child the instant she makes a sound, you deprive both of you of the opportunity to learn to communicate effectively. There are of course considerations of physical safety that must be taken into account—I'm not suggesting that you restrain yourself from intervening if there is any question whatsoever about illness or danger—and I realize that for first-time parents there's a fear that any cry may be a signal of serious distress. So it'll take a while to get over the panic. But that is the goal—for your own well-being as well as your child's.

Ultimately the child's security will not come from knowing that you will be there to offer protection against every minor problem, from the slightest pang of hunger to the cuts and scrapes of early walking days. Though every parent seeks to minimize danger, there's not a two-year-old in the world who doesn't know that no one can protect her from falling, or magically make the pain of an earache go away. If security depended on never facing difficulty, no child would ever feel secure. It's better not even to try to offer that kind of protection (if only because your child needs to *know* when to feel fearful or anxious, so she can learn how to deal with the inevitable problems she'll face). The best way of enhancing feelings of security is to teach your child the skills, beginning with self-calming, self-control, and self-entertainment, that will make her feel capable of dealing with problems on her own, while always letting her know that help is there if she needs it.

Mutual trust and security are not promoted by dependency, but by the parent's belief in the innate competence of the child, and the child's feeling that her parent is doing everything possible to facilitate that competence—which is the purpose of the survival skills I write about in this book. A feeling of control over her own environment is what the child most longs for, and what those skills will give her. In fact, much of what we call separation anxiety seems to me to be a control issue. It's a given that the child will not want her primary caretaker—mom, dad, or whoever—to leave the room. After all, that's her most important social relationship. So until she starts playing the sophisticated push-pull games of the two- and three-year-old set, she's not likely to invite or welcome mom's departure. In fact, even in families who have cultivated good self-regulatory skills in their children, there is likely to be an initial howl of protest from the one-year-old when mom does leave. For the child who does not have these skills, whose parent has set herself up more as protector than facilitator, the cries are likely to go on much longer. But are they really cries of fear and anxiety? Or is something else as well? Let's look at a typical scene.

"But I can't stand not to be with her. What if she needs something? I feel like I should always be there." It was the last appointment of the day, and Alison was at the door leading into the hall while her mother talked of the conflicts of feeling the requirement to be everpresent, but having no life of her own. (Alison was a sprightly little girl whose idea of a long nap was forty-five minutes on a good day, but those days were alternate Thursdays of the Blue Moon.) Nancy did have a good case for feeling tired and trapped. She was always on call.

"What happens when you leave the room?"

"Sooner or later she cries. It varies."

"Well, what is she saying?"

"I always think she's mad because I'm not there. I never hear anything else. I just respond immediately."

"Instant service?" Nancy was certainly attentive and available. Alison was now out in the hallway pursuing small pickings from the carpet.

"Maybe. She always stops as soon as I enter the room, even if I don't do anything like pick her up or talk to her. That says to me she feels abandoned."

I was about to add that Alison's recovery seemed a little quick if she actually felt abandoned, a feeling that would provoke truly anxious crying and would not subside with just an appearance at the door. While I saw the instant shut-off as a sign that Alison simply wanted to be in control of her mother's every move, Nancy took it as an indication of her absolute indispensability. At the same time she realized she also heard the trapdoor on the rest of her life slam and lock. I had no other explanation to give her so I tried a different approach, literally following Alison's lead. As she inched out of sight, one orange sock still visible in the door, I asked with as much innocence as I could muster, "Does she ever leave you?"

"No, but I keep the door upstairs blocked with the pillow, and there are gates on the kitchen, so she doesn't have much chance. Why?"

"Well, if she leaves on her own, then it would seem to belie the idea that she has separation anxiety."

Nancy looked around. "Where is she?"—worry having replaced the whole gist of the conversation. She started out of her chair toward the door.

"Wait. She's out in the hall. The doors to the exam rooms are all shut. She can't get beyond Denise and Marguerite at the front desk." It wouldn't be the first time a crawling infant or a toddler had played out this scenario in the office, so the two ladies were used to such impromptu social visits.

"She just left?"

"Yep, and I'll bet she'll be quite happy if you facilitate these explorations at home. Let her crawl around—just poison/ accident-proof the place. You'll see her come and go, not that she values the relationship any less. And hopefully you can get back to a normal amount of freedom and initiative in your half of the relationship as well." Alison on cue appeared at the door, clearly delighted with her foray. "See, she can even find her way back."

If you watch closely, you'll see this happening over and over again at the classic age of separation anxiety. Clearly the reaction to separation varies with *who controls it*. More often than not, when mom leaves, the child will protest: I didn't give you permission. That's an attempt to exert social control. But she loves crawling off on her own. That's *self*-control.

Unfortunately, for many families the age of separation anxiety, typically commencing at nine to twelve months, never ends. Every week at Red-Tae (see addendum, page 294.) I get calls for help from parents who have a three- or four-year-old whom they can't leave or can leave only at the expense of great emotional travail. These are parents who have been available, have been responsive. As I've heard over and over again, "I did everything I was told was right." They were just never told to listen to the child's request to help her do it herself.

If neither parents nor children believe in children's competence everybody pays a heavy price—the parents in ways that severely limit both their emotional and professional lives, the children perhaps even more profoundly. Anxious and fearful, children suffer through sleep problems, act out more often, and stage self-destructive adolescent revolts. They also have to struggle all the harder to become self-sufficient. Nor are their problems at an end once they achieve adulthood. Aside from the psychic scars this kind of upbringing can create, they have a lifelong debt to repay their parents. After all, these were parents who invested everything in their children, as many an obligatory Mother's Day or Father's Day card is quick to acknowledge.

Of course, giving up these stereotypes of parenting, the ones we experienced as children, entails developing our own ways of doing it. This process means fathers have to understand that they have an active role to play at every stage of their children's lives, and mothers have to acknowledge the competence of both father and child, thus escaping the impossible burden of taking on too many roles. Children too will face challenges. I don't pretend that your two-year-old will applaud the idea of your leaving her with her godparents while you go on vacation. But if you have worked together on the self-calming, self-control, and self-entertainment skills she needs, you won't worry so much when she protests, because you know she has the ability to handle the situation. Like any person who faces the absence of a significant other, a child has feelings of loneliness, but that doesn't have to mean experiencing abandonment. Even a one-

or two-year-old who possesses the survival skills can cope—I've seen hundreds of children over the last decade who aren't traumatized or distraught by their parents' short-term absences. You may not feel like a savior when you walk in the door after that vacation, especially if your child decides to punish you by giving you the cold shoulder and holding on tight to her godfather, but it won't be long before she's hugging and kissing you and telling you what a wonderful time she had while you were gone.

Why do I feel so sure that this will be the outcome? Because children love experiencing their own competence. The demise of the glorified mother role, and its complement the distant, authoritarian, breadwinner father role, is as freeing for the child as it is for her parents. The child who wants to do it herself—and can, thanks to your belief in and encouragement of her—is a happy child, whether or not you're always there.

Perhaps you fear that you'll be creating a monster if you take all this stuff about your child's innate competence seriously. Don't you run the risk of having one of those obnoxious two-year-olds who dominate the dinner table (and every other aspect of adult life)? Not if you really believe she's competent, you don't. You'll see that if she's capable of controlling what happens at dinner, she's also capable of understanding discipline. Your job then is to establish and communicate the rules of mealtime behavior to her; her job is to understand and obey them. And don't underestimate your child's ability to outwit your rules—another sign of her competence. If you tell her to stop throwing her peas on the floor and she replies no, that's a sign of autonomy, which means competence, not of a failure to understand, which would be incompetence.

But you anticipate that you'll get frustrated with this response or you worry that no will become defiance, not just autonomy. What do you do to redirect this competence? That's the whole point. The two-year-old who has been taught the rules and been encouraged in the skills that will help her to make acceptable choices about her own behavior—self-calming, self-control, and self-entertainment—is likely to do so rather than to act out. She behaves not so much because she wants to please you as because she exults in her ability to make these choices.

Ultimately, that's what my ideas about parenthood boil down to—choices: the choices you can make, the choices you enable your child to make. You make personal choices about what matters to you. A three-year-old coming and going at the dinner table may not bother me at all, but be intolerable to you. You will need the courage to define your own values, and the humility to allow your children to define theirs *within acceptable limits that you have set.* It's not easy to watch your child make choices that seem to you to be the wrong ones— whether it's the method the fourteen-month-old uses to get down a flight of stairs, or the person your twenty-year-old chooses to marry. But children whose autonomy has been acknowledged from early on, and who have been enabled to make good use of it by careful fostering of their self-mastery skills, are likely to make choices which work for them and you.

I see parenting as an art form, not a science. It's sort of like cooking. The good cook feels free to adjust the specific ingredients in a recipe to his own tastes. The great one is the chef who has mastered the basic techniques of food preparation so well that he can take the raw ingredients and fashion a memorable meal without any recipes at all. Thankfully there will never be a cookbook for parents, but all parents can learn to be facilitators and life-long allies for their children. My goal in this book is to give you the techniques that have proved successful over the years. You take it from there.

I'm not pretending it's easy. Parents who grew up in the technical/scientific atmosphere of the last several decades may feel more comfortable with step-by-step approaches to child rearing based on universal stages of development that have been identified, verified, and quantified. My own feeling is that parenthood doesn't reduce quite that way. Just as there is no one right recipe for fried chicken, there's no one right response when a child wakes at three A.M.

Is your primary goal as a parent to do everything for your

child and hence have a feeling of indispensability, or to help
your child have a feeling of competence because she has learned
how much she can do for herself? If you have begun to question
the old models of parenting, and you are looking for techniques
that will provide new options, new choices at three A.M., then
I hope you'll read further. You'll see that much of the art of
parenting is learning to enjoy the abilities of your new ally—
the small child in your home who says, steadfastly and legitimately, "I wanna do it myself."

Temper Tantrums

The Grocery Store Classic

Slam. The car body rolls a bit. Shutting the door with more force than usual, you flip on the radio and try to gain a little perspective. An hour ago this had been a fabulous day. You'd gotten your work done on time and your daughter was squealing with enthusiasm to see you and chattering with delight after you picked her up at day care. You even beat the Friday afternoon rush at the market. Perhaps you didn't feel like Supermom, but everything did seem right with the world. Glancing in the rearview mirror, you ask your reflection, "Didn't I feel like that? Wasn't that today?"

But that was then and this is now. Right this minute your neck aches and your underarms are wet, and no, you can't clench your teeth any harder. Just to drive home the point, the oldies station provides an ironic choice by the Shirelles:

"Mama said there'd be days like this, there'd be days like this.
. . . ." But like what: the first part of the day, which was a
dream, or the last hour in the grocery store, which was a nightmare?

Glancing to your right, you can see two-year-old Kate looking out the window, swinging her foot in tune to the music,
licking the last crumbs of cookie off her fingers. She's not exactly
smiling, but she's certainly not contrite either.

Thwunk. The sliding door of the van shuts and you wave
at the boy who loaded the bags in the back, putting a maximum
effort into smiling politely and trying to look under control.
His expression seems to indicate that he's very relieved to get
you and your daughter out of the store at last. Apparently he's
in the group who thinks she's a brat, while the other group,
equally sizable, is undoubtedly talking right now in the checkout
line about what kind of terrible mother you must be to make
such a cute adorable little angel behave that way. Since there
are no horns on the top of her head, and regretfully no halo
either, you realize, even in your rage and humiliation, that both
groups are mistaken. But whatever the cause, this tantrum behavior can't go on. It's becoming painfully obvious to you how
child abuse can occur. Though so far you've taken all the parent
abuse she can dish out, you're not sure how much longer your
restraint can last.

The question is: Why does she do it? What's so enjoyable
about creating a scene with a tantrum? The box of cookies wasn't
really worth it, was it?

Later that evening, when Kate's in bed, you talk it over
with your husband.

"The day was going great. I was able to stay focused at
work, I didn't feel tired out, the weather was really uplifting.
Kate was in a terrific mood when I picked her up. But we had
one of those godawful scenes at the grocery store again."

"I thought the two of you were a little at odds during
dinner. So what happened?"

"Well, nothing at first—in fact things went very smoothly. We had gotten almost everything we needed and I thought we were doing a fabulous job of working as a team. Then just as we were heading for the cashier she grabbed some cookies. I told her we had cookies at home, and we weren't getting those. She went to put them back, and then started to sob, saying, 'I want these.' An older lady who heard that patted her on the head and said, 'Won't your mommy buy those for you? You're such a nice little girl. I'll bet you she'll do it if you say please.' "

"Well, Kate sure knows how to put you on the spot. I wonder if she saw the lady and then the cookies, or vice versa."

"Thankfully her ally didn't stand there to watch, but Kate turned and said, 'Please, Mommy,' clutching the box of cookies to her chest. In my most reasonable but firm manner I said no. Then she sat down in the aisle and started crying—and I don't mean whimpering. One person walked by with that incredulous look that says, 'Lady, can't you keep your kid under control?'—while someone walking the other way was wearing an expression that carried the message 'You have to be the meanest person on earth.' I figured I could give in to her and she'd stop, but I knew that wasn't right. So I said, 'Kate, put them back. You have cookies at home. I'll even let you have one before dinner.' She could tell that my offer meant as a compromise actually indicated weakening on my part, so the crying increased. That made me angry. I said, 'Fine, stay there and cry,' and started to walk down the aisle. She just sobbed and looked at me, so I pointed in the direction I was headed and kept going. As soon as I disappeared, there was a wailing of, 'Mommy, Mommy,' reverberating through the store, so I stopped while she ran to catch up."

"At least that strategy seemed to work."

"She was still clutching the cookies."

"Oh."

"If it hadn't meant coming back for a late-night trip I would have just walked out of there then, before I got angrier or more embarrassed. I took the cookies from her and went back down the aisle to put them back. Running after me she yells, 'Please, Mommy, I want the cookies,' in her best outdoor voice while making it sound like a perfectly reasonable request. People at the checkout counters were turning to look as she declares in the same loud voice, 'I hate you.' So I decided I'd have to figure out a way to handle this later, and I gave her the cookies to shut her up."

"Did she say thank you?"

"No, but the tears went to instant smiles, and she hugged my leg like I was her best all-time buddy, and I thought maybe it wasn't so terrible to have given in."

"Yeah, sometimes it just doesn't pay to fight."

"Unfortunately, this feeling didn't last long. She was parading behind me as pleased as punch carrying her cookies, when I hear this crash of boxes. I don't want to look. By now I'm so mad, nervous, and on edge that I've got the shakes."

"What had she done?"

"She'd found those candy dinosaur things she likes, pulled out a box from the bottom of the pile, and brought the next half dozen down with it. The next thing I see is Kate running down the aisle with the dinosaur box in one arm, the cookies in the other, shouting 'Mommy, dinosaurs,' like she's just discovered the New World. I wasn't going to give in on this. I told her that she had the cookies, she wasn't getting candy too. Immediately we were back to a mournful 'But I want them.' I tried to pick her up as a move of reconciliation and she pushed my face away. I think I would have smacked her except that literally everyone was watching me. It made me want to cry in desperation and scream with rage that a two-year-old could manipulate me on the public stage like that."

"I'd probably have just opened the package and given her the cookies at that point, forgetting about the promise of one when she got home. The war was over, why not let the battle go too?"

"I did just that but it made me feel terrible, even though she was instantly Ms. Congeniality, flirting with everyone, contentedly munching cookies. When we got in the car, I was fit to be tied, but she was smiling, and kicking her feet in time to the music on the radio. She knew I was mad, so she pretended to ignore me, but more in a way to say that she was putting me in my place than that she was worried about my being upset with her."

"It's funny how she can calm herself down so fast. She works herself into such a state that I'm sure people think we've been beating her at home, or that she's so starved for attention that she has to focus on getting the cookies, since she can't get what she really needs, and then she's all smiles as soon as she gets what she wants. It all makes you wonder what you're doing as a parent."

"I just don't get what's happening. If she's really upset or really not getting something she needs emotionally, how come she can turn off the waterworks so fast? A cookie can't make up for love and attention."

"I don't think that she lacks for love or attention. She gets tons of both—and cookies."

"Part of me says you're right, but then why this kind of behavior? What's her motivation? Why are tantrums worth it? I can't believe this is really all about cookies."

What Causes Tantrums?

Practically every parent I know has had moments of wondering whether tantrums are simply inevitable—one of those awful but inescapable burdens of parenthood—or whether they're a sign of some deep psychological problem. After all, they're so intense it's hard to believe the child is not in some serious distress. And if there isn't an underlying trauma of some sort, then why doesn't negative reinforcement put an end to the problem? Why

do children persist in these displays in the face of parental opposition—which is often just as intense as the tantrum itself? Is
something wrong with these children? Does Kate's saying "I
hate you" mean that there is a serious flaw in the parent-child
relationship?

For a long time in the 1970s and early 1980s I wondered
if these conclusions weren't true, since I didn't know how else
to account for what was happening. Certainly the form of the message—the screaming and yelling and kicking and head-beating
—was inappropriate, but perhaps the message itself was legitimate.

I was in good company with this kind of thinking. Doctors
and social workers and psychologists are always ready to blame
parents, and parents are so fearful of making mistakes they're
only too ready to be blamed. So parents played along—especially
parents who were trying out new ways of doing things, with
both parents working outside the home or the mother going
off to work and the father staying home with the child. Everybody
was feeling so insecure about these changes, and how they might
affect a child's long-term development, that people forgot that
tantrums had been around long before the social changes that
were supposedly causing them. And there were certainly plenty
of strident voices and critical glares, coming from everyone from
Grandmother to Phyllis Schlafly, to reinforce all the doubts that
any parent in such circumstances might have had. "Of course
your child is desperate for attention" was the message given. A
child needs a full-time mother—not a live-in or day care or
even a father. How would a man know what to do with a child?

I for one began to doubt the conventional wisdom. Like
Kate's parents, I felt that if tantrums such as Kate's bravura
performance in the grocery store could be settled with first the
purchase and then the consumption of a cookie, it was unlikely
that the underlying cause was real emotional distress. On the
other hand, there did seem to be some evidence that if the so-
called natural order was restored, things got better. Many concerned parents changed their behavior, some even left jobs that

they enjoyed, and they did report changes. The tantrums decreased, and in the initial elation, they felt that the decision to spend more time at home was the right one. But the euphoria never seemed to last long. Soon—sometimes within days, occasionally weeks—I'd be getting the same panicked calls. Parents were more confused than ever. Anytime their attention was directed elsewhere or they tried to stand fast on a limit, the tantrums returned. Once again they were caught facing their own familiar reincarnation of Napoleon, only this time no one was betting on the outcome at Waterloo.

Neither the traditional family arrangements nor the unconventional ones resulted in a solution to the problem. Between myself and these caring parents we came up with endless variations on positive and negative reinforcement. There were star charts and other gimmicks to acknowledge individual actions, and even more elaborate schemes to reward good behavior for three or four days in a row. Alternatively, sometimes we put the emphasis on punishment for bad behavior, rather than rewards for good, so each tantrum episode would result in a loss of bedtime stories, no TV, no computer time, and so forth in some graduated hierarchy of deprivation we adults thought made sense. But whether the system was skewed toward reward or punishment, the results were always mixed. When the tantrums continued, as they nearly always did, we'd have long discussions about how to calibrate incentives and/or disincentives more exactly. Was one cookie enough of a reward, or did such behavior deserve two cookies? Should a minor tantrum be punished by one hour of no TV, or the entire evening? Why did the whole system usually collapse around birthdays and the Christmas/Hanukkah season, and what did it mean that in certain situations, with specific people around, tantrums never occurred, regardless of reward and/or punishment? And what was the best move when parents admitted that they couldn't do the impossible—trying to ignore tantrums when all else failed? It was questions like these that devoured hours of office time and kept me awake many nights too.

Sooner or later many of these parents, especially those who

had made big sacrifices, would say "Enough." There would be a major attempt at reassertion of parental authority—or what people thought of as authority. If spending more time with the child and transgressing more limits hadn't made up for the supposed parent neglect, maybe what the child needed was more direction. People who had been very giving in every sense of the word suddenly felt they should now be sterner. If they just said no and meant it, perhaps that would make the child obey. It didn't, but you couldn't blame them for trying. Others, unable to make such a reversal, tried ignoring the behaviors, but, much like Kate's mother they found that an unworkable solution too. Perhaps, as many experts said, tantrum-throwing really was a phase that every two- or three-year-old had to go through. Eventually the child would outgrow the phase, but nothing could make that happen before the child was ready. The only problem with this theory was that it seemed to me from watching many of my patients, the children of my peers, and even some of the peers themselves, the tantrums didn't always disappear. They changed forms—I didn't see any thirty-five-year-olds or even thirteen-year-olds blubbering and turning purple when they didn't get what they wanted in the grocery store—but they persisted, sometimes in behavior that wasn't all that far removed from Kate's. I just couldn't seem to make any headway in understanding the tantrum issue, nor did any of the other doctors or professionals I consulted have much to offer, other than advice either to adjust the system of rewards and punishments more carefully, or to wait out the phase. Unfortunately I was failing to consult the actual experts—the children themselves.

Intensity: The Real Issue

The person who caused the sun to rise and brought me out of the darkness of confusion was three-year-old Peter. A plucky child, he was very talkative and rambunctious, which stood him in good stead when he wanted to hold his own against his twin sisters, who were six. Almost every time I saw him he was bright and smiling. He'd mastered self-calming early and hence was a great sleeper. His nursery school teacher thought of him as a leader, even though he was younger than most of the kids in the class and not at all bossy, because he seemed to know how to get others to do what he wanted them to—by getting them to have fun doing it. Now this was a child whom I could in no way label as insecure or troubled. He was much loved and he obviously knew it. Nor were limits a real problem with him. He was certainly not defiant in most situations. I had only two concerns about Peter. The first was his weight. He had been born at about the fiftieth percentile, but over the next eight months, while his height stayed at the eighty-fifth percentile, his weight sank to the third percentile and it stayed there. He had no other signs or symptoms of problems, but every time I'd look at his growth chart I'd get pangs of concern— was something physically wrong? More pressing in the immediate sense, and not unrelated to this issue, was the other problem: tantrums, which almost always took place at the dinner table these days.

One afternoon in June of 1982, Peter came in with his parents for his yearly checkup. I realized that while his parents and I had talked in front of him about the tantrum problem, we'd never actually discussed it with him as an equal participant. So, out of the blue, I decided to ask him about it.

"Pete, can you explain to me something I haven't been able to understand—why do you keep throwing food and yelling at the dinner table?"

Peter raised his left eyebrow and gave me an incredulous expression—whether it was amazement that I asked, wonderment that it had taken this long for someone finally to put the question to him, or some combination of the two I don't know. He was clearly pondering an answer when his mother interrupted and said, "We've asked a number of times, and all he says is 'because.' "

"But that's usually in the heat of the moment, and I'd like him to tell me, now when everybody's calm." Peter shifted in his seat, scratched his knee. At the time I thought he looked like someone who was about to disclose state secrets. He certainly was going to get the maximum dramatic effect out of the moment. "How about it, Pete?"

Suddenly he jumped out of his chair, landing solidly on his feet in a stance like a fighter. "Nothing else gets sooo . . . *big* a reaction," he announced, flinging his hands up over his head and then throwing them to the side in a big circling motion at the very moment he pronounced "big." The body gestures and the smile did indeed say that it was a very big, very predictable, and very controllable reaction he was accustomed to eliciting. That was a revelation in itself, but I still didn't see the point.

"But doesn't everybody get angry and upset with you? And doesn't that mean no dessert and no stars on the chart?"

"Yep. But everybody is paying attention to me. I'm the star." The enormity of what Peter had said began to dawn on me. It enabled me to understand that although tantrum behavior is often extreme, especially in those situations where he, like other children, used screaming, head-banging, breath-holding, and even vomiting as ways to bend the limits, it's usually *not* out of control. In fact, the child is in total control. That's why a tantrum can be stopped in mid-explosion with one cookie. Like most adults, I'd assumed the intensity of the behavior indicated some kind of profound emotional distress—and therein lay the temptation to give in. Even if the cookie or whatever was only a symbol *of* a need, it seemed important to acknowledge that the child *was* in need. But that wasn't the case, Peter seemed to be suggesting. The child *wanted* something—mainly attention—but the technique he used for getting it was not an indicator of need. It was simply a very successful manipulation.

Second, and of greater general importance, Peter had finally clarified why all the intricate schemes of positive and negative reinforcement were coming to naught. It was not whether a response was positive or negative that mattered to Peter and his contemporaries. What was important was the degree—the more intense (big) the attention he got, the better. No wonder nothing seemed to work. In fact, many of the elaborate plans that various parents and I designed together were playing right into this—which explained why the tantrums didn't go away, or sometimes even got worse. Peter was talking about one of his (and all children's) central motivations—the urge to get the most intense attention possible. This seemed to explain just about everything I'd found puzzling about tantrum behavior in children (and on further reflection, in many adults too). My mind was racing so fast that I thought I was going to experience meltdown.

I'm sure it was almost a full minute before I said anything. Finally, trying to rise to the occasion, in a style that on the basis of what Peter had just said I thought would please him, I jumped up, clapped my hands, smiled at him, picked him up in the air, and swung him around onto the examining table. "Pete, that's great. You've finally helped me understand. What you said is so important it's hard to put into words." The more I thought about it, the more I felt like doing a jig.

Liz, Peter's mother, said, "I'm not sure that Tom and I get it."

"I'm not sure I do entirely, either, but let me try to explain. When all this started, back more than two years ago, when dinnertime became a daily battle, we assumed that Peter's tantrums were a sign that he was out of control. In fact I now see that the opposite was the case. He must have picked up on our concern about his weight, and figured out that by refusing to eat, he could create situations that would get him endless amounts of attention."

Tom interjected, "But it's not the right kind of attention."

"Ah, *you and I* don't think so, but he just told us that what matters to him is how *big* the reaction is, not whether it's what we think of as the right kind of reaction. Let's look at some of the typical incidents in your house. For instance, since we acknowledged that it would only backfire if we tried to *force* him to eat, we tried to make him feel more in control by giving him a choice of *what* to eat. So Liz would ask what he wanted to eat and he'd say hot dogs, but as soon as she started to cook them he'd change his mind. This might happen two or three times before Liz would get fed up and refuse to make anything else, and then he'd start yelling about wanting peanut butter or some other new choice. Everybody in the family by that point would be fed up with him—but he'd have each person's attention and he'd usually get his way. As soon as he ate the peanut butter, then everyone would be praising him. But even if he didn't get the peanut butter, he got plenty of attention.

"And all those star charts and other things you tried that we figured would serve as such great incentives. It's really laughable. Think about it: he sits there and behaves. For the first day or so that's great. He gets praise and he gets a star. By the third or fourth day, though, the novelty has worn off, and he realizes he'd much rather *be* a star, courtesy of a tantrum, then *get* a star."

"But we don't want him to be the star . . . do we?" Peter was listening to all of this, so Liz was tentative.

"No, we don't want him to be the star, but I think I'm beginning to see how we can use his desire for attention to get him to eat." Liz and Tom looked eager, but dubious. Their three-year-old son weighed all of twenty-eight pounds, and they were getting tired of trying endless numbers of new strategies, none of which seemed to work. Nonetheless, they were all ears.

The Solution: Time-Out

"How about whenever he starts a scene, you give him a choice: He can stay at the table if he behaves, or he has to leave."

"With no dinner?" Tom wasn't sure that this was advisable. "Won't he just not eat?"

"Not if not-eating doesn't get him all the attention he's been using it for during the past year—or that's my guess. Let's give it a try and see if it works."

It did take some tinkering to get this approach to succeed. "Time-out," as it's known, was not a new disciplinary technique. I had heard about it, but been taught not to use it because it made a lot of people uneasy since it seemed so extreme—a form of isolation, something that would be experienced by the child as an emotional rejection. (I suppose it could be used that way, but I don't expect that any of the people interested enough to read this book would be likely to reject their child.) Peter, along with Gillian and Edward, whose contributions are told in the following pages, helped me find out how to use "time-out" so that it is an effective means of disciplining a child, because it speaks to both of his primary motivations—the desire for intense social attention and the desire to master new skills— yet does not get misinterpreted by the child as rejection.

It was Tom, Peter's father, who came up with the idea that time-out had an analogy to absolute numbers in math. The concept—numbers without a positive or a negative sign in front of them—is one that many of you probably got exposed to sometime in high school and then forgot because you couldn't see how it related to your checkbook, or any other part of real life. Well, it does have relevance, although in ways that your math teacher probably never anticipated.

When it comes to gaining attention, I now understand, children live in a world of absolute numbers. Each interaction, each social experience they have, has an impact on them, depending on its intensity. As adults we've been influenced by the moral/ethical values of our culture to believe that children desire positive feedback more highly than negative—in other words, that they'd rather be praised than yelled at. I still cling to that premise at times, but Peter has a point that parents ignore at their peril: Children want intense attention, and they'll persist in whatever behavior gets it for them.

Let's go back and look at how this applies to Peter. In order to keep the numbers simple I'll assume that Peter will value any interaction with another person on a scale of zero to one hundred, with zero representing no social response whatsoever from that person, and one hundred representing either maximum rage and fury, or pure delight, joy, and enthusiasm.

In a scene typical of those that used to occur before Peter tipped us off, he sits at the dinner table and refuses to eat. Liz asks, "Peter, aren't you hungry? This is one of your favorite meals."

"Kind of."

"Then eat, please." A minute goes by and Tom says, "Pete, let's not have an argument tonight." Peter picks up his fork and spears a piece of meat but it never reaches his mouth. His sister Heidi chimes in, "Peter, can't you let one night go by without trying to ruin everybody's dinner? I was talking about my recital. Now everyone is worried about what you're eating."

Peter grins as he plays the group like a dexterous puppeteer. "But I don't like it," pointing with his fork toward the plate.

"You can't know without trying." Liz is getting sterner. "If you don't eat at least some of it, then no dessert." Already she's compromising, since the terms she had laid down as she put the plates on the table at the beginning of dinner required a clean plate as a condition for getting dessert.

"I don't care." Peter is emphatic, back stiffening, folding his arms. He knows he's winning.

"Young man, you won't be allowed to leave the table unless you eat. You'll sit here a long time." Tom sternly tries another tack to little avail.

"No I won't!" Peter yells, hitting the table, mimicking his father.

"I can't stand this anymore." Heidi finishes her plate, and she walks off. Lucy grabs two pieces of bread and says she'll have something later. Having worked the family from asking, to pleading, to bribery, to despair, Peter is not only the focus of attention, he's also controlling everyone else's behavior.

"Happy now?" Tom is clearly sarcastic and irritated, jabbing his fork toward Peter. Some children might stop here, but Peter is a real master at this game.

"I don't want this." Peter pushes his plate away. "I want hot dogs."

"No. You said earlier you didn't," Liz barks.

Screeching loudly, "But I'll eat them," he hits his plate with his fork. Crack. A chip flies off. Both parents glare at him. "I don't want this," and he flips over the plate.

Tom launches into a tirade, "I wish there was some way to teach you . . ." Then he thinks better of it and says to Liz, "Let's clean up. I don't feel like extending this." As Tom picks up the dishes, he glances over at the refrigerator door where there's a chart with hand-drawn pictures of animals, nine of which now have stickers on them—Peter's achievement chart. Five more and he'll have earned his way to the circus. Until a few days ago, the chart had still seemed like such a promising ploy. Tonight it's totally forgotten. Is it that Peter doesn't really care about the circus, or that he knows they have the tickets already? Muttering to himself, Tom says, "I wish I could figure out why he does this." A few minutes later, everyone is eating chocolate cake. Peter wants some. He gets it.

On a scale of zero to one hundred such an episode might be a 60. True, you might think of it as minus 60, but remember this is absolute numbers, so it's [−60]. That's the same thing as [+60]. Now let's look at the reverse—a scene in which Peter behaved very well, apparently because of positive reinforcement. It was only a week ago Monday night that Peter's parents had put up the big chart on the refrigerator and explained to him that if he ate his dinner every night for the next two weeks, he would get stickers to put on each of the fourteen animals his sisters had drawn for him, and then he would get to go to the circus with the rest of the family. Peter jumped and screamed for joy.

Indeed for almost a week everyone had thought this was going to be the solution (although they did wonder what the next incentive would have to be). Four evenings in a row Peter cleaned his plate, and the whole family clapped when he went to put his sticker on the chart. Not bad from Peter's perspective. He wasn't getting quite as much time or energy from everyone as he had during the height of his tantrum-throwing days— each night seemed to be averaging out at around 50 [+50]— but it was enough to keep the system working, given the additional incentive of the circus.

Then the fifth night Heidi had a practice to go to and Tom had a business call he had to make just as soon as dinner was done. Liz told Peter how proud she was of his change and Lucy did clap—briefly. So this was maybe a [25].

Saturday night they'd rented two movies. Dinner was early, the popcorn was ready to go, and everyone was in a rush, excited to see the flicks. Peter was as excited as the rest, but that didn't mean he wasn't disappointed when Liz gave him the sticker while everyone else was headed toward the TV, so that he had to put it on the chart by himself, with no applause. Liz and Tom had said something positive during dinner about his eating, but he wasn't the center of attention for even a moment. Total score: [10].

The numbers don't look good from Peter's point of view. The next night he plays with his food, eats little, and his parents encourage, remind him of the circus, and give him a sticker for eating almost nothing. Hard to score. So far as Peter can see, no one seems to care very much anymore—not the way they used to.

Monday—they should be halfway there. Seven stickers are up. But obviously the situation isn't as promising as the chart suggests. Peter decides at the last minute he wants bologna, not the lasagne everyone else is having. Liz hesitates. It is easy to fix, but dinner is ready. She reminds him about the circus,

and he screams back, "I want a choice." She's uncertain, and
Peter throws himself down on the floor, rolling over and over,
howling loudly enough for even some of the neighbors to hear,
"You're not fair. I hate you." Liz tries to stand her ground,
thinks about the circus outing and how much she wants everyone
to have fun, then grudgingly says okay. At the end of dinner
Peter announces, "All gone." He did eat two pieces of bologna,
while artfully shoveling the rest to the dog. "Well, I have to
agree that your plate is clean, which is what you get a sticker
for, but the idea was that you *eat* your food, not play with it."
Peter didn't say anything but his grin clearly did: "Got you."
Liz scowled. Tom growled, "Don't push us." Everyone felt better
when Peter ate the rice pudding.

After the dishes were put away Peter stood by the refrigerator
pointing at the chart. Tom stared at him. A complex calculation.
He wasn't pleased, felt manipulated. "I'm not sure you deserve
this." Peter snapped, "Clean plate," imperiously, and then in
a more calculating tone added, "I ate the rice pudding." Outma-
neuvered, Tom added, "I'm giving you this because I want the
family to enjoy this outing." He gave Peter the sticker with a
peremptory motion, and left him to put it up himself. Total
score 15 or 20 [−15 or −20].

Tuesday—this was almost a repeat of the previous night,
with Peter eating very little and both of his parents irritated,
discouraged, but trying to avoid any kind of blowup so they
won't have to call off the circus. Net effect: [−15].

The following night produced the original incident recounted above. Does the circus matter to Peter? Of course. But
the stickers don't replace attention, and when he can get a 60—
plus or minus—he'll go for it. As will every other child.

Time-Out: Putting It to Work

What Peter so aptly indicated in the office was that rewards
and punishments, as they are usually understood, are not the

answer. I've only seen failures with that approach. The question was how to apply Peter's insight—how to use time-out so as to test the idea that the most effective deterrent to tantrums and other forms of misbehavior would be some form of social zero. The two big unknowns were: How long should time-out last? And where should it take place? Could you use the child's room for time-out, or were there emotional complications to that? I certainly didn't want to have the cure end up being worse than the disease.

What became evident from our initial experiments with Peter was that time-out had to be very carefully designed if it was to impact on the child's two primary motivations: the desire for intense social interactions, and the urge to master new skills. If there was any possibility of social activity, Peter exploited it. If there was any possibility of his being able to divert himself by mastering new skills—which is what playing with toys and games enables a child to do—he was great at that too. The goal is to come as close to zero—which means total isolation and total boredom—as possible. If time-out is not a zero, then it won't work.

In Peter's case it took us a while to discover exactly what constituted a boring, isolating zero. Sending him to the corner, the easiest thing to do, left him too much in the social scheme— he still talked to people, and he's so charming they often couldn't resist responding. Sitting on the stairs he would play with the dog. Neither option amounted to a social zero, and neither worked. If sent to his room where he really was alone, he had a cornucopia of different toys and games with which to entertain himself and compensate for the lack of social activity. Since his parents were reluctant to undo his room, even up to thirty minutes in there didn't work either. But one day they discovered that fifteen minutes in the guest bedroom was like a miracle.

It was dinnertime. A typical scene had started. Peter was protesting the dinner menu and Tom gave him a choice: Be quiet or have time-out. Not unexpectedly, Peter yelled, "I don't want to go." Nothing happened for a minute, then Peter grabbed Heidi's bread. "It's mine." Heidi resisted the temptation to yell at him (since her parents had enlisted the girls' help) and reached for another roll. Peter beat her to it, grabbing the last one. "Pete, they're not all yours." Heidi prized a piece away from Peter as Tom demanded, "Stop it!" Peter responded, "No, they're mine." Realizing that he needed to turn up the intensity level a little to break through everyone's restraint, he screeched, "I never get what I want to eat," and whizzed the other piece of roll at Heidi. It glanced off her cheek. "Daddy." Heidi was all plaintive indignation. Things were falling apart again.

Tom had had enough. "You're going to your room, Peter. You can come out when I say so."

Peter recovered quickly, "I'm sorry. I don't want to go there, I'll be good."

Tom was taken aback by this sudden display of contrition. He almost bought it. But then he remembered how they'd given in on the circus, which had only made everything worse, and how they were running out of options to try. If time-out didn't work, what was left? He also reminded himself, he later told me, that Peter's quick switch from antagonist to apologist was a sign of exactly how in control of these situations Peter really was. It now seemed obvious to him that if Peter could exercise that amount of control when he was facing punishment, he could have made a different decision about how to behave before the fact, not afterward. "Think about that the next time you're tempted to do this. Right now you have to go to time-out."

"No."

"Then I'll take you." Tom rose from his chair, and Peter scampered down the hall in the opposite direction from his room, sobbing, "I hate you." When Tom caught up to him, they were standing outside the guest bedroom. Suddenly it occurred to Tom that since the guest room had only a bed, nightstand, desk, and chair it was a better spot for time-out than Peter's bedroom. In he went. "Can I come out?" echoed down the hall as Tom walked away. "No! And more talking will get you more time." The clock ticked off fifteen minutes, most of which Peter spent singing to himself and talking to the moon (after a brief howl of protest followed by a short silence). For the final moments there had been a couple of "Can I come out? Isn't it time yet?" pleadings, and much less physical activity. When he did come out he behaved wonderfully.

The next night was chicken casserole—a favorite of everyone in the family except Peter. Liz had therefore offered him a choice before dinner, but he declined peanut butter and jelly or toasted cheese, as well as her usual standby, hot dogs. So Peter was given a small portion of chicken casserole (Liz knew he wouldn't eat much) which he proceeded to play with. Nobody said anything, following through on the agreement to try to avoid making an issue of his mealtime habits. Everyone else was busy eating and commenting on the glorious sunset when Peter broke the calm. "I want my hot dogs . . . *now!*"

"You said no when I offered them to you before," Liz reminded him.

"I want them now, now, now!" The first "now" was loud, the last painfully commanding. Peter reached toward his plate, palm up, his usual maneuver to flip it. As he raised the edge, however, he stopped in mid-action, glancing at Tom, and said, "But I don't want to go to the room." Tom choked, since Peter had anticipated the very words about to come out of his mouth. Heidi and Lucy, both incredulous, said, "I don't believe it," in perfect unison. Liz later told me that she thought the whole thing was choreographed. Tom said, "We're happy to have you stay, but you've been told how to behave. Anything less and you're gone." Peter gently lowered the rim of the plate and grabbed his fork. Turned out that Peter thought the chicken was good enough to have seconds.

That was it. The whole food escapade collapsed. From then on he ate more or less normally, gained enough weight to assuage any health concerns we might have had, and turned out to be quite the charming dinner table conversationalist.

The Extremes: Breath-Holding and Vomiting

Needless to say, I was ecstatic with our results. But was Peter an anomaly? Had Peter told me about Peter, or all kids? I knew how to find out. Gillian looked every bit the blond-haired princess at eighteen months; no one would even dream that for almost a year she had been persecuting her parents with breath-holding whenever the world wasn't just right. While we've all seen episodes like Kate's in the grocery store, and Peter's at the dinner table, breath-holding seems to most of us extreme, maybe even bizarre, and it causes parents intense anxiety. Is the child feeling unloved, they wonder, are their limits too harsh, is there something terribly amiss with the parent-child relationship that is forcing the child to resort to such drastic measures?

In the office Gillian seemed so happy that her temper tantrums—especially the extreme form they had taken—were a particular puzzle to me. Her mother was a pediatric nurse who had worked in a day-care center before going to nursing school. Despite her initial intentions, Hildy had not gone back to work after Gillian's birth, so she devoted most of her time to her daughter. When she did leave Gillian with a babysitter, usually her aunt, there was some separation protest but no big deal. Nighttime behavior was rarely a problem, although bedtime had recently been more of a struggle. Gillian was quite verbal and motorically advanced as well—scotching two of my earlier hypotheses that tantrums were due to frustration caused by the child's inability to succeed at certain motor skills or to express herself verbally.

Though Gillian could be quite charming to be around, there was no saying no to her. Whatever she wanted had to be done and done immediately or else Gillian would squeal, then take a big breath and hold it. At about thirteen months she had even passed out during an episode. After that, I'd done a more thorough cardiovascular and neurologic workup, but had found nothing out of the ordinary. Still, her behavior was certainly cause for concern, even if her health wasn't. So I was anxious to try Peter's lesson on her.

Though Hildy was dubious when I described what I wanted her to do, since time-out sounded like such an extreme measure to her, she was distressed enough by Gillian's behavior that she decided to give it a try. She told Gillian about the new rules, explaining to her that whenever she held her breath she would have to go into her playpen and do time-out by herself. There followed two days of complete uneventfulness, and I began to think that for some children the mere threat of time-out was enough. But then Sunday arrived. . . .

It was time for the midday meal after church, and Gillian toddled into the kitchen to join her mother and both grandmothers, who were all busy with last-minute preparations. When Gillian said, "Bottle," the roast was just coming out of the oven. Hands full, Hildy said, "I'll get it for you as soon as I can," turned back to her cooking, and then heard the dreaded yelp followed by a kerplunk as Gillian sat down on the floor for added emphasis, her face already slightly blue around the gills.

"Mom, can you take care of the roast? I have to take Gillian to her playpen for this. I've decided to try that to stop this breath-holding."

"But, Hildegarde," her mother protested, using Hildy's given name as she always did when she was going to be critical. "She wants her bottle. Don't you think it's a little unfair to punish her?"

"Oh, Mom, we've talked about this before. The person who's unfair is Gillian. Every time she doesn't get instant attention, or there's some limit that doesn't happen to fit her whim, she holds her breath. This has to stop." With that she swooped Gillian up and walked into the other room. Realizing that her mother was actually going to follow through on this plan, Gillian started to cry. Hildy cleared out all the toys from the playpen, put Gillian in, and reminded her what this was all about: "No breath-holding." Then she rushed back to the kitchen before the pouting expression could make her relent. Gillian continued to cry for about a minute, until everyone came through to the table, and then there was silence.

Hildy spent about ten minutes fending off questions like "How can you be sure she hasn't passed out in the playpen?" Appetite waning by this time, wondering whether the breath-holding wouldn't be easier to endure than this inquisition, Hildy went to get Gillian—and found her playing with a stuffed bear.

Returning to the dining room with Gillian, Hildy asked in as mild a manner as she could muster, "Who gave her the bear? That's not supposed to be playtime in there." Glancing around the table, she found no one willing to meet her eye. Finally Hendrick, her husband's father, said, "We did," nodding to his seventy-two-year-old confederate Otis. "We thought it was too harsh a punishment, and even though you said you talked to her, I'm not sure she understands you. She's got to be lonely in there. Besides, in our day, we just told kids what to do and it happened."

More than slightly miffed, Hildy replied, "Grandpa, if children at this age can't understand, then how did it happen that they did what you told them to do? Look at her now." Everyone glanced toward Gillian, grinning widely beneath her mashed potato mustache. "Tell me she doesn't know exactly what's going on."

Hendrick smiled embarrassedly, but Hildy's mother took up the cudgel. "I still think it's too cruel."

Nels, Gillian's father, finally entered the fray. "But you all spanked us as kids. It may just be personal preference, but that strikes me as just as cruel. Besides, if it was that bad, why isn't Gillian more upset?" Everyone agreed to call a truce, and Gillian had no more breath-holding spells that day.

Monday morning, however, she grabbed for a knife, and when Hildy took it away and said, "No knives," that set off another episode. Hoping Gillian would stop on her own, Hildy hesitated, then said, more as a warning than a prelude to the act, "You're going to the pen." Gillian got dusky. Her bluff called, Hildy picked Gillian up and put her in the playpen. Gillian started to sob a little, and, as Hildy finished evacuating the playpen, begged pathetically: "Bear." Hildy hesitated, but then gave her the bear. She just couldn't shake the grandparents' disapproval, even when they weren't there.

When we talked at the end of the week, Hildy reported on the various time-out episodes, but didn't let on that the bear had become part of the deal. She said she thought that maybe there were somewhat fewer spells, but she wasn't convinced. With a certain hesitancy in her voice she said, "I don't think it worked that well."

Sensing something amiss, I asked her to review the previous week's events again, this time in more detail, and that's how I heard about the bear, the grandparents, and Hildy's weakening of resolve. Once she'd confessed, Hildy reaffirmed her commitment to trying time-out, this time the right way.

In fact she got her first chance almost immediately upon hanging up the phone, because Gillian had tired of waiting for the end of what by then had become a fairly prolonged conversation. When Hildy explained that she couldn't play with her just then because she had to get dinner started, it took Gillian about ten seconds to decide on her reaction—another round of breath-holding. Without hesitation, Hildy reminded her that that wasn't allowed and put her in the pen. Gillian didn't even protest until the bear went out too, then she howled more out of amazement than anything else, according to Hildy's interpretation. After just that one time-out, Hildy thought she could see a change. Gillian seemed sort of cautious in her demands. "On occasion I thought that she actually waited until I was done with something or in some kind of transition before she tried to get my attention." But Hildy's first success with time-out had occurred while she and Gillian were alone. What would happen when other people were around, she wondered.

Of course the big test would be at the weekly family dinner—which that week was being held at Hildy's mother's. Hildy and Nels went prepared, lugging the playpen with them. "I thought my mother was going to have a fit when we unloaded it," Hildy later recounted to me, "but my father came to our aid and told her that this was our business, not hers."

"Did you have to use it?"

Hildy laughed. "This is Gillian we're talking about. Of course we had to. Being at her grandparents, she thought she was safe. But in fact it was a scene with my mother that got her into trouble. She kept going near the oven while Mom was cooking, until finally Mother lost patience with her, telling her in a very strident tone of voice to stay away from the oven. Overhearing this from the den, I went running in to help, but by the time I arrived Mom was holding a gray-faced Gillian, apologizing to her for yelling at her and begging her to stop holding her breath."

Hildy hesitated for only a moment before plowing ahead. She gathered Gillian out of her grandmother's arms so fast that grandmother didn't even have time to protest—unlike Gillian, who smacked Hildy in the face. "You may not like this," Hildy told Gillian, "but hitting me won't change anything"—whereupon Gillian screeched and held her breath again. "You're going to the pen, Gillian, and you're going to keep getting sent there every time you hold your breath."

Predictably, Hildy's mother tried to intervene at this point, but this time Hildy held fast. "Mother, as long as breath-holding works for Gillian, it's going to continue. She's going in the pen now and I don't want any interference from anyone."

I congratulated Hildy on her courage—it's very hard to persist in the face of such opposition, especially when you yourself aren't convinced that what you're doing is right—and then asked what the outcome was.

"Best family dinner we ever had. Gillian's become a different girl, and our parents respect us as parents now." I was delighted to hear this, of course, especially since I had already started a third time-out investigation, this time with parents who were new to my practice, whose son Edward was using vomiting as his form of temper tantrum. Or that was how they explained the problem to me.

As a baby Edward had been a "spitter," despite varied diets of breast milk, regular formula, and predigested formulas. Since the problem didn't go away, the special diets continued. Short, frequent feedings were recommended, in the hope that he could keep smaller amounts down more easily, and he was always very carefully kept in an upright position during feeding. Over the course of the first year some days he'd spit up or vomit many times; other times he'd go four or five days with no problems and everyone would say, "It's the bananas that cured him." Only the next week, the bananas didn't work any longer so they'd try something else.

When I met him, his digestive problems were getting worse, not better, though in every other way he seemed healthy and happy. Whatever the original cause of his spitting—and this was still not clear—somewhere along the line Edward had learned he could control it (and everyone around him). His parents, Anne and Hoyt, thought that he might have been as young as two months when he'd first begun to see its potential as a protest. The frequent-feeding regime he'd been put on at that time meant that Edward was often forced to eat when he wasn't hungry, and it seemed to them that the vomiting he'd done then might have been a way of voicing his unhappiness. Unfortunately, it had become a means of expression he'd been using ever since, as well as a technique that got him lots of extra attention. Not only would he be bathed and changed whenever he got sick, but held and caressed and talked to, in the hope that the affection lavished upon him would decrease his acting out. Because his parents seemed like very level-headed people, I was inclined to trust their interpretation of Edward's behavior as deliberate, and as I explained to them I thought he would make an ideal candidate for another trial use of time-out.

While we talked, Edward's attempts to interrupt us indicated that he understood much of what was going on. Edward went from pulling on Anne's shirt to hitting her on the leg to throwing up again—this being the third vomiting episode of the day. I watched carefully as Anne grabbed him, cleaned off the front of his overalls, and rocked him. "Eddie," she said pleadingly, "we're only trying to find a way to help you." Eddie didn't look convinced. But I went on with my questions.

"When does the vomiting usually occur?"

"It's starting to happen more and more often as a response to any kind of limits," Hoyt said. "We've probably made matters worse by giving in to him so much. Since he throws up whenever we try to make 'no' stick, we've responded by playing distraction games with him. Over the last few months, however, we've run out of distractions and we're both pretty angry with him because he's really in control of our lives. The truth is, though, since we've always had this fear that something is really wrong with him, and we've never been entirely sure whether the vomiting is in his control or maybe just a bad reaction to the stress of being disciplined or told no, we've never been able to make our limits stick. And obviously we're paying the price for that now." Hoyt looked drained—thirty-four going on fifty.

We talked about ways to establish various kinds of limits, but the first step toward any self-control for Edward obviously involved putting an end to the willful vomiting. So we came up with the following: Whenever Edward vomited, whether it was an attempt to bend a limit or just a ploy for attention, such as had happened in my office, his parents would clean him up, address any other immediate physical needs that arose in the situation, and then put him in time-out. They asked me if I thought ten to fifteen minutes would be long enough for time-out, and I suggested about half that, but, as it turned

out, I was wrong. By chance, they found out on the very
first try—which happened right after their visit to my office.

The telephone was ringing when Anne walked in her front
door with Edward. Although it was Saturday, as dean at a small
liberal arts college Anne had to be available whenever crises
developed, and it was just her luck that a problem requiring
her instant attention had developed that very morning. It was
the president of the university on the phone, and he was eager
to talk—now. Eddie also wanted her attention, so she held him
in her lap for a few minutes, until his whining made it impossible
for her to focus. Having a portable phone allowed her to drag
out a puzzle to distract Edward briefly, after which she found
him a few toys which gave her another few minutes of freedom,
but then the whining started again, and she could see another
vomiting episode was imminent—the fourth in one morning,
for an all-time record.

"What a mess this was," Anne recounted later. "The president wanted me, Edward wanted me, and Hoyt was off running
errands. I held my hand over the phone and tried to reassure
Edward that I'd be off the phone as soon as I could—but then
it happened. He threw up again. Suddenly I was feeling sorry
for him. He'd had to sit through the long session with you,
and I knew he was expecting me to make it up to him now.
Meanwhile the president was getting more and more irritated
and impatient. I almost screamed because I was feeling so torn,
but then the whole situation got very focused and I knew what
I had to do. 'Excuse me,' I said to the president. 'My son is
sick. I have to deal with him, but I'll be back in one minute.'
Then I turned to Edward and said: 'You heard everything we
talked about in the doctor's office and I know you understood
it all. You're not really sick and you can control this—the timing's
too obvious.' I peeled off his shirt, wiped his mouth, and put
him in the playpen in the next room. He grabbed for the bear
and the ring set, but I took them away, reminding him and
myself that this wasn't playtime. Having found my resolve, I

was much better able to deal with the school situation, and ended up spending another thirty minutes on the phone. I hadn't meant to leave him that long, so when I got off the phone and realized how much time had gone by, I was almost sick with worry about what state Edward would be in when I went in to get him. Would he be covered in vomit, would he hate me, would he be hysterical? Quite the contrary, he was calm and cheerful. I spent the next hour playing with him, until the chairman of the history department called with the latest report on the crisis, and while I talked to him Edward did a superb job of playing by himself."

So by happenstance they ended up with a time-out lasting thirty minutes, and they were reluctant to change, since it worked so well. The vomiting stopped, and they now had the foundation of a discipline system that made everyone, Edward included, much happier. It may be that the same results could have been obtained with a shorter time-out, but we'll never know, since they stuck with what had worked, and it continued to work.

If you're going to make time-out work, there's no room for compromise or being "nice" as the parents of Peter, Gillian, and Edward all discovered for themselves. And don't underestimate the challenge. Creating a real time-out for a small child can tax your creativity, especially if the child is good at self-entertainment. My son Red, for example, needs nothing more than a look at the sky to be happy. During the day he sees horses, pigs, clowns, and trees in the clouds, and he loves watching the stars and moon come out at night. Even if the sky is empty, there's a bird feeder he likes to look at right outside his window, and the ferries that cross Lake Champlain, so when Red goes to time-out we always draw the blinds shut. Each child is different, of course, and you'll have to customize a time-out arrangement that works for yours. It may take some experimenting, and it will almost certainly require some prep work—but it *can* be done. Following are some pointers that may be helpful to you.

Where Is Time-Out?

Do you need a special environment? Yes and no. Any room or place in the house has possibilities so long as it can be cleared of all items within reach as well as made childproof. One family in my practice has a huge walk-in closet that the children sometimes play in. It's a perfect spot for time-out when there's nobody else in there for company. In other homes there may be a guest room or other seldom-used space with very little in it. Just remove any breakable items that might fall victim to curious investigation, make sure the electric sockets are plugged up, and roll any curtains up out of reach.

The major goal is to guarantee that there is nothing of any conceivable entertainment value within reach or sight of the child, and no human or animal companionship available either. This of course means that the child is physically separated from other members of the family—not parked in a corner where she's still part of the family scene.

Can you use the child's room? Yes, but it requires some work, as many of us have discovered. Given the layout of our house, we don't have much choice. So if Red goes into his room for time-out, the blinds are closed, for the reasons described above, the books go on the top shelf, and the toys and stuffed animals get locked in his closet. I worried at first that using a child's bedroom for time-out would set up negative associations that might cause sleep problems or other emotional stresses when he was sent to his room for bed or naptime. But if you remove all the play items and strip the room of all its pleasures and comforts, you create such a different physical setting, and general ambience, that there doesn't ever seem to be any confusion in the mind of the child. The only time trouble arises is when parents use bedtime as a punishment (which is *not* supposed to be part of the deal), because then the time-out and bedtime distinction does get blurred. Otherwise the differences in environment, and in the parents' attitude, make it easy for the child to understand when his bedroom is a cozy, comforting refuge, and when it's a time-out space.

What's Time-Out Like?

Above all, boring. There's an absolute minimum of social attention directed toward the child—no yelling before sending him to time-out, no communication during, no conciliatory displays of affection after. The time-out environment contains no books, no toys, no games, no stuffed animals, no dolls, no baseball bats or gloves, no puzzles, no tapes, no musical instruments, no mobiles, no pets. The bottom line is that the more boring the setting, the shorter the time-out needed to create an effective zero—and hence end the problem behavior, whether it's tantrums or any other kind of limit-testing.

How Long Does Time-Out Have to Last?

If you don't compromise on time-out—I call it cheating—then it will be shorter, not longer. However, as soon as you allow the child to have a toy, or a drink, or communicate with her in any way, even if only to answer a question about when she can get out, then time-out has effectively ended. Either you start over again from the beginning or it won't work. (If going to the bathroom is an issue, ask her if she needs to go *before* time-out commences, and then don't get manipulated.)

It's the people who cheat on time-out who have given it a bad name. We've all heard horror stories about putting a child in her room all afternoon without its having any effect. If every tantrum required hours of time-out, then this would indeed be a hopeless, unrealistic strategy. But every time I've been able to get to the bottom of one of those stories it turned out the child wasn't really in time-out at all: she was talking with the birds, *and* playing with her blocks, *and* reading stories, *and* listening to tapes.

At the other end of the spectrum from the stories about time-out marathons that have scared people away from even trying the technique, there's the one-minute-per-year-of-age rule. I find the latter as unrealistic as the former. I have yet to see the determined, competent two-year-old who will respond to two minutes of time-out. Her facial expression tells you it's a joke, and so does her behavior, because it won't change at all in response to such a brief period of time-out. Most one-year-old children will respond to five minutes of time-out, and it's rare for a three-year-old to need more than fifteen or twenty minutes. But times vary widely. You have to find each child's individual threshold—how much time matters to her. However much that is in adult terms, five minutes or thirty, often has nothing to do with parental feelings about what ought to work for their child, or any author's pronouncements about what has worked for other people's children. As we'll see in more detail in the next chapter, you know you're over the threshold when the problem behavior starts to wane. Rapidly. The child who is stubborn, persistent, determined, or assertive (different parents prefer different adjectives to describe their progeny) may require more time than her peers, but unless there's some hidden (or not so hidden) loophole in your version of time-out, it need never extend to hours; it's always a question of how many minutes.

Often you can use the sounds coming from the child's room as your guide. There's usually a brief period of protest (crying, yelling, etc.) when the child is first sent to time-out, followed by a quiet period, and finally another vocal outburst which seems to be the child's way of saying, "That's enough time."

When you discover that twelve minutes works for your eighteen-month-old, is there any point in using more time? No. Once you're over the threshold, pushing harder won't make any difference and may even backfire. Then time-out becomes excessive, a punishment that is resented, rather than an opportunity for the child to gain self-control.

Now that you have worked out the optimum time span, it usually only takes one or two episodes of time-out to stop a particular behavior. It doesn't take endless repetitions. In the case of the child who has been allowed to get away with certain behaviors, like tantrums, however, sometimes it does require four or five episodes of time-out to get her to change her behavior.

Once you know the child's time threshold, will it always remain the same? Doubtful. As children get older I've occasionally had parents tell me that they can decrease the time, but that's the exception. Usually the time must increase. So while five minutes produced wondrous changes in behavior in your fifteen-month-old, a year later the same duration of time-out will probably leave him unfazed. I'm not sure exactly why this occurs. To some extent it may be an assertion of will, but more often than not it's a reflection of the child's increasing ability to self-entertain. Let me give you a home-grown example: Red can be a stubborn, blockheaded person (numerous individuals have assured me this is the result of a genetic legacy that doesn't require Gregor Mendel to figure out), so he's seen his share of time-out. When he was about two-and-a-half I remember one period of four or five days when his behavior was getting worse by the minute. And time-out wasn't making much of an improvement, so I kept making it longer, with no effect. The next time I had to send him to time-out, I decided to check for possible loopholes in my system. Sure enough, when I listened carefully at his door, I could hear him chortling merrily away, talking with imaginary clowns and bears and elephants and tigers. He may have been alone, but he sure wasn't bored. If he could manufacture a whole world in his imagination, then time-out would never work again. But it turned out that even Red couldn't entertain himself in a total vacuum. When after ninety minutes he finally began to fuss and cry—the signal that he really was over his threshold and needed to come out—I went to get him and discovered that he'd found a couple of blankets in a chest at the foot of his bed and used them to erect a tent. Aha, I realized: a circus tent! That explained the clowns and the animals.

After that I saw to it that he couldn't get to the blankets, and his time-out threshold was dramatically reduced.

That day Red taught me something. Now I always advise parents whose children's time-out seems to be lasting extraordinarily long to check for hidden sources of entertainment. Even a highly imaginative child will usually require some kind of prop to set in motion a fantasy elaborate enough to keep him happy beyond the hour mark.

Time-out, if used properly, is an amazingly effective strategy. As you have seen, it was able to stop tantrum behavior in Edward, Peter, and Gillian, and in my own son as well. Thanks to Peter's honesty, over the last decade I have used this strategy with families in all parts of the country. I have found it to be the only consistent and effective enforcer of limits that doesn't rely on compliance and obedience, and therefore does further the child's desire for independence and autonomy without putting him in conflict with his family, or in physical danger. Time-out enables parents to let their children make choices, and over time to develop self-control, which is the real goal of discipline, as we'll see in the next chapter.

Oh, and just a bit of follow-up. Now, approximately a decade later, Peter is tall and still thin. He takes great delight in reminding me how brilliant a psychologist he'll be if he's not an airline pilot. Gillian is an aspiring ballet dancer, and at a recent recital her instructor told me she has just the right dramatic flair—to which I responded, "If you only knew how long she's been practicing." And Edward is an extraordinary athlete who loves basketball, but says that his stomach is always grumbling when he steps up to the foul line. No doubt. But his coach says he's got nerves of steel—and he's by far the best foul shooter on the team, leading the league.

Setting Limits— Shaping Behavior for the Future

"You can't make me." Standing at the top of the stairs, towering above you, he's an impressive figure—not at all the same person you knew even a few months ago. With his head cocked defiantly, hands on hips, brows knit sternly, a slight smirk on his face, this is not someone to be taken lightly.

As a parent your thoughts and emotions are mixed. While part of you feels a certain ironic pride in your child's determination, you're tired of the big scenes that come with it. You know from past experiences that reasoning with him won't work, and you exhausted most of your bribes yesterday.

"I don't want to have to tell you again," you threaten for the fourth time, "I'm getting really mad." Still hoping to avoid physical violence, you play your trump card: "If you don't do it *now*, you'll lose TV." Instantly you remember that yesterday afternoon you revoked TV privileges for today. You feel embarrassed and admonish yourself to keep better track of these things

in the future. Such slip-ups just make you feel and act ever
more out of control.

"I don't want to."

"I don't care. You don't have a choice!" you scream at the
top of your lungs, brandishing a fist. Are you really going to
be reduced to such pathetic bullying? the little voice in the
back of your head says. You're hardly a model of adult behavior.
Who's in charge here? Outwitted by a two-year-old for the third
time today, and it's not even noon.

The real voice of your child snaps you out of your musings.
"I want ginger ale, . . . please."

At least one message got through: He did say please, after
a very long and considered pause. But this is clearly a distraction.
"Stop changing the subject."

"But I'm thirsty."

No longer faced with an impasse, you decide to compromise.
"Okay, but *then* we'll pick up your toys." Of course you, not
"we," end up doing it, after playing step-and-fetch-it for the
ginger ale of which your son drank only a sip. Since this type
of episode gets repeated many times, by the end of each day
you've lost a little more respect for yourself. Worse still, you've
started to feel ambivalent about your child. Maybe going back
to work *is* a good idea. Whatever your fantasies about being a
parent, in reality you spend most of the day yelling at him,
and feeling guilty because you've overreacted—like the time
you swore at him, or the long-regretted time when you hit
him a little harder than you intended.

As a parent who spent many days at home with a two-
year-old, I've had all of these emotions and thoughts. I also
know firsthand that it doesn't have to be like this. Two-year-
olds are not inherently negative or terrible; they are marvelous
people, with tremendous capacities to solve problems and to be
delightful companions. Going back to work full time won't
resolve anything. (And, alternatively, neither will staying home

full time.) But none of the kinds of discipline attempted, contemplated, or recollected in the above scene will work either. Before moving on to what will work, let's dispense with what won't, since all parents will find themselves in similar or far worse situations. And yet many parents are fearful of using the time-out technique I described in Chapter Three because they think it's too severe.

Types of Discipline That Don't Work

Many of the commonly used techniques for dealing with problem behavior are destined to fail, most because they play directly to the child's primary goal of getting an intense reaction—positive or negative—from the parent. I discussed this extensively in the previous chapter, and will expand upon it in this one. Let's look at the child's perspective on each of the following:

Hitting

Yelling

Ignoring behaviors

Distraction

Being denied certain rights and privileges

Ultimatums

Hitting

Hitting is the way most parents try to make a point when they feel that all else has failed. They rarely succeed. They won't teach the child to abide by limits when they break one of their own—the one that says "Don't hit." Adults strike children when they are angry, usually out of control. Being out of control is itself a problem, because it sets such a bad example. And the physical violence is an even greater problem. If the parent really hurts the child, then fear lowers the child's self-esteem by making him feel like a victim. Fear also supplants the respect that parents want from their children, and results in devious behavior, since the child's main goal will be to escape detection. Alternatively, if the hit is just a light tap on the hand or the backside, accompanied by strong words, the message is mixed and the child will probably not take the discipline seriously. Worst of all, when hit the child almost always retaliates. This kind of exchange produces escalating physical and emotional conflict, which can be profoundly upsetting to the child. Some ex-hitters explain why they abandoned that form of punishment:

> I was never comfortable with hitting Liza, but I didn't know that there was any other way to get through to her when I was trying to steer her away from something dangerous. So I'd either hit her so hard that I'd feel guilty or tap her so gently that she'd smile at me as if I had praised her. And her behavior never changed much in either case.

Other parents come to the realization that physical punishment won't work only when the child hits them. Even more dramatic is videotape, which I've suggested to many families.

> Two neighbors and three books told me to hit back when Jimmy hit me. That way he would understand that it hurt. But hitting only seemed to make him more difficult—almost as if he enjoyed the pain. Then one day my wife took a movie of what was happening between us. I didn't like the expression on my face or Jimmy's. He wasn't learning the lesson that I intended.

Frank felt that Ronnie could be trained just like a dog. When he broke a rule he was told what he'd done wrong and hit. I argued but to no avail. No matter how much Frank hit him, Ronnie never learned the rules. Ronnie grew to both hate and fear his father. One day when Frank wouldn't pay attention to him, Ronnie really walloped him. I thought Frank was literally going to explode, but that was the last time he ever hit Ronnie. Our second son was two months old then. Ronnie and his father still have trouble, but Frank has learned. He has never hit David and he realizes discipline is much more complicated than dogs.

Yelling

This attempt at discipline usually precedes and later accompanies hitting. Screaming is another out-of-control reaction, and, like hitting, it is also ineffective.

I'd yell and rant and rave, and Gayle would smile as if to say, "That was quite a show, Mom. What else can you do?" She became pretty good at copying my act. She probably even learned her first swear word from me.

At first I'd try to be reasonable. Then I'd change my tone of voice, and David would grin. When I turned up the volume, he'd simply repeat the behavior. When I was yelling and jumping up and down he'd laugh. I now see I was just adding fuel to the fire. Not only was he getting the intense reaction he wanted; I was serving as a superb model for the temper tantrums which started about that time.

Since the child's action has produced an intense parental reaction, which is what children want, the behavior will remain unchanged.

Not to mention that there may also be emotional damage, since words spoken in the heat of the moment are often extreme and may leave lasting scars. Yelling creates an atmosphere in which the child will almost certainly not listen to what the parent is saying—and for good reason, since out-of-control adult behavior usually has more to do with the parent's own fears and projections than with the child's actions. From the child's perspective the reaction is inappropriate to the offense. The end result is often the same as hitting. The adult encourages behavior that no one wants to live with while becoming more and more frustrated. The behavior pattern not only doesn't change but often deteriorates, with the child yelling and screaming right along with the parent.

Ignoring Behavior

While yelling and hitting set an example that undermines everyone's self-esteem and doesn't strengthen self-control, ignoring unacceptable behaviors is equally ineffective. Any breach of the limits requires an appropriate response. If the behavior isn't acknowledged, the child is free to repeat it again. If, however, you have decided to ignore it because the limit set isn't very important, then it wasn't worth setting in the first place, and should be abandoned. Ignoring even one established limit is contagious. This is an area in which the domino theory really does hold true.

Another problem with ignoring bad behavior is that it's impossible. Many parents may like to think that they have considerable willpower in such circumstances, but few if any think they could win an Academy Award for acting. And that's the kind of acting skill it takes to ignore a two-year-old on a rampage. Even if you don't say anything, the child will notice the stiffening in your body posture, the tortured facial expression, or your attempts to avoid yelling. He knows he's won. And even if you do on occasion fool him, this is certainly not a technique you can use at the grandparents', the neighbors', the supermarket, or any other social or public situation.

Perhaps the worst aspect of trying to ignore behavior is that it confuses the child.

> Some days I would let something pass by, and then I'd feel frustrated and powerless, so the next time she'd do the same thing I'd punish her. Even though I was trying to be nice to her on the days when I ignored the bad behavior, Gina understandably felt I was unfair. Why did I let her do it four times and then explode at her the fifth time? I wonder if she even realized what part of the behavior I was really mad about. The other problem was that if I held it in all day, then I was furious by the end of the day. I would get angry at everybody else since I was feeling so sorry for myself. When my husband suggested I go back to therapy, I knew that my discipline technique didn't work. Since then I've realized that ignoring Gina's breaches of discipline is no favor to any of us!

Distraction

Some parents, when they can no longer ignore a child's actions, seek to distract him with another activity, instead of making it clear that the present activity is unacceptable. Like trying to pretend the behavior isn't happening, this is another way to avoid setting limits. In fact, since the parent responds to undesirable behavior by trying to engage the child in an even more enjoyable activity, he is rewarded for his bad behavior. Nor is that the end of the cycle. Once the child is distracted, the parent often leaves him alone. Since the child will then usually seek further attention, he is likely to return to the original activity. So the cycle repeats itself.

This pattern is destructive for three reasons. First, the child rarely develops positive ways to get attention. Second, the emotional message is confusing in much the same way that consoling a child after punishing him is, i.e., an unacceptable behavior induces intense positive reactions from the parent. Finally, distraction is a major effort for the parent. It consumes vast amounts of time and energy on behalf of a self-defeating enterprise.

I swear Gwen waits until she knows I'm looking at her before she misbehaves. And it's not because she's defiant. By using distraction I've only succeeded in conveying to her that any time she does something I don't like I'll find something that she'll enjoy doing even more. Gwen's delighted—and she should be. The problem is I never get anything else done. Of course if I leave her alone she just goes back to doing what got me to come get her in the first place. It is the classic situation of damned if you do and damned if you don't.

Distraction seemed to be a way to avoid confrontation. I'd threaten to put Joey in the crib and then try to get him to do something else. Joey would just grin—and obviously not take me seriously. Then I'd get upset and isolate him—sometimes on the first threat and other times on the tenth. So he'd get angry too. From his point of view I was always changing the rules. He needed me to be more predictable. That meant no threats, no distraction. Things are much better around here now.

Denying Privileges

With older children this can often be an effective means of shaping behavior, a workable variation on isolation. For a teenager, taking away the car keys for a week *is* isolation. For a grade-school child, depriving him of his favorite TV show is another viable form of isolation—as long as the parent does not allow any alternative entertainment. Nevertheless, for any child under three or probably four years of age, such a system does not work because it's so hard to fit the punishment to the crime with any consistency. The result is that the child feels outraged and the parents end up feeling both angry and guilty—a terrible combination.

> George is a good kid. He rarely acts up, and I was hoping that if I took away his toys I could avoid having to isolate him. I enjoy his company and I didn't want him to spend long periods of time in his room. One day after I had just removed all of his favorite toys, he got mad and hit me. I didn't have anything left to take away, and the whole process had only resulted in his being violent. He was angry, I was angry, and we were both in a jam.

> The problem is that what you take away from them depends as much on your mood as anything else. That will get you into trouble. The other day, for example, I was irritable, so every time Jared did anything that interrupted my concentration on work I took away another toy and told him he'd have to play by himself and not bother me. The problem was that I'd made that impossible for him. By two o'clock I had taken away all his toys, told him he couldn't have his bike for a week, and said no to *Sesame Street* for that afternoon. Then at three o'clock I found myself going out for ice cream to make it up to him, even though I knew that would only make the whole thing worse.

Ultimatums

Many parents feel that the child should "do what I want him to do." This attitude is based on the idea that adults are all powerful and all knowing, and that children are the reverse. In fact, they are so convinced of the child's incompetence that when the two-year-old doesn't automatically obey, they think he must not understand what he was told. But disobedience is rarely due to incompetence. Rather, it's a form of noncompliance, which is in fact a statement of competence—of the ability to make a choice.

The two-year-old wants to do it himself. He wants to make choices. The parent who demands unquestioning obedience is acting out of a need for the child's compliance and adoration as well as out of insecurity about whether his way of life is worthy of the child's respect and emulation. So when the obedience is not absolute, the parent feels threatened or tested, and is likely to respond with physical punishment, emotional estrangement, or both. The result is a frightened child, unsure of his parents' love, whose actions are determined not only by fear of punishment but by an ever sharper sense of what he might be able to get away with (often by lying and subterfuge). Such a child has no inner control, hence little self-respect, and certainly little respect for the parent.

Effective discipline takes time, and the process is not aimed at producing automatic obedience. To be controlled so totally by others denies the child's sense of individuality and forestalls any possibility of learning self-control, since the parent exercises all the control. For the two-year-old such compliance may seem to be quite appropriate—it may even earn him the title of being a "good little boy." But the price is high. On the one hand there is a burning desire to escape what can only be called oppression. On the other hand, he's wholly dependent on the parent. Any separations from the parent therefore feel very risky and frightening, as there is no one there to tell him what to do. Since this pattern often continues into adulthood, he will be left vulnerable to the whims and desires of others, unable to act in his own best interests.

Competence: The Foundation of Discipline That Does Work

As a parent and as a pediatrician I've found only one answer to the dilemmas created by the kinds of discipline that I've just been describing, and that is to redefine discipline itself. Instead of being the means by which an all-powerful, competent adult enforces compliance on his offspring, any successful system of discipline must accommodate the competence of both parent and child.

You have an important role to play, but so does the towering figure at the top of the stairs—all thirty-eight inches and thirty-two pounds of him. After all, you're in this confrontation because that two-year-old can walk, talk, and think as well as you can. Maybe better. Trying to control him, yelling at him, hitting him, telling him he has no choices, no matter how "correct" your limits are, only provokes what you'd reasonably expect from anyone so capable: a defiant and resolute no. From his perspective he can with equal justification tell you he's tired of being bullied, or ordered to do everything *now*. In fact you both have the same feelings.

Your two-year-old doesn't like being pushed around any more than you do. So as a parent you must set up choices, and a means of enforcement, you can both live with. It will take effort, but in a few days you'll both feel better and you'll like each other more. And since effective discipline is self-reinforcing and perpetuating, the effect continues, so you won't fall back into the same old habits.

In thinking about discipline remember the following:

1. Effective discipline puts the emphasis on freeing the child to make acceptable choices of his own, rather than imprisoning him in a straitjacket of your restrictions.

2. Effective discipline involves saying yes more often than you say no.

3. Kids don't like limits and, whatever the experts may say, don't inherently want them. Even if the limits you impose do acknowledge the child's competence, don't expect him to welcome them. They will be tested.

Setting Limits

The Purpose and the Promise of Limits

Limits enable your child to identify a range of appropriate choices, and to avoid unacceptable and ineffective actions. Do limits stifle your child's curiosity or inhibit her motivation? No, exactly the opposite. Discipline—setting limits and backing them up with action—lets her lead a happier, more fulfilling life. You do have to say no sometimes, but in turn that allows you to say yes more often. Your child has tens of thousands of behaviors to choose from, and you find a couple of hundred at the extremes unacceptable. That still leaves her with a huge range of behaviors that can bring her joy and make her feel that she's capable of selecting the right actions without your telling her what to do. Such repeated experiences of success are the foundation of her self-assurance and sense of security, and of her feelings of trust in you.

Don't, however, expect her to applaud the limits you set, no matter how appropriate they are. We would all prefer to do whatever we want, where and when we want—whether it's the two-month-old who cries to nurse every hour in order to calm herself, the six-month-old who desires company three times a night, the three-year-old who never seems to accept anything you say, or the thirty-three-year-old who resorts to acting like a two-year-old whenever she feels frustrated or anxious. But your child will accept your limits when she believes that you will enforce them in a trustworthy, consistent fashion, and when by using them she starts to build on the security of a pattern of successes. Adult praise is an added incentive, but not, it is hoped, the primary one. And even when she gets praise, some part of her still won't like limits. That's human nature.

So when she protests—which she will do—you'll be asking yourself, "Am I being fair?" If you've followed the guidelines in this chapter, the answer is probably yes. The limits will be challenging and demanding, but attainable, and they will change with time as your child herself changes and as a result of the interaction between you. They will also be specific to your child and your family situation, so they won't exactly match the ones that apply (or applied) for her older brother, or her younger sister, much less those that your neighbors have devised for their child. Being fair does not mean doing what all the other parents do or what some expert tells you to do. The limits you set will be determined by your own judgment of your child's capabilities and what will enhance her happiness—and that of the rest of the family as well. It's your obligation to make such judgments, and to reestablish limits that reinforce them.

What Is a Limit?

The answer to that question seems obvious. Yet parents often talk about setting limits and then make a mockery of the idea. Limits must be clear and unambiguous, or they don't work. For the six-month-old newly liberated by the ability to crawl, or the thirteen-month-old who now possesses the thrilling ability to walk in combination with an insatiable desire to discover everything in less than a day, a limit defines the choices that will offer maximum freedom with minimal danger. Therefore a limit is marked by a stop sign, a fence, or a barrier, not a yellow light (i.e., a signal to proceed at risk). Although the grass may look greener on the other side, the child must learn that she just doesn't go there. Conversely, she's free to go anywhere at all on this side of the barrier. Without your guidance on limits, however, every step, literally, is high risk.

There are two types of limits that parents decide upon. One set ensures physical safety. It varies with the age of the child, and is defined by rules such as "Don't touch the knife." (In addition to setting such limits, you will of course childproof your house and do whatever else you can to anticipate and avoid dangerous situations, such as remembering not to leave the knife on the counter edge when you go to answer the phone in the middle of preparing a meal—for no observance of set limits is ever one hundred percent effective, alas; children are too ingenious at figuring ways around them.) The second set of limits is just as important. These are the perennials, many of them as valid at eighteen months as at eighteen years. They tell children how to interact with other people and how to behave within a relationship, and these limits will stand them in good stead for the rest of their lives.

To be effective, limits must first of all be *enforceable*. For the infant and young toddler this means that the parent can prevent certain behaviors from occurring, with or without the child's cooperation—for example, you can keep the eleven-month-old from climbing onto the counter. With the toddler and older child "enforceable" generally means that the parent achieves the desired end not through direct intervention but by using the kind of punishment described in this chapter as a deterrent—e.g., you don't have to physically remove the forty-five-pound four-year-old from the counter, because, knowing what the consequence will be, she doesn't get up there in the first place. The classic example of an unenforceable limit, on the other hand, is telling the child she has to go to sleep. It is possible to tell a child to go to bed, and to enforce that, but parents can never make a child go to sleep no matter what they do or what punishment they resort to (as we'll discuss in some depth in the next chapter).

To be effective limits must also be *specific,* and this is an area where we all get into trouble. Too often when imposing limits we don't say exactly what we mean, thus opening the door to behaviors that are unacceptable but have not been prohibited. If a limit is specific, it's not a complicated matter to determine whether the rule has been broken, and once broken, it doesn't matter whether it's broken by a hair or a mile, the punishment is the same. If, however, your limits are ill defined, any child is bright enough to see through the loopholes you've left, and to come up with behaviors that don't really break these vague limits but are nonetheless quite irritating. This is what is known as testing. Testing can lead to manipulation, and even perhaps defiance.

Is there an identifiable difference between these three behaviors? Absolutely. Testing is actually an abused term. Many people say testing when they mean manipulation or even defiance. But from the child's perspective testing is her means of defining the limits. That's why it's more common among one-year-olds than three-year-olds—for the latter have generally tried out just about everything at least once, and they know the limits (whether or not they abide by them).

When my son was almost eleven months old, I watched him struggle hard to define (and of course to evade) what was off limits. He was determined to sample the dog's food, and I was trying to establish that it was off limits to him, even though it wasn't in the same category as an electrical outlet or other things that had been made off limits for reasons of physical danger. When for the third night in a row he crawled over to the food and looked up at me, waiting for my reaction, I said, "You don't eat the dog's food." He gave me a big grin. Realizing from past experience with that grin that he wouldn't be daunted once I took away his primary objective, I quickly tried to cover every imaginable option he might be considering or had tried on previous evenings. "Don't play with it, don't throw it, don't kick the bowl, don't stand in it, don't pour it on the floor or tip the bowl over." For about one millisecond I felt secure, until he grinned again, staggered to his feet, turned around, and sat in the bowl, hands held high so as not to touch anything while squealing with delight. He'd found the loophole. He didn't go beyond any of the established limits, and this was clearly a way to show off his new skill of being able to walk—not to mention his powers of understanding and reason. This to me spelled ingenious testing, so I applauded—quite literally. But in stating my rules the next night I added "sitting in the bowl" to my list. That night I apparently covered all bases, because once he heard the list, he simply watched the dog eat and that was the end of that round of experiments.

Once a limit has truly been defined and understood, however, you shouldn't need to make a speech each time you want to enforce it. A month later, if Red had gone over to the dog's bowl and in response to my telling him not to touch the food had dumped it on the floor without ever actually touching it, I would still consider that to be manipulation, not testing. When the limit has been made clear, the testing time is over.

Let's look at another example of the way your failure to say exactly what you mean when establishing a limit can lead to testing and manipulation. One day your son is playing with the stereo receiver, changing stations. This may be irritating but it's not until he turns up the volume so that your ears hurt and the speakers crack that you say something. If you say, "Don't change the volume," and he immediately turns it up, that's defiance, and it's clear that you must punish him for breaking a rule. A much more problematic response, however, which confuses many parents, is the following: He pauses, thinks, cocks his head, smiles, and carefully touches the case with just one finger. That's testing, an activity to be encouraged and applauded because it's part of his endless quest to explore the world and to determine what the limits really are. His ingenuity has enabled him to make an allowable choice, since all you said was that he was not to change the volume—and he didn't. On the other hand, if when the volume was turned up you said, "Don't touch the stereo," which doesn't really specify what you want, and he chose the action of touching the cabinet with only the very tip of his finger, it's no longer testing, but it's not quite defiance either. It's manipulation. Nonetheless, it too must be punished. Why? It's such a minor infraction, and in any case doesn't cause the loud noise which is what you were really trying to eliminate when you said, "Don't touch the stereo."

The reason it must be punished is that limits must not only be clear, enforceable, and specific, but they must be *consistent*. Or, more precisely, *you* must be consistent in backing them up. If you are not consistent in your enforcement, if you get into the habit of tolerating minor transgressions, you'll undermine your own established limits and eventually make them meaningless. In the case of the child who touches the stereo when told not to, even though he didn't blast out the music at 110 decibels, it's important not to let the infraction go, because you'll be giving him the message that rules can be broken. Touching the cabinet with the tip of a finger after he's been told not to is breaking a rule just as surely as if he had hit the stereo with a hammer—and he knows it. If you tolerate it, not only will you open yourself to further manipulation but, when he moves on to open defiance, you'll quickly discover that the rules and limits don't mean much anymore.

Manipulation is a conscious attempt by the child to break or stretch parental limits without incurring punishment, and it can only occur with parental complicity. While testing is a manifestation of curiosity and exploration, manipulation is a calculated move. You can tell by the child's body posture, furtive glances, and sly grins that he knows this is an affront and that he's calculated he can probably get away with it. The only way to change this kind of behavior is to make sure that he *doesn't* get away with it.

I'm not underestimating the difficulty of being consistent. Consistency demands great self-discipline. It's no small feat to care for a vigorous, energetic, inquisitive eighteen-month-old who sees options where you thought you had eliminated all the unacceptable and dangerous choices. And if you've just returned from a long day at the office, or are tired out from a comparably long day at home with your child, it's tempting to not be so rigorous. So what if she played with the papers on your desk—a no-no—she didn't really do anything worse than shuffling them a bit, and it only took a minute to get them back in order. Do you really have to punish her for that? You'd so much rather relax and try to have a good time with her. But yes, you *do* have to punish her. Once you don't enforce an established limit, regardless of your "valid" reason, you say to your child that your limits are negotiable. And since she doesn't like limits, she reaches her own logical conclusion—that every limit may be extended or even ignored. The inevitable result is the oft-heard lament: "She's impossible to live with this week. Out of the blue I'm seeing behaviors I haven't seen in months." Almost certainly it wasn't the child who changed, but the enforcement of the rules.

But what happens when you want to change a rule because you've decided for one reason or another that it's not valid? Parents stay awake nights wondering, "Won't I ruin the whole system with that kind of inconsistency?" Thankfully no, or the parent role would be so impossible that it would have been phased out long ago. Sometimes we mistakenly establish limits that are inappropriate or unfair. If you have lingering doubts about a limit you've set, you must resolve them—either by changing the limit, or by sticking to it after you've thought the issue through more carefully, but *not* by enforcing it waveringly and inconsistently. And if you need to change it, do. Tell the child what the limit was intended to accomplish, why it doesn't seem to be adequate, and what the new one will be.

What Is a Phase?
(And Why Doesn't It Go Away?)

When parents aren't consistent, when they aren't specific or they fail to enforce limits, they usually compromise on the spur of the moment, and as a result they end up tolerating multiple behaviors which make family life unhappy. Suddenly the child seems like a different person. "I don't know what's gotten into her," we say at such times—as though we ourselves had had nothing to do with this change, when in fact we bear the major responsibility for it. The problem can escalate even further, and become what we commonly refer to as "a phase she's going through" (thus implying that neither we nor she can be held accountable for this supposedly inevitable stage of development) when lapses in discipline happen to coincide with the appearance of a new skill in the child's developmental repertoire. The ability to walk, for instance, demands dozens of new limits, as does an added inch or two of height and reach, and if the child comes into these new abilities at a time when limits have been compromised, the stage is set for a wide appearance of problem behaviors. Yes, a new "phase" occurs, but there's nothing inevitable about it. Phases involve a family reaction—it's not just how the child behaves, but how everyone else reacts that contributes to the creation of a pattern sufficiently sustained to warrant the term "phase." Your reaction also determines in large part when such a phase will end. Children don't automatically outgrow phases of behavior. To say "It's just a phase, she'll outgrow it," as a means of evading the responsibility for imposing discipline is just that—an evasion of responsibility, not an accurate psychological picture of how children grow up.

Typically a phase begins because some new language or motor skill catches you unprepared, so you don't react when a rule is broken. Or, startled by the new display of competence, you distract the child rather than try to enforce a set limit. As parents we've all stumbled into this situation. You see it as a one-time affair, the child does not. As far as she's concerned, the rules have changed. Wanting as much freedom and independence as possible, unchecked by limits which weren't enforced, hoping for other breakthroughs, the child sees opportunity everywhere, and with her new skills or new physical range she's better equipped than ever to make the most of it. This is straightforward logical thinking, and it happens in every age group.

Since you, as a parent, tend to forget the one incident that set this chain of action in motion, not understanding its significance to the child, just as she doesn't understand that you never intended a one-time lapse to become a precedent, you become adversaries in an escalating battle. So the backtalk continues, the hitting episodes increase, the bedtime routine becomes no routine at all, and so on. During this time parents often feel manipulated.

This happened in our family when Red was around eighteen months old, and was suddenly developing all kinds of new physical skills, due to improved coordination and two new inches in height. One of the rules we had at that time, which (after a few episodes of time-out) he'd been very good about observing and which I'd therefore come to take for granted, concerned knives. All sharp knives were off limits to Red, and he knew it. Nonetheless, one night when I'd just come home, I walked into the kitchen to find that Red had five knives perfectly aligned along the edge of the countertop—a countertop he could barely reach at that time! Furthermore, the knife drawer was behind a cabinet door, and all the cutting knives were at the back of the drawer in their own compartment. Frankly, I was so impressed with the energy and ingenuity he must have expended, first to get the knives out, then to align them so neatly on a countertop he couldn't even see, that my first reaction was just that—I was impressed. Even so, I should have—and would have—punished him on the spot, except that just at that moment he said, "Fix dinner," and made me laugh. As part of our evening ritual together Red is given a very dull butter knife to chop things like peppers as I make dinner, and he was clearly in a state of high anticipation. I love my time in the kitchen with Red as much as he does, so I chose to interpret his defiance of our rules about not touching knives as an innocent sign of his eagerness to get started on our nightly cooking chores. Without saying so, therefore, I compromised: "Thanks for trying to help out. Are you ready to chop up the peppers?" He grinned as he took the butter knife out of my hand.

As we started to work I reminded him of our rules about knives, but since he hadn't used them to cut anything, but had only arranged them in a neat row and left them alone, I decided not to make a big deal out of it or punish him. I just wanted us to have a good time in the kitchen, and we did. He frowned slightly when I reminded him that knives were off limits, worried about going to time-out, but kept working on the peppers once he saw I had no intention of punishing him. When he made no further attempts to use or reach for any of the cutting knives that night, I reassured myself that I had gotten away with this one incident, that previous well-enforced specific limits and Red's basic common sense had rescued me. What a joke!

For about a week afterward there was one inexplicable incident after another of acting out, with Red trying to evade limits he'd long since accepted. Suddenly I seemed to be yelling at him all the time. The change in his behavior wasn't confined to home, either. When I heard that Sarah, one of his teachers at day care was upset with him, I began to think seriously about this phase, since Sarah was perhaps Red's biggest fan, often joking with me on Fridays about wanting to kidnap him so she wouldn't have to wait until Monday to see him again.

What was going on? I began to think that maybe Carol wasn't disciplining him while I was gone, or conversely that— as Red's grandparents were always trying to tell me—we were being too hard on him, and he'd finally had enough and decided to rebel. Maybe I'd gone too far with my insistence on limits, I thought. But then Red himself put me straight. One night before dinner, Red walked over to a chair and, in full view, with none of those sneaky looks or coy gestures that tell you when a child knows he is doing something wrong, he climbed up on it, reached into the drawer where the knives were kept, and proceeded to line up two knives—one sharp, one dull—on the counter, before announcing: "I'm ready." Furious, I was about to yell at him—something along the lines of "Red Sammons, you know very well you're not allowed to play with knives"—when I realized that he no longer did know that. For several nights he'd been punished for his bad behavior by not being allowed to help out in the kitchen, and tonight he'd decided to try to get back into our good graces by showing just how helpful he could be. I could see from the look on his face and from the openness of his behavior that this wasn't defiance, manipulation, or even testing. Because of the way I'd handled the knife situation the week before, limits had become unclear, which in turn had precipitated his attempts to get all the other limits clarified. I knew then that I would have to confront this situation head on.

"Red, remember last week when you lined up those knives?"

"Uh huh," he said expectantly.

"Well, somewhere in the talk we had that night I'm sure I told you that the sharp, dangerous knives were still off limits, but I didn't make it very clear and I didn't back it up with time-out the way I always did before. No doubt that made it confusing for you. But from now on if you touch the sharp knives we're going back to our old system of time-out. I'm all for you doing ingenious activities and showing off your skills, and I love having you help out in the kitchen—just do it with the dull knives. Do you understand the difference?"

He nodded his head yes, opened the drawer, and put the sharp knife back. "Can I help now?"

I hesitated a second. He had touched the sharp knives. Technically that called for time-out but he understood the lesson. I went over and hugged him. "Yes, you can help, but you only use your knife to cut the carrots for salad. I appreciate your putting the sharp knives back, but they are off limits from now on, regardless of the situation." He nodded his assent and proceeded to get slices, sticks, and chunks out of those carrots with his dull knife. While knives have never been an issue again, that wasn't quite the end of the string of problem behaviors, of course. But two days plus half a dozen episodes of time-out later, when I picked him up at day care Sarah said, "He's all better. His usual, lovable self has returned." Indeed it had. And I'd learned a valuable lesson.

Fortunately he never cut himself with those knives, but he, like other children, probably wouldn't have stopped playing with them even if he had. Children never automatically outgrow phases. As long as a behavior is allowed or even encouraged by receiving ever more intense reactions and added attention (precisely what I was giving Red during that week when he was behaving so badly), then it will continue to be used. Children only outgrow a phase when parents clearly reestablish (or in the case of new behaviors, *establish*) what the limits are.

Unfortunately, recouping lost ground often makes a parent feel foolish and humble. The tendency is to try to compromise your way back to how things were before. In the process, however, limits become all the more unclear, enforcement more erratic. Compromise only begets more compromise. Sometimes you just have to admit the error of your ways and explain to your child that though you were lax in the past, things are now going to be different.

Enforcing Limits:
Time-Out and Recognition

Setting reasonable limits, making them clear and specific, and communicating your seriousness about them by enforcing them consistently, without compromise or negotiation, day in and day out, is only half the battle. The other half is coming up with an appropriate enforcement strategy. Many of the inappropriate ones described at the beginning of this chapter—yelling, hitting, trying to distract the child from one activity by offering another even more enjoyable one, and so forth—have one factor in common, different as they are in other respects: They all focus a lot of attention on the child. And attention, as I discussed in the chapter on tantrums, is exactly what every child wants. That's why none of those techniques work. The key to getting a child to behave acceptably is to appeal to her primary motivations, which are two: first of all the desire for attention, and secondly the drive to gain new mastery in the world around her.

Time-Out

As you'll recall, the father of one of my patients and I developed what we think of as the absolute-number theory of child psychology, to describe the fact that children go for the most intense reaction they can get from the outside world, whether it's positive or negative. Startling? Not really. Many adults behave in the same way. And even those of us who have managed to get our behavior under control are still likely to crave attention, though we are generally well enough socialized that we have a strong preference for positive attention. But children will take any attention they can get.

Imagine the following early-morning scenario involving your four-year-old daughter. For the last several days you've been fighting the battle of the finger paints. They're a wonderful diversion for her, keeping her occupied for as long as several television shows but producing much more interesting results. Of course she's had to learn how to use them properly—which means only in the kitchen on the washable linoleum floor in a corner that you've set aside for that purpose, and only on the special finger-painting paper that you gave her. She now understands the limits very well, and this morning she faces a choice. She can score a [−80]: you scream and yell and turn blue in the face and cry when you find her at the desk in your study smearing finger paints over a legal brief you stayed up half the night to finish; or she can get a [+10]: you're tired from having stayed up to finish that brief last night and so when you see her playing quietly in the corner of the kitchen with her finger paints, you give her a perfunctory kiss and pat on the head, say, "Good girl," and then sit down to a cup of coffee while thinking over further refinements you might be able to make in your brief. You're barely considering that the youngster in the corner has made a conscious choice not to smear paint over your papers, and is hoping for someone to notice how good she's being. Which do you think will be more tempting—the hysterical tirade or the quick kiss?

The point here is that the only adult reaction which does not reinforce a behavior is whatever comes closest to a social zero. In this case an absentminded kiss and pat on the head are very close to zero. So let's say that, on the basis of past experience, she's chosen to break the rules and your papers are now awash in purple paint. I do of course understand the temptation to just let loose and explode. But an explosion is great from her point of view. It's lots of attention, directed at her, and quite a show besides! When faced with situations like this, you need to remember that children are not simply perverse beings endowed by Mother Nature with a negative streak which is always going to be there. No. Children are extremely competent human beings, and one of their great competencies is in getting what they want. What they want most of all is attention. To change their behavior you must speak to this primary motivation, which means creating a social zero.

As discussed, time-out, or isolation, is the closest to a social zero you can get. If you send the mad finger painter to her room—instead of throwing a tantrum to rival one of her own, instead of trying to guilt-trip her by talking about how her action is going to ruin your day, instead of explaining how this is going to take up hours of extra time that you might otherwise have spent on her, and so on ad infinitum—then you will be depriving her of what she most wants: attention from you. And that's the primary purpose of time-out.

If, moreover, you confine her in a place without any kind of toys or other stimulating environmental distractions, you will prevent her from fulfilling her next most important motivation in life—the drive to make new discoveries and master new skills.

Recognition

Let's imagine a third version of the finger-painting scenario. In this one you walk into the kitchen, still in a daze from last night's marathon work session, dying for a cup of coffee, and there's your daughter, sitting quietly in the corner doing her finger paints—the first time she has done this on her own. If you want to reinforce this behavior, you'll delay that cup of coffee and give her the benefit of the same amount of attention and energy for being good that you used to give her (before you learned about time-out) for being bad. First you offer her a big hug and kiss and tell her how pleased you are that she chose to play with her paints in the area set aside for that purpose. Then you start looking at her stack of paintings. And don't just say how pretty they all are. Really look at them, and engage her in an in-depth conversation about them.

"Which one of these is your favorite?" you might ask.

"I don't know." The eyebrows are arched a little, her body posture is coiled—more coy than indifferent. She's waiting to be drawn out.

"What about this one? I know how much you like purple and orange, and this one has great colors in it."

"Uh huh."

"I like this one with all the pink in it even better, because it reminds me of the flowers outside. And I bet this face with the whiskers is that cat from down the block who I chased out of the flower bed yesterday. Am I right?"

"Yes. His name is Smoke."

"So is the one with Smoke your favorite?"

"No, the one with the whales."

You look but don't see any whales, until finally she takes pity on you and hands you one with a big gray blob and a big black blob. "See, he's chasing the boat because he has to protect his family," she explains, and in fact now you can see that there are three little gray forms behind the big one, and that the black blob is a boat. "I made it be black because the bad guys are in it," she elaborates. Not quite Moby Dick and Captain Ahab, but Herman Melville would get the picture.

"You're really fascinated by whales, aren't you? I can see why this one's your favorite. You should save this picture for your scrapbook. But do you think I could have the one of Smoke?"

"Okay." She grins up at you.

"Thank you for my present, and thank you for doing your finger paints here! Do you want to bring a few more pictures over and tell me about them while I get my coffee?"

Since intense social interaction is the child's goal, even a few minutes of focused attention will be wonderfully effective— much more so than telling her she's a good girl and wandering away. It's what you do, more than what you say, that carries the message. When you react quickly and intensely to acceptable behavior, you let her know how much you value it.

Not that words aren't important. But they should be the right ones. One thing we all tend to do is to fall into the habit of labeling a child a good girl or a bad girl because of something she has done. It's the behavior, not the child, that is good or bad. And it's the behavior you should comment on, particularly in terms of how it makes *you* feel. Here's an example:

A few days ago I got mad at you when you wouldn't pick up your toys before dinner, so I sent you to your room and told you that's what would happen from now on if you didn't clean up by dinnertime. I'm really delighted to see you got the message. Tonight when I saw the usual unbelievable mess I thought we were going to have a repeat of the other night. Instead you picked it up without even a word from me. You can't imagine how happy that makes me. It means we'll have time to read stories tonight before I have to make dinner. That's a lot more fun for both of us than my yelling at you or sending you to your room.

Accompany these words with much clapping, jumping up and down, and excitement—comparable to the energy you might once (before time-out) have put into shouting or yelling or hitting.

And remember, the older the child, the more important the feedback is. Because if she doesn't get signals from you to reinforce the values you're trying to instill in her, she'll certainly be getting plenty of them from her peers, and from television and the movies—and they probably won't be giving her the messages you'd like her to get.

Time-out and recognition are the two most powerful ways of communicating your values to a child, from toddler age on into the teen years.

Time-Out: Mutual Gain, Mutual Reinforcement

Many parents are reluctant to use time-out because they think it is psychologically cruel, sure to result in damage to the child and to the relationship between parent and child. But reinforcing limits with isolation is not abandonment and will not be interpreted that way. Children respond to it very quickly because while it is a real punishment, they know it does not mean the withdrawal of emotional support or love; otherwise it would not be effective. Even the one-year-old understands that his mother is in the next room, available to him if he really needs her. If your child continues to yell during time-out, it's precisely because he knows that someone is there to hear him. If he really felt abandoned, this would be a shattering experience and, like hitting or other physical punishment, would not lead to an acceptance of the limits you have set but to anger and even worse forms of acting out and unacceptable behavior. But unlike other forms of punishment, isolation is a message that is clearly about limits and doesn't create any uncertainty about your feelings for him. Still unsure? Think about the child's behavior. When he's mad, the fifteen-month-old pretends not to hear you, the twenty-month-old stomps off to the other room, the four-year-old threatens to run away. In fact, whether you use isolation on him or not, your child will use it on you. Children clearly know what it is. They won't get confused when you use it for discipline. The parent who can use isolation for the mutual good of himself and his child is the parent who will create a sense of security in his child.

Does time-out really work that fast? Believe it or not—yes. The message it gives is clear, the parent-child relationship remains intact, the unwanted behaviors disappear. This may seem hard to believe if other forms of discipline have been unsuccessful for your family. Just because you've been saying no incessantly or punishing your child for months without any impact on his actions does not mean that his behavior is unchangeable, however.

The primary reason isolation works so quickly is that it utilizes the child's dual motivations—his desire to discover and to master the world around him, and his quest for intense attention. The other major reason isolation is so quick and effective is that it is as reinforcing for adults as for children. Just as it enables children to make more and more acceptable choices, this strategy relieves parents of their constant doubts about both the appropriateness and the effectiveness of what they're doing. There are no more angry shouting matches motivated by your fear that the eighteen-month-old is eventually going to be kicked out of school or get caught stealing from stores if he persists in his present behavior. Nor will you suffer the embarrassment of wondering what other people think of you in the grocery store.

Isolation defuses explosive feelings and puts them in perspective. Since isolation enables you to control the spiraling, escalating reactions that typically occur in battles with a child, your own self-esteem will be enhanced as much as your child's. You too will be feeling a sense of self-mastery. Many adults gain almost as much self-control from the use of isolation as their children do, and in the process become better models for their children as well. The end result is that you feel more competent as a parent: your limits are being obeyed, your time with your child becomes more enjoyable, and your child also seems to enjoy life more. This is what happened for Harvey and his three-and-a-half-year-old daughter Carrie during the first week they were left on their own together.

Pam, Harvey's wife, had to leave town on business that week. She was rightly concerned that Harvey would let Carrie get away with murder, or its equivalent, and she explained to him that his only hope of getting through the week without having Carrie turn into a hellion was the time-out techniques she'd been using with great success for the past several months. Though he could see that they worked well for Pam, he'd been reluctant to employ them himself. The truth was he liked having Carrie be daddy's special girl and was afraid she wouldn't feel the same way about him if he were to put her in time-out. So while congratulating Pam on her success, he'd stayed on the sidelines. This week, however, he's moved to the front—taking complete responsibility for his daughter for the first time since she was born.

The week did not begin well. "Most of the guys at work told me I'd never live through it," Harvey said, "and by Monday night I was already beginning to agree with them. In fact I was beginning to wonder what kind of man, what kind of father, what kind of human being I am."

Yes, children can do that to you, and Carrie, knowing that she could twist her father around her little finger, had really pushed Harvey to the limit that first night. "After she ignored five or six warnings to leave my blueprints alone she spilled some of her milk on them. Next we had a long negotiation over dinner. She said she wanted scrambled eggs, but when I served them she demanded hot dogs. I didn't want her to starve, so I ate the eggs and made her hot dogs. When I gave her the hot dogs she said they weren't the right ones and she wanted Frosted Flakes. I ended up letting her eat ice cream, rationalizing that at least it had a lot of calcium in it. Finally it was bedtime, and that was yet another negotiation. After I read her the usual two stories, she begged for two more 'just tonight because Mommy's gone.'

"I felt exhausted and foolish from being pushed around, but she looked like she was having the time of her life—until I got mad and told her I was leaving that minute and she had to go to sleep. You can't imagine how awful the rest of the night was—up, down, up, down, all night long—stuff she never does when Pam's around, but I felt sorry for her because I was afraid she missed Pam, so I kept getting up and going to her every time she called out."

To Harvey's dismay the next morning continued the downhill slide when Carrie stalled about getting dressed. He threatened her with no TV, then no going to Burger King for onion rings after school. Still no results, so he went to pick out her clothes for her. "Nothing I chose was right. This one was the wrong color, that one felt scratchy, until finally I just dressed her myself. I was a little rough with her because I was so exasperated. Here I am, six feet four inches and two hundred and fifteen pounds, pro football career and all, and I've got this thirty-five-pound brat running me ragged. Yeah, suddenly I'm thinking of her as the brat—this kid I've always bragged about. It was all I could do not to call Pam and beg her to come home."

By Wednesday things were worse still. Harvey was so tired he made mistakes at work. Carrie, however, was raring to go, having had a long nap to refuel from the interrupted sleep of the night before—something which Harvey could have used himself.

"She was running around with this Zube Tube—one of those things that make a lot of noise—and when I asked her and then finally ordered her to stop she just kept shaking it, until I grabbed it out of her hands. She started screaming hysterically, 'It's mine, you can't have it,' and I didn't know how to get her to stop, so I told her we'd go out for onion rings, even though I'd taken that treat away the day before. While we were at Burger King I had a serious talk with her about how I was giving in to her this one last time, but her behavior had to change. She looked at me with the sweetest smile and said okay. So what's the first thing she does when we get back to the house? Goes straight for the Zube Tube! That was it—I told her she was going to time-out. You should have seen the look on her face. She was outraged that I would do such a thing to her. And frankly, I couldn't believe it myself—but I did it.

"The whole time she was in there—I don't think it was more than five minutes, but it felt like a century to me—she sobbed like she was being tortured. When I went in to get her she told me she hated me, and I felt awful. Especially since it didn't help any. The whole night was one scene after another. Absolutely nothing went right, and I was furious at myself because I felt time-out only made matters worse. I figured it wasn't right to use isolation on her when she was probably already feeling abandoned by her mother."

Luckily for Harvey, Pam called and listened to his tale of horrors. She explained that the reason time-out hadn't worked wasn't that Carrie felt abandoned; rather, she knew he wasn't serious about it. He'd only left her there for five minutes, while Pam had been leaving her for twenty; he hadn't locked up her toys; and he'd only used time-out that once, even though she had misbehaved continuously afterward. "Either get serious about it or don't bother with it at all," she said, and Harvey began to think she was right.

The next morning Harvey informed Carrie, "This wasn't the way I wanted to spend the week," and that he didn't want her to keep taking advantage of him, so he was going to start using time-out—but this time for real. Things went pretty well after that. She dressed herself—everything but the boots, anyway, which she got him to do for her—and was ready to leave on time. But back at home that afternoon she openly defied Harvey when he told her to take the Zube Tube outdoors. She grinned and ran around the room with it, just like the day before.

When Harvey ordered her to her room, she refused to go. "If you don't go now, you're in there for more time," he told her, and she took herself away, wailing with every step and making him feel miserable. "I steeled myself for the sobbing I was sure would follow, but it lasted maybe a minute. Twenty minutes later, when I went to get her, there was none of that 'I hate you, Daddy' stuff she'd pulled on me the day before."

The rest of the evening went fairly smoothly. Each time there was a potential confrontation, Harvey warned Carrie about time-out and she backed down. Friday began with a scene about getting dressed, but Harvey told Carrie she'd do time-out after school if he had to dress her, and she quickly pulled on her clothes, boots and all, scowling at him the whole time. "I felt like kind of a heel—I mean, she's just a little girl and her mother's gone—and I was expecting her to be mad at me when I picked her up at school that day. But she was bright and happy as could be, gave me a big hug, and was great all afternoon and evening. When Pam called that night to say she'd been delayed and couldn't get a flight back until Sunday, I thought Carrie would cry, but she was less upset than I was—started chattering about the things we were going to plant in the garden the next day, just the two of us.

"When I told her it was bedtime, there was no funny

business at all. I guess she knew this wasn't up for negotiation anymore. I'd changed—my successes of the last two days had really given me a lot of self-confidence—and she knew it. I still can't believe how much we accomplished in just two days. Or how different I am as a parent. I'm really lucky Pam put up with me all those years I was just playing at being a father."

What's the Right Age for Time-Out? And How Do You Start?

Setting limits starts in the first few weeks—as you decide when and how you are going to respond to the baby's various demands for physical comfort and social interaction. But when do you start using time-out to enforce your limits? Actually the most common trigger for most parents is being laughed at. They say no and the child chuckles and goes right ahead doing what he was told not to. That's a critical moment, because the laughter says that the child understands the words that specify limits, and the social rules as well. Does this occur at a specific age? Unfortunately, no. It usually happens toward the end of the first year, although I've seen children as young as seven or eight months who were clearly laughing at their parents, and I've heard of, but never seen in the flesh, children who didn't do this until eighteen months of age or so.

The defiance, and the need to do something about it, usually become obvious to parents when they try to enforce a limit having to do with physical safety. Crawling may produce some early confrontations at seven or eight months, and climbing even more, but it's walking that provides the height (reach) and mobility that make any conscientious parent aware of the need for vigilance. And suddenly this formerly tractable ten-month-old, who only last week either retreated or dissolved in tears when ordered away from the forbidden area (a hot stove or an electrical outlet or a staircase), laughs at you when you say no to him. What causes the difference? In part it's his innate desire to explore and develop new skills. Walking is such a boon in this regard, fueling self-esteem and literally opening new vistas, that it's hard for him to resist its possibilities.

But the new physical skills are only part of the development occurring in the child. That figure towering at the top of the stairs is not just able to walk; he's beginning to form words and to be able to understand your words, newfound powers which make him feel he can take on the world and win. Because these feelings of empowerment tempt him to assess the limits of his parents' power, this is a dangerous time in the life of a child. So I'd suggest you consider the ability to stand and walk, and even more importantly the ability to understand what you say, to be signals that it's time to start using discipline. There are also many other behaviors which say it's time: bedtime feels more like a power struggle than an enjoyable winding down at the end of the day; the dinner table is a battleground; you're always tired because your vigilance is up and your antennae are working overtime. The day you made five excursions to get him away from the electric outlets, grabbed him off the stairs three times, pulled him out from under the sink after twice telling him to stay out of there, and then got into a screaming match when you told him not to pull the cat's tail—that's the day enforcement must begin. Defiance is in the air, and danger too.

Do you lower the boom suddenly? Not at all. Even if you're so mad that you *want* to do something dramatic, the ideal response is as low key as possible while still being firm and decisive. Remember, you're trying to create an absolute zero. So don't scream and yell, don't lecture, don't try to guilt-trip him. Just tell him matter-of-factly what's wrong with his behavior and how it makes you feel. "Pulling the cat's tail hurts the cat, and it upsets me because you know I don't believe in hurting either people or animals." Then describe time-out, and tell him that the next time he hurts the cat that's what's going to happen to him. Time-out works best when there's no surrounding drama.

Talking to the child first and telling him in advance what he can expect when he misbehaves means that you respect him and wish to treat him as someone capable of making intelligent decisions about his own behavior if given good guidelines. You're probably looking at the eleven-month-old cherub in front of you and wondering if I'm really serious. Talk to him? You bet. As I said, you're doing this because part of you knows that he does understand. He may not get every word, but he will get the gist of it.

When you think it's time to start using time-out, prepare your child for what is to come by doing the following:

1. Identify a code word which gives the child a clear verbal signal. Pick a word like "don't," "can't," or "mustn't" to indicate limits. "No" is *not* a good choice because nearly all parents overuse it and after a while the child no longer hears it. Explain to the child that this code word is his warning sign.

2. Make it clear that there are no second chances. One verbal warning, and then—if that's not obeyed—time-out.

3. Tell the child where he's going to be during time-out.

4. Assure him that after time-out is over you'll always come back and get him. It's important that the person who initiates time-out also ends it. You want the child to understand that it's his behavior you don't like, not him. Your feelings for him remain unchanged.

In our household the discipline moment came when Red was nine months old. He couldn't walk yet but that didn't stop him from going wherever he wanted to investigate the world around him. Like any parent I was only guessing that he could now understand what I said, so when for the third night in a row I told him to stay off the stairs leading down to the deck, I was alert for signs that verbal reception was available—and I saw them.

Red had been sitting over by the stairs in the opposite corner of the kitchen for about a minute. Going by my own rules I decided to try to preempt the move he seemed to be contemplating. "Red, don't go on the stairs."

He grinned, played with his foot, edging closer to the stairs each time I looked away. Finally, he made his move. Too quickly, however, because it caught my eye. "Red, get off the stairs," I yelled, "the stairs are off limits." I came toward him, he shrieked and crawled away, trying to start a game of catch-me. Again all the cues indicated that he was well aware of what I was saying to him. He certainly wasn't contrite. So I decided the time was ripe.

"Red, life is going to change. From now on when I say 'don't' you need to stop what you're doing. So if I say, 'Don't touch the plug,' that means don't put your finger on it, or try to poke anything in it. If I say, 'Don't touch the cat,' you leave Albert alone. If I say, 'Don't go on the stairs,' then that means stay away from them." He was staring at me, no smile. I didn't get the feeling that this was startling information to him.

"If you go ahead after I say 'don't' then you'll get put in the playpen to be by yourself." (The "pen" as we came to call it, was on the next floor down in a guest bedroom where there was a bed and a table and nothing else. In preparation for time-out, we'd even taken down the pictures so there were only white walls.) Since he was unfamiliar with this room, I picked him up and we went to see it. "I want you to know what this looks like."

Downstairs I put him in the playpen and stood there. "See, nothing to do." His lower lip went out, and I picked him up. "If you listen, and you decide to do something else when I say 'don't'—like crawl away from the stairs and play with a toy—then you won't have to go to the pen." He was pointing and waving toward the doorway, obviously wanting to leave. "I brought you down to see this. If you come down to the pen for time-out, as it's called, then you'll be left here alone. And you'll stay here until I come back to get you. But I'll always come get you. And if your mother puts you in the pen, then she'll come get you. It won't be fun staying in the pen by yourself, but when you do something like going on the stairs, or hitting Albert, then I want you to remember what will happen if we say 'don't.' "

Red was quite delighted to get back to the kitchen. Did he test out the system? Repeatedly. But like all children, he was quick to learn to choose other options when he heard "Don't or you'll go to the pen."

And how do you know you're doing things right? Because your child is. Properly used, time-out and recognition cause problem behaviors to end, and positive behaviors to replace them. This transition will bring pleasure to you and your child. Here's another story about a family who tried many tactics before opting to use time-out. Both Peter and Marcie had been reluctant to make this change because they thought Jackie, eleven months old, was too young. But now she's mastered walking. This development, in combination with the danger posed by their wood-burning stove, now a constant attraction to her, has forced them to talk to Jackie about time-out. But they haven't tried it yet, and like all parents they're faced with the task of finding out what Jackie's threshold is—how many minutes of time-out are required to change her behavior—in this case to prevent her from getting burned. Peter and Marcie are motivated, but still unsure exactly what to do.

"How do you determine how much time is enough?" Peter demands as he squeezes his arms around Jackie, who squirms in his lap, anxious to get back to pursuing her primary goal in life, to reach the red ceramic stove—in the middle of an Idaho January a hot, ominous presence. Of course Peter's asking himself the same question as well, because countless threats, attempts at distraction, even spanking her lightly, haven't deterred Jackie. Now, since it's snowing too hard to take her to the church day care while they tend the ranch, Peter's faced with sitting there all day holding Jackie in his lap or trying time-out.

Jackie wriggles free, totters, and then starts toward the stove. "Stay away from there. Don't touch the stove," Peter bellows. Jackie turns, laughs, and keeps going. Peter jumps out of his chair ready to spank her again. Frustrated, concerned, and worried, he grabs her a few feet from the stove. Hesitating, he turns to Marcie. "Well?"

"I don't know either." Peter marches into Jackie's room, puts her in the playpen, and stands out in the hall for a minute, literally sweating, listening to her cry while reminding himself that this is necessary even though he fears he's being cruel. The problem is that it doesn't work. Three more times in the next hour Jackie goes back into the playpen, leaving Marcie mumbling to Peter, "I don't know what to do now. All the books say one minute per year of age. Do we dare put her in there longer?"

"I'm beginning to doubt anything will work, but what choice do we have? I'm going to try for five minutes." When he does Peter finds out that he's still too lenient. Jackie squawks for about two minutes, but then calms down, and she's hardly contrite when he goes to pick her up. An hour later he tries five minutes again. Clever child that she is, Jackie waits awhile until Peter is busy before she moves toward the stove. Luckily Marcie walks into the room at just the right minute. "Jackie, don't," which again elicits a grin and a provocative chortle before Jackie keeps moving toward the stove. And off she goes for ten minutes.

Everything sounds the same: initial crying followed by chattering and running her feet along the slats of the playpen. Peter wonders out loud if they really removed the toys, since she sounds as if she's enjoying herself. Then after eight minutes she starts to cry. Marcie and Peter watch each other and the clock, determined to wait it out. Finally it's over. Marcie rushes in to get Jackie, who immediately stands up, wants out, and clearly seems to have gotten the message. Marcie reminds her, "If you go near the stove you're going back in the pen, even

longer this time." Much to her mother's delight Jackie looks
somber, but she remarks to Peter, "Does she really understand?"

The answer is yes, and the proof is in her behavior. All
afternoon Jackie never approaches the stove. Then just before
dinner there's another incident. Ten more minutes with the
same pattern of crying, silence/play, then crying. The next day
it's mid-morning when Marcie sees Jackie edge toward the stove.
Just as she's about to put her back in time-out, contemplating—
horror of horrors—going to fifteen minutes, Jackie shakes her
head no dramatically and, with a satisfied grin, grabs a book
which she brings to her mother. Amazed and delighted, Marcie
applauds, hugs her, thanks her for deciding not to touch the
stove and then proceeds to read her three stories—a real bonanza.
The lesson is: For Jackie one minute doesn't work, nor does
five, but ten minutes of time-out will stop unwanted behaviors.

Tips on Using Time-Out

Following are some guidelines to help you enforce your limits:

- Keep statements simple and direct—"Don't touch the plug."
  Don't add "Okay?" at the end, don't apologize, don't overex-
  plain.

- Try to anticipate problem behaviors and preempt them before
  they occur. Don't wait for the trash can to be turned over.
  When you see the child headed toward it with trouble
  written over her face, "Don't turn over the trash can" is a
  valid response. If she does it anyway, she's off to time-
  out.

  If you didn't get a chance to issue a warning before
  the fact, then you'll explain that the next time she does it
  she goes to time-out. Once the precedent is set—she's been
  sent to time-out several times for turning over the trash
  can and you feel confident, on the basis of her body language
  and facial expression, that she understands the limit—you

don't need to keep issuing warnings before using time-out. It's time for self-control to kick in. And don't worry—it will.

- If the child breaks the limit, react promptly. Delay only confuses. Giving second chances and using threats—such time-honored statements as "One more time" or "I'm sick of telling you," etc.—won't work. Say what you mean and mean what you say.

- Don't compromise time-out. If you think the child may need to go to the bathroom or be changed, ask her before you take her to time-out or check her diaper. In the summer get her a drink on the way in if necessary. But don't let cries for help—"I'm thirsty," "I need to go potty"—interfere with the isolation that is the whole point of time-out.

- Time-out means the child's alone, with no play toys, preferably in a separate room. Sitting on the stairs, in the hallway, or facing a corner, rarely works the first time, and never works over the long haul.

- The necessary duration for time-out—what I call the threshold—varies from child to child. One minute for every year of age doesn't work. Expect a one-year-old to require five to ten minutes, a three-year-old double that. If your child is blessed with a stubborn, persistent temperament, then it may be longer. Once you know the threshold, then you never need to use more time than that. You know you're over the threshold—whether it's five, twelve, or twenty-five minutes—when the problem behavior stops.

- When you first use time-out, the child may cry the whole time. Some of it is protest, some affront. For the child who's been through this routine a few times, especially in the eighteen-month and older group, the pattern is likely to be different: initial crying followed by silence (the length of the silence often determined by the child's ability to self-entertain), followed by another bout of crying or fussing. That second round of crying is often an indication that you've found the threshold, and it's time to end the time-out.

■ The person who sends the child to time-out is always the person who retrieves her at the end. The message is that the relationship is unaffected, the slate is now wiped clean. On the other hand, that doesn't mean giving the child extra TLC to make it up to her—for that implies you did something wrong.

■ At the end of time-out, you should review why it occurred. Go over the episode to make sure the limit is clear. For the child who still can't talk, you tell her why she was sent to time-out. For the child who can talk, time-out doesn't end until *she* tells *you* why she went in there. That's more important in terms of changing behavior than wringing out an unconvincing "I'm sorry."

■ Recognize good behavior as well as bad, remembering that intensity of response is the key. When you say, "Don't ————" and the child then makes an acceptable choice, make sure there's no doubt in her mind that you noticed. And comment on the behavior, not the child. "I'm happy you petted the cat instead of pulling his tail," not "You're so good" or "You're the best boy." Hugs, kisses, smiles, applause, or whatever other signs of animation you're capable of will help make your words convincing.

■ It helps to review established limits, and your response, after vacations or other periods during which discipline got lax. Get back on track by talking.

■ When limits have to change because the child develops new skills or your expectations are different, say so; don't fume about it. Consistency doesn't mean rigidity.

- If you lapse on enforcing some limit, perhaps because you've been taken in by protests of "I love you" or "I'll never do it again," then tell the child you've realized (finally) what's happening and that you're now going to respond differently.

Isolation for Aggression

When you see your ten-month-old sticking his hands into the mashed potatoes, your two-year-old using his plastic bat to poke Christmas tree decorations a little too zestfully, or the three-year-old on the verge of dumping over a waste basket, you've got the time and opportunity to issue a verbal warning, to say "Don't do ———— or you'll be going into time-out." The child then makes his decision, and suffers, or enjoys, the consequences. But I recommend making one exception to the rule of one verbal warning—giving one chance for the child to choose a behavior before time-out—and that's when physical aggression against another person is involved. Anytime a child hits, bites, kicks, or in any other way commits or contemplates an act of violence against anyone, he must go to time-out immediately.

You don't need to change the system much. You just have to establish that, regardless of the provocation, biting, hitting, kicking, punching, pushing, and scratching are not acceptable. So the very first time you or anyone else is attacked, I'd respond by saying some version of "Don't hit, that hurts. Any time you do that you're in time-out, starting now." And then put the child there. That may seem a little extreme, but it's the only move that works. Unfortunately, since aggression is a basic part of the human personality, this behavior never stops unless you attack it preemptively.

Now some people will argue that since aggression is a natural means for the child to express anger or frustration, it's wrong to interfere with it. (This is an argument you hear mainly about boys, of course.) If, however, you refuse to use violence and see to it that aggression never meets with success in your home, but instead is an immediate ticket to time-out, you give your child a powerful message—strong enough to counter both his innate tendency toward aggression and the attitude promoted by television and much of the society around him. Often, as in the following story, it is necessary to take a stand when your child is still at a very early age.

Eleven-month-old David reached out for his mother's cup of hot coffee, only to have her grab his hand away just in time. David scowled, then leaned toward her and bit—hard.

Yelping in pain, Anne managed to squelch the curse words that rose to her lips and said in her firmest tone: "David, no biting." However, she was not convinced by the almost smirking look on his face that her words had any effect.

Sure enough, a day later when Anne removed David from her lap to go answer the telephone, he bit her again. "No biting, David, I don't like that," she said sharply as she picked up the receiver and, to her delight, heard the voice of her college roommate whom she hadn't spoken to in a long time. Soon, lost in her conversation with Sally, Anne forgot all about David, until he reminded her of his existence by biting her so hard that her scream of pain alarmed Sally. "Oh, it's just David," Anne reassured her. "He bit me again. For the third time in two days. And now he's grinning about it. I don't know what to do. I'm beginning to think this is part of a pattern that goes back to when he was nursing. Then I was able to stop the biting by refusing to nurse, but now I don't know what to take away or how to respond. How can I punish him when he's not even a year? I still feel a little guilty about stopping the nursing. After all, he was just a baby—what did he know? Maybe he's expressing some leftover anger from that period."

"I wouldn't beat up too much on myself, or get too elaborate in my interpretations, either," Sally interjected. "Getting bitten is no fun, and if he was able to stop then it was clearly intentional, even if all he wanted to do was get a rise out of you rather than actually hurt you. I think that the important thing is not to get sidetracked by all those theories and guilt feelings, because they can keep you from making appropriate decisions."

"I'm not sure what you mean."

"Well, when Hal was about eighteen months old he started hitting and biting, and Bill and I were very upset with him. But we were uncomfortable about punishing him because we felt that we might have set a bad example by doing a lot of roughhouse playing with him, and with the dogs as well. So we decided to deal with the problem by changing our behavior. We stopped all the roughhousing, we gave him a bunch of warnings, and we figured he'd eventually get the message about hitting."

"So did he outgrow it?" Anne had to smile at herself. She'd always found that such a lame excuse for an idea before she had David, and now here she was hoping for the easy way out just like all the parents she'd silently criticized.

"Good Lord, no. I kept hoping he would, and I'd ignore him if he hit me, or try to distract him. But finally one day he clobbered Bill's mother, and I was so embarrassed and upset that I actually hit him back—figuring maybe that was the only way he'd learn a lesson."

"Sally, I can't believe it! After what you told me about how much you resented your parents for hitting you."

"I swore I'd never hit my kid, and I meant it. I was so ashamed I cried. I hugged Hal, apologized, told him I loved him. Everything my parents said to me. Then two minutes later when I didn't immediately go get him the drink he'd asked for, he swatted me on the cheek. Well, I went from remorse to fury in a split second, and hit him again. I knew right then that things had to change—fast!"

"But how?"

"Bill and I talked that night and we realized that there were two issues: the behavior and the emotions. We weren't doing anything about the behavior because we were too tied up with suppressing the feelings connected to it—his and ours. We decided we'd better get the behavior under control before dealing with the emotions. So we sat down with Hal that night and we told him no more hitting, biting, kicking, scratching. Nobody—not us, not other people, and none of the animals. No excuses; no warnings. As soon as he did it, he was in the isolation room. We hadn't wanted to use that technique because I was worried about damaging him emotionally, but suddenly I realized it might help all of us get back under control."

"And did it work?"

"Quickly."

"That's fine for Hal. He was almost two, but David's not even a year."

"Believe me, they understand plenty, even if they can't talk. We've started using time-out with Damian at ten months since he's a biter too, and the message got through immediately. We talk to him afterward including what we think his feelings might be as well as our own. When he learns to use words to express his feelings he can say he's angry and *why*. Just the way Hal did, he'll find it works better than hitting or biting, and when he has a good case, we'll change our limits and he'll avoid time-out. It's a marvelous incentive and certainly builds their self-control. But with David my advice is act now and talk later."

Anne decided to explain time-out to David and warn him that she'd be using it the next time he bit her. He tested the system very soon after that, but changed his behavior so rapidly in response to only two episodes of time-out that Anne realized he did indeed understand, and that all her worries about the possible underlying causes for his behavior had been off base. The point is, many people, like both Anne and Sally, have such strong, conflicted emotions in response to their child's aggression that they tend to overanalyze and underreact (or react inappropriately, anyway). But there's no need to get caught up in amateur analysis. Whatever the underlying reason for aggression, the action itself must be stopped. Only then will you be able to deal with whatever caused it—which is usually nothing serious. The child uses biting or hitting because it works to get his way—not because there's something troubling him that he can't express in any other way. As soon as he realizes it doesn't work, he'll stop. If he's helped to find other means of expressing his feelings, he'll do just that. Physical aggression rarely means that a child is bad or disturbed; it means his parents haven't enforced limits against it.

When "Isolation Doesn't Work for Me"

Isolation will always work because it uses the child's primary motivations to shape behavior. If you've tried isolation but find that your family life is still dominated by conflict since the child's behavior isn't changing, then ask yourself the following questions:

1. Are your limits clear? Make sure limits are explicit and that there are no second chances.

2. Is the time-out space really isolation? Sitting on a chair or the hall stairs is not isolation, and rarely keeps the child out of the social action. If she's not isolated, she'll be creative enough to get the attention she wanted to begin with.

3. Is the isolation enforced by a securely shut door when necessary? Parents who can put the eighteen-month-old in a crib suddenly balk at closing the child's door when she masters climbing out of the crib or the playpen. The crib is justifiable, they feel, but the door seems like a prison cell. If the child willingly stays in the room, then shutting the door isn't necessary. But if she doesn't stay there, you will have to shut the door. And if, as often happens with the three-year-and-older set, she still won't stay in, then hooking the door is the only solution. Don't use a lock, because locking handles are too dangerous, whereas an eyehook can always be undone quickly in an emer-

gency. And there is no reason to start using it in a sudden fit of temper or as a surprise to the child. When she's not in trouble, show the child the hook and how it works, and explain that you'll start locking her in if she leaves her room the next time she's given time-out, which will frequently enable you to avoid ever having to do it. Always end the demonstration by clearly stating that whether or not the door is hooked is entirely her choice, because she can decide whether she's going to stay in the room voluntarily—it's part of her training in self-control. If she chooses to come out, then she knows what the consequence will be. The child makes the eyehook a necessity, not the parent.

4. Is isolation too much like playtime? Remember, for isolation to work, the room environment can't be a play area. Books to read, favorite toys, or cherished games all make isolation a joke.

5. Has the isolation lasted long enough? The answer to this question varies from child to child. Each child has an individual threshold, which depends on both her ability to self-entertain and her stubbornness. You can tell when you're over her threshold because the behavior for which you have isolated her stops.

The duration should not change with the seriousness of the offense. If fifteen minutes is sufficient to keep your two-year-old from throwing her food on the floor, then it will also prevent her from hitting her baby brother; putting her in her playpen for thirty minutes, as you may be tempted to do for the more serious offense, has no additional impact. On the other hand, the amount of time required for effective deterrence does usually change as the child gets older, so that the number of minutes in isolation must increase—for two reasons. First, her growing independence makes it more valuable than ever for her to be able to assert herself, so she will be ever more willing to endure a certain amount of isolation if she can just continue to do as she pleases; secondly, new motor skills and language abilities improve her capacity to self-entertain, so it will take longer for the isolation to become unpleasant.

How do you know when to increase the duration of time-out? There are two reliable guidelines. The first is when, although the time period you're using seemed to work in the past, isolation is not stopping a particular behavior. This often happens, for reasons previously discussed, as the child gets older. It also very commonly occurs when parents initiate a variation on time-out called the parole system, which allows the child to come out of his room at his own discretion—i.e., "when you think you've learned your lesson." If you offer the opportunity, even the most precocious child will come out of his room because he wants to leave, not because he's learned anything. In very rare instances this technique does succeed, but it's a policy that has to stop if the problem behavior recurs.

The second indication of a too short time-out is when you find you're sending the child to his room numerous times, sometimes in the dozens, each day. The sheer number of episodes strongly suggests that the time per incident is too short. It doesn't mean that the child is negative, manipulative, or defiant—just that his threshold is higher than other children's, or that his own has changed. But how can you increase the time? As one mother said, "If I put him in his room for double the amount of time he'd never be able to even go to the bathroom." Once you've found the optimum time span, he won't need to go to his room for dozens of separate isolation periods. Four periods at twenty minutes per episode can be much more effective than, say, twenty episodes of ten minutes. So go ahead and start upping the time. Soon the problem behaviors will lessen dramatically, and the total time spent in time-out will too.

6. What do you do with the child who goes to sleep during time-out? This is an admirable choice on the child's part which may have advantages for everyone, but rarely solves the behavioral problem. I'm not sure why—perhaps there is some association with waking up to the sound of an alarm each morning—but I do know that this seems to happen in a disproportionate number of families who use timers or alarm clocks to signal the end of

time-out. Awake and refreshed when the bell goes off, your child is ready for another round, but time-out is not for sleeping. Tell him and then reset the alarm clock/timer and start all over again.

     7. How do I know that time-out isn't failing because of some fundamental emotional problems that are disturbing my child? Or conversely that he's become such a brat that only therapy will work? If things are really out of hand, then one or both of these worries will occur to anyone, and such concerns must be taken seriously, even though they usually turn out not to be warranted. There's only one way to find out if things have gone too far for time-out to be effective, and that's to spend a couple of days steadily increasing the time your child spends in time-out for each episode of bad behavior. This is better than sending him to his room dozens of times for shorter periods. Maybe he will have to spend the better part of a day and a half in time-out, but he'd be doing that anyway with these innumerable five- or ten-minute sessions that create such an endless battle. If after a week's worth of experimentation with ever longer periods of time-out the problem behaviors end, then you can relax. The only problem was that you hadn't determined where his threshold is. Your child isn't deeply disturbed, he's just persistent, stubborn, and resourceful—admirable qualities, albeit challenging ones. If, however, time-out shows no signs of having an effect, it would be a good idea to seek professional help.

Avoidance of Discipline

Parents and children are equally ingenious at trying to compromise the time-out system. If limits are not clear or isolation is compromised in some way, then the system won't work. Its effects will be lost or possibly even reversed.

Ways That Children Avoid Isolation
—Manipulation

At one time or another every child experiments with ways to distract the parent and avoid discipline. Most parents fail to recognize what is happening because they underestimate the creativity of the child. Some of the more typical means of avoiding or undermining discipline are:

▪ Remorsefully saying "I'm sorry";

▪ Emphatically stating "I don't care";

▪ Hysterically pleading "I love you";

▪ Putting on an extreme show by acting outraged, humiliated, or distraught at being isolated, as if the punishment was unjustified;

▪ Pleading an accident or else playing deaf and dumb at some critical moment;

▪ Adamantly shouting, "I really, really, really want to come out";

▪ Hitting oneself, head-banging, or engaging in some other distressing activity like vomiting or breath-holding which refocuses the parents' attention;

▪ Declaring allegiance to the *other* parent, as in "I want my daddy."

The following scenarios are but a few of the many stories parents have told me over the last ten years to illustrate the ingenuity of children determined to sabotage limits. See which ones remind you of what goes on in your own home.

I had avoided thinking about discipline, but I was absolutely delighted with this whole idea of time-out. I could give

Leah a clear choice, and then she could decide. The isolation was a very dramatic message to her. When my mother-in-law came to visit she was amazed at how much Leah's behavior had changed. Suddenly, however, Leah regressed. I would tell her not to do something and she would go right ahead, looking at her grandmother and grinning while she did it. When I went to isolate her, with her grandmother protesting loudly, she started a new trick. I would pick her up and she would go totally limp. Since that reminded me of the time she had to be hospitalized I didn't want to do anything with Leah except hold her. After three days of this, Leah's behavior was awful. I had to go back to using isolation. She was brilliant—combining the go-limp response with the support she knew she could get from her grandmother. Next step: acting school.

Dan has both selective hearing and selective understanding. But like many first-time parents I didn't know kids knew how to use these adult ploys so effectively. For a while I thought I was just expecting too much of Dan, but then I realized he's incredibly bright and he understands things I would never expect him to be able to comprehend. So why wouldn't he be able to understand 'Don't play with Mommy's face powder'? His other trick is sudden convenient total 'deafness' that he can turn on and off. When I ask if he wants ice cream I get an immediate response, every time. But if I want him to wash his hands before dinner, he suddenly can't hear me. I don't buy these stories anymore.

Of course there may not have been any visits from the relatives recently, and you recognized selective hearing, but perhaps you've been involved in long discussions justifying what you're doing or maybe your child simply bluffed you successfully.

You get this false sense of hope when they're three or four and you can start to reason with them. The problem is they can start to reason with you too. Suddenly Charlie had an excuse for everything, and many of them were plausible enough that I had to stop and think. That was all he needed to be able to get away with anything. He would start talking about something new, and I'd never be able to find a way back to the original issue. He knew he could distract me that way. It is helpful to talk with him—but only *after* he's been isolated. He gets my point, and I can listen better to his.

One day Andy came out of his room and announced that he didn't care about time-out; in fact, I could keep him in his room for double the amount of time. Of course this was a bluff. So I called him on it and left him in isolation for over an hour. That was the last time I heard "I don't care if you send me to my room."

And don't forget that words have great power. I don't know any parent who hasn't been tripped up by one of the following.

The performance was unbelievable. Sally would do exactly what I told her not to do, and then as soon as I went to put her in her room she would be so remorseful. She'd use words that I never heard her use before like "apologize." I found it very difficult to isolate her while she kept up this refrain about how she would never do it again and couldn't I forgive her just this once. She was so cute it was all I could do not to laugh. But I stopped being amused when I noticed how badly she was behaving. It was back to time-out, and this time for real.

"I want my daddy" nearly stopped all of my discipline. Eddie knew exactly how to get to me. I had been working very hard on the playground committee, so I was away from home some nights and he was with his dad. Then one afternoon I sent him to his room for something, I can't remember what, and he started to cry and moan, "I want my daddy." I felt terrible. I thought it was his way of telling me I'd been away too much. But then that night, my husband reminded me that "I want my mommy" was how Eddie had avoided discipline when *he'd* tried to send him to his room. In fact this was no different. Women just aren't used to hearing it.

Ways That Parents Avoid Discipline —Rationalization

Parents are no less inventive than their children at devising ways to shave limits or to make time-out slightly more tolerable and therefore less effective. They often have their reasons for letting the child have one more chance or not really isolating her, such as the following:

- Limits frustrate children, and that can't be good.

- When a child is tired you have to go easy on her.

- Discipline will quash a child's curiosity.

- When you work you don't have the time for discipline.

- There are so many rules in life children should be allowed more freedom while they're young.

- Limits should always be subject to compromise.

All of these reasons sound plausible enough, but they aren't true and they will only work to undermine discipline, not make for a richer or pleasanter life for either you or your child. As a result of such rationalizations for not enforcing the limits you've set, the child no longer understands what a limit really is or why you feel so disappointed, angry, or frustrated when it's not maintained. In every instance, avoiding discipline weakens trust and undermines security. Family life is never what it could be because the child gains little self-control and continues to stage incidents which provoke intense negative reactions from the parents.

> I used to take pity on Charles when we had a long day. He was tired and I would tell myself that I just couldn't expect as much from him. There were other days, however, when he'd use my sympathy as an excuse for awful behavior even when he didn't really seem that tired. So, depending on whether I bought his story or not, one day I'd be understanding and solicitous, and the next day I'd get angry, even though the behavior was the same both days. At that point I was being totally inconsistent and his cries started to sound like he was not just tired but angry. I am sure he thought I was behaving like an unpredictable witch. All of his whining and fussing was really unacceptable behavior regardless of whether or not he was tired, and I had to learn to react accordingly. Now when he starts to act that way I put him in his crib, and if he needs to, he sleeps; if he doesn't, then I figure he was just acting up and needed to be isolated anyway.

> I wanted to go back to work because I have a great job, and when Katie was about two I did. I just wasn't meant to be a twenty-four-hour-a-day mother. But I had read dozens of books that put a heavy load of guilt on my shoulders about this decision, so for a while I was always trying to make up to Katie for this terrible thing I was doing to her. We started to have dinner with the TV on because she wanted it. I would give in and buy her all the cookies she wanted at the grocery store, and in general I just started

to give in to her on a lot of things. After ten days she reverted to being a nine-month-old, throwing food at the table and screaming at me every time she wanted something. I was almost convinced that the books were right and my going back to work really was doing her some harm. Until I discovered that she was an angel the nights she was home alone with her father. Katie was picking up on my guilt and playing on it. As soon as I reestablished the limits by using time-out to enforce them she was fine. Now I concentrate on spending time with her in ways that we both enjoy. Interestingly enough, she continued to behave very well with her father and her grandparents the whole time she was being so awful with me. They never changed the rules; I did.

More Ways That Parents Avoid Discipline
—as in "Do You Love Me?"

The above are some of the rational (or, rather, semirational) reasons parents use to avoid discipline or sabotage it so that it's ineffective. The biggest stumbling block, however, is emotional. Every parent at one time or another avoids discipline out of the fear that it will carry an "I don't love you" message to the child. Equally daunting to parents is the question "Will *he* love *me* after all of this?" which tends to come up as they watch their child shuffle off to his room in tears because they've condemned him to isolation. At such moments it's hard to convince yourself with absolute certainty that he really did deliberately disobey you after you warned him, and that it wasn't an accident as he's now pleading. Perhaps some of these feelings linger because of your own childhood memories, or maybe you're not clear about the difference between making him go to his room, and losing control and yelling something horrible at him or spanking him. After all, he looks just as miserable now,

even though time-out is supposed to be more humane. And it
is. Yelling and spanking episodes are emotionally as well as
physically threatening: both people in such transactions eventually
feel unloved and unloving. However, there is no need to play
emotional Jeopardy. Time-out, used appropriately as a discipline
technique, is not threatening to the relationship. It works quickly
and leaves no emotional aftereffects, since there are no outbursts
you later regret, no physical pain, and no false threats which
ultimately are a type of emotional blackmail.

Make no mistake about it, however: feelings can be at
risk with certain other kinds of discipline—not just your child's
but yours as well. Love, even a parent's love for a child, is
rarely unconditional, although it can withstand many blows.
Enough transgressions will injure any relationship. If your child
repeatedly engages in temper tantrums, confrontations, or total
noncooperation, then negative emotions will build within you
until you erupt in the type of explosion that says, "I don't love
you." In turn this behavior will threaten his feelings for you,
since the love of a child, like our own, is not unconditional.

In part the technique for discipline outlined in this chapter
is so successful because it allows you to express your anger and
disappointment in an appropriate, nonthreatening, nonhostile
way, following a cooling-off period for both of you. No lingering
hard feelings remain afterward.

There is one final way that assertions of and questions about
love undercut discipline. Sometimes parents unwittingly create
insecurity when they fervently reassure the child of their affection
after an isolation episode. "I love you" in such circumstances
says that the parent feels he may have overreacted, or imposed
an inappropriate limit, and is now trying to make up for it.
Some parents in these circumstances become so fearful about
the possible threat to the relationship that they even request
reassurance of the child, as in "Do you love me?" Remember,
discipline is in part teaching, and a role model who asks for
approval will be much less effective. If parents use the methods

described earlier in this chapter the child will not be in any doubt either about the parents' feelings or the lesson to be learned; nor should the parents have any doubts (though we parents have much longer histories, therefore larger neuroses, than our children, alas).

"I love you" is implicit in effective discipline. Parents are saying, "I care enough to discipline myself, to put in the effort, to show my child the enjoyable, useful, socially acceptable behaviors that will make for a good life." And the child will love them in return, for children love those people who help them succeed, not those who do things for them or try to make things easy by fudging limits and encouraging behaviors which are not viable. Nor do they love adults, especially parents, who expect approval or affection as a payback for what the grownup supposedly believes is right. Effective discipline, through the use of mutual self-control and a consistent, reliable behavior pattern, enables parents and child to say "I love you" to each other in more ways, more often.

5

Sleep

"**D**addy, daddy." Normally music to your ears, that squeaky voice from the other room, out in the hall or the other side of the bed, certainly evokes concern, and perhaps a touch of anger or skepticism as well. Blinking your eyes, you roll over to peer at the digital clock: three-fourteen A.M. No wonder you have such a mix of emotions, your head aches, and you feel slightly nauseous.

Should you answer? If so, what should you say? If she's calling from her room or the hall, should you go to her, or take the path of least resistance and let her climb into your bed? Maybe if you had read her one more story at bedtime, for a total of seven, not six, she'd still be asleep. Or is this happening for the third night in a row because your spouse is away on a business trip? As you get both eyes open, you recall that it does happen some nights when your wife is home, but you usually sleep through it, according to her. Didn't your macho pride say you would handle this better?

What do you do? Answers are hard to find, especially in the middle of the night. Your two-year-old may be *compos mentis* at three A.M., but you're *non,* so she has a definite advantage. Unfortunately, as parents, we all forget the lesson of Sleeping Beauty (who, you'll recall, woke up after that fateful kiss). One more kiss, one more hug, another story, or even sleeping in your bed or on the floor of your room, will only result—like the kiss from the prince—in everyone's being awake even longer. And if perchance, on a given night, your child does get back to sleep quickly, you probably can't, especially if she's in the same bed. And you certainly won't feel rested come three o'clock the following afternoon, although she may be showing no effects of having gotten up at that ridiculous hour. In fact, three P.M. is probably just about the time she's taking a nap to refuel so that she can be up at three A.M. again tonight.

No problem causes more family stress than sleep disturbances. For a parent, sleep is vital. Without adequate sleep your career and your marriage will suffer. Other children in the family will be affected too, not just the one who is up in the middle of the night. Furthermore, sleep—long blocks of effective, restful, sleep—is essential to everyone. Fatigued and disorganized, your child doesn't get the most out of her life, can't realize her true potential. Think what a boost it is for a child to sleep soundly at night, to be revived by napping in the morning and again in the afternoon.

If sleep is so crucial, why isn't it automatic? No one knows. Surprisingly, we understand little of how sleep works, why you feel rested in the morning, why a child is suddenly alert, vibrant, and fun after a nap. On the other hand, we all know what lack of sleep can do to an individual and to relationships.

Unfortunately, many children never develop the skills that let them sleep soundly. In almost all families the patterns of behavior that cause sleep problems start early, usually in the first six months. Being a good sleeper doesn't just happen. It has nothing to do with age, body weight, or how much the child eats. Nor is it simply luck or genetics. The three-month-old who wakes at night uses self-calming skills in order to go back to sleep on his own. The two-year-old not only has to be able to self-calm, but she needs sufficient self-control not to go into your room or call out at three A.M. The three-year-old may wake up at five A.M., and unless he can entertain himself until you wake up, then both he and you have a sleep problem. A child can master the skills necessary to go to sleep or go back to sleep with much less effort than a thirty-year-old. It may seem paradoxical that this is easier for the infant than for the school-age child or the adult. We always assume the older person is the more competent. Not in this situation, however. The infant has no bad habits to break, and none of the intense, deepseated emotional dependencies which make sleep disturbances in older children such a seemingly insoluble problem.

This chapter is about the sleep skills children can master and the types of decisions parents must make to help them do so. The result will be a child who rests quietly through the night at two to three months of age and who will in later years be able to deal effectively with stress, fatigue, emotional upsets, and all the other factors that can influence sleep in infancy as well as childhood and adulthood.

How do parents teach their child that daytime is the time to be awake and night the time to sleep? What bedtime and naptime behaviors can parents expect of their child? How do children actually go to sleep, and what determines when they wake up? What should parents do in order to help their child go to sleep at night, and what determines when parents should get up at night?

I will answer these questions, and others, to show you how what you do during the day is a major part of stopping those wake-up calls for attention at night, as well as preventing a wide range of other sleep disturbances. Since your actions do influence how well your child will sleep, and hence how well you will sleep, does that mean you're doomed to years of sleeplessness if you've already established a bad pattern? Not if you're willing to change. The solution for your mutual sleep problem will always involve enabling the infant to be more self-sufficient by nurturing her abilities to self-calm, and helping the older child not only to self-calm but to establish self-control and devise means of self-entertainment. Rather than such ad hoc measures as extra stories at bedtime or desperate actions at three-fourteen A.M., these are enduring skills that any child can master and that will ensure a restful night for everyone. Fortunately, these are also skills that you nurture during the day, which is much easier than sorting out problems in the middle of the night.

What Do We Know About Sleep?

Like all elements of family life, sleep is surrounded by falsehoods about what children can't do and what parents can do. For instance: no matter what any book or baby doctor tells you, there is nothing you can do (short of administering sleep-inducing drugs) to make your son or daughter go to sleep at a specific time. Equally significant (and misunderstood) is the fact that while you may be able to sleep through the night, infants and young children *never* sleep through the night. Typically a child wakes up or comes into light sleep a minimum of two or three times between bedtime and breakfast. There are many other misunderstandings as well, folklore about the ways that feeding, age, body weight, and so forth can affect sleep, the result being that many parents believe their child's failure to sleep through the night means that the child has a sleep problem and that they have failed as parents—neither of which may be the case.

Over the last twenty years research has begun to clarify many of the reasons why children sleep the way they do. For instance, even though our days are twenty-four hours long, most people have an internal biological clock which runs on a twenty-five hour day, and for some individuals their natural day may be even longer. This is one reason why it is often easier to stay up late at night than to wake up early in the morning. There are many other unknowns and uncertainties, but understanding what we do know about children's sleep will help you avoid creating unnecessary problems.

Different Types of Sleep: REM and Non-REM Sleep

Like everyone else infants have two types of sleep, called REM (rapid eye movement) and non-REM.

Non-REM sleep is what we usually think of as deep sleep. Although the brain is still working and controlling respiration, heart rate, and other body functions, there is almost no muscle activity. Breathing is slow and regular. In infants there may be an occasional startle response. Actually, non-REM has four stages progressing from drowsiness to very deep sleep. The characteristics of each stage differ by EEG and other physiologic measurements, but are difficult for parents to identify. In the stage called light non-REM, certain types of sleep disorders such as night terrors and sleepwalking occur. It is also during the light non-REM (and REM described below) that short cries and body motions may occur, which many parents mistakenly identify as signals that the child is awake. This can be confusing, and I have been amazed at the level of noise and the amount of activity my son can generate and still be asleep.

REM sleep is very different, and not just because most dreams take place within REM sleep. REM sleep is characterized by small twitchings of the hands, legs, and face. Although the eyelids are closed, eye motions are apparent beneath them, whereas in deeper non-REM sleep there are no eye motions visible to the observer. These differences enable parents to distinguish between REM and non-REM sleep, which is important, for example, because the child who is in deeper non-REM is less likely to wake when moved than the child in REM sleep. Many infants spend at least fifty percent of the night in REM sleep, and

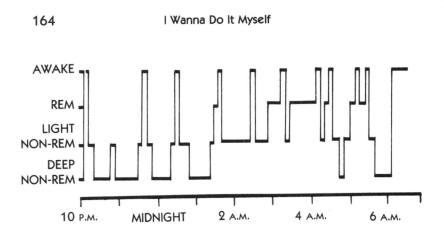

DIAGRAM 1
Sleep Cycling During the Night in an Infant

children who are fatigued or do not sleep well at night have even more periods of REM sleep, which is why they are easily disturbed and not as well rested.

Sleep Cycles

Sleep is made up of different periods of REM and non-REM sleep. These occur in a pattern which changes as the child gets older, especially as he starts to sleep in longer blocks of time at night. Children in a stable nighttime sleep pattern typically have more non-REM sleep shortly after going to bed, and more REM sleep toward morning.

The increased frequency of REM sleep is associated with more periods when the child is actually awake or in extremely light sleep. This is why the child often seems to sleep from ten P.M. to three A.M., and then is up every hour after that.

Diagram 1 clearly shows that children do not sleep through

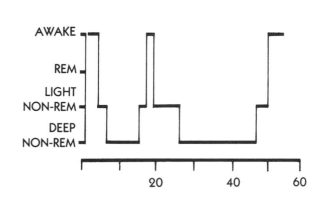

DIAGRAM 2
Sleep Cycles After Arousal

the night. Even from ten P.M. to three A.M. the subject of this study awoke, or was in a light sleep state, but was able to get back to a deeper sleep state. The period from one near-waking or waking event to another is called a cycle. Within what might have appeared to the parents as a solid block of sleep time lasting from ten P.M. to three A.M., there are typically about five cycles. In infants each one of these sleep cycles lasts about fifty minutes, and they gradually increase in length with age. There are also changes within a cycle. While many newborns will go into a deep non-REM sleep right away, they often come back to very light sleep after just ten or fifteen minutes.

During these periods of light sleep, over the course of the night (Diagram 1) or within a single cycle (Diagram 2), the child may wake up, especially if she is overfatigued, hence disorganized. In essence the infant has to fall asleep all over again. The child who has good sleep skills can accomplish this easily regardless of whether she wakes at the end of a complete cycle or during light non-REM fifteen minutes into a cycle. The child who is dependent on being nursed or rocked to sleep, however, needs the parent to come in and begin the whole process over again. At both bedtime and naptime, this can result in a series of mutually exhausting repeat visits to your child's bedroom every twenty minutes or so.

Sleep Rhythms

One of the most exciting areas in medicine is the research which has identified the complex rhythms affecting the way we live and the way we feel. Our body clock is primarily determined by the secretion of a hormone called cortisol from the adrenal gland. Newborns don't have a daily rhythm, but a child's body clock, the one with a minimum twenty-five-hour day, is usually set by his first birthday. In addition, there are other rhythms which determine fluctuations in hunger, body temperature, and activity. Usually we fall asleep in the evening at a time when we have been fed, our activity cycle is low, our body temperature dropping toward the lowest point of the day, and our cortisol level decreasing. We wake as our temperature starts to rise and cortisol nears a daily peak. Because of these built-in rhythms, waking at an unusual time or trying to fall asleep at a different point in the cycle is a psychological and physical struggle.

When travel or illness disrupts the usual rhythm, a child's sleeping pattern may change. If on top of this disruption the child is offered incentives to be up at night, especially in the form of any kind of social attention, he may continue in this unfortunate new pattern, which does not provide enough restful sleep for him or his parents. Repeated every night for weeks or months, this pattern may alter the balance of REM and non-REM sleep or change the normal fluctuations of cortisol and hence the individual's whole body clock. These potential long-term changes are one of the reasons to settle sleep disturbances quickly so your child maintains a consistent sleep pattern that reflects natural body rhythms.

Total Sleep Time

Endless magazine articles and numerous books state that all normal children sleep a certain amount of time at a given age; e.g., the two-month-old sleeps sixteen hours a day, the eight-month-old fourteen hours a day, and the two-year-old eleven or twelve hours a day. Whether directly stated or just implied, such numbers are set as standards which parents should strive to meet. In my experience, however, there is tremendous variation in the amount of time that individual children sleep from one day to the next—just as there are variations in adult sleeping times.

Actually, total sleep time is relatively meaningless. What is important is how long the child sleeps at any one time, and, from the parents' point of view, how long a block of time is available to them to sleep at night.

Many parents can tell you that total sleep time is very deceptive. Their newborn may appear to sleep for a total of fourteen to eighteen hours a day, but no one is rested, including the baby. Everyone is tired for two reasons: First, the baby rarely sleeps longer than one or two hours at a stretch because she doesn't have the sleep skills to string together four or five individual sleep cycles (see Diagram 2, page 165). Second, while she may sleep for a total of fourteen hours each day, just as she's supposed to, nine separate one- or two-hour blocks don't work for her, or for anyone else in the family.

Judging total sleep time in the newborn is also complicated by a phenomenon known in professional research as habituation, which I call playing possum. (See Chapter 3 of *The Self-Calmed Baby* for a more complete explanation of this phenomenon.) When external stimulation gets to be too much, the baby habituates, which is her way of tuning out. What makes this confusing is that habituation looks like sleep (the eyes are closed, the body still), but unlike sleep it leaves the baby fatigued and irritable rather than well rested. Parents who think their one-month-old was snoozing all afternoon are suddenly faced with a wailing, inconsolable, very tired tiger at five P.M. rather than the well-rested, sociable, smiling cherub they were expecting. Furthermore, since that kind of fatigue generally results in light sleep and increased wakefulness during the night (see Diagram 1, page 164), everyone in the family is up more often—one of the reasons that parents sometimes mistakenly think that naps interfere with nighttime sleep. They may also worry unnecessarily that something is wrong with their child. Why else would she be so miserable when she seems to be getting plenty of sleep?

Total sleep time may be an equally specious concept for the two-year-old. He may sleep for twelve hours a day, but if he's wide awake and crying for you twice a night, even if it's only for five minutes at three A.M. and again at four A.M. before you get him back to sleep, he's likely to be tired and his behavior less than sparkling. Furthermore, you'll be exhausted, even though you may actually spend eight hours in bed each night. Getting up for five minutes, even if it's just once, can wreak havoc on both of you, psychologically and physically. The same is true of naptime. Your two-year-old may take a nap for two hours from roughly two to four P.M. each day, but if that requires your going in to resettle him at two-fifteen, when he wakes from light sleep and can't get resettled on his own, and again at three, when he can't make the transition from one sleep cycle to the next without five minutes of intervention from you, then he won't be well rested, and you won't get the uninterrupted block of space and time you need.

None of this is to dispute that children do need adequate sleep time. On the other hand, as in the case of the two-year-old above, getting a long block of sleep time during the night is much more important than the total amount of sleep during any typical twenty-four-hour period. But what causes the differences between getting and not getting enough sleep?

Building Sleep Skills

For years I thought that the answer to this question lay in the child's need for a set routine, transitional objects, and lots of parental help (like rocking or even lying down in bed with him), combined with a dash of parental authority, a dollop of ingenuity, and just plain luck. Nothing could be further from the truth. Parents can have tremendous impact on how well their children sleep by the types of physical and emotional sleeping environments they create, the bedtime routines they establish, and, most critically, the discipline they use during the day. In the next few sections of this chapter I'll discuss how to create an environment which encourages sleep, and the types of decisions which make bedtime, nighttime waking, morning wake-up escapades, and naptime all manageable and reasonably hassle free. At issue is how to encourage the three skills that are the focus of this book, self-calming, self-control, and the ability to self-entertain, for they are as crucial to nighttime as to daytime behavior.

What most parents really long for is to help their child develop ways to go to sleep and to go back to sleep that he can continue to use as he gets older. If you establish some type of prop system, whether it be nursing, rocking, a pacifier, or anything else, some conflict will inevitably result. A time will come when the crutch is not available; you can't or don't want to be there; the pacifier is lost; and so forth. While you may think you're being nice by getting up every night for months or years on end, this is actually setting the child up for an eventual and inevitable withdrawal. Having been encouraged to be dependent, he now feels abandoned. He cries not just because he can't go to sleep on his own and feels vulnerable; he's also angry. Do not delude yourself into thinking that you can avoid this crisis because the child will outgrow the need for the prop. Why should he? How is he to know that the prop system won't continue forever? What incentive is there for him to change?

Building sleep skills ought to start in the very first weeks to prevent creating such dependencies. The ultimate goal is to give your child the security of being able to sleep on his own, when he needs to, regardless of the situation. That may seem to be impossible when faced with a fussy three-week-old or a two-year-old who has never slept through the night, but it's not. Self-calming, the basic sleep skill, is not only an innate competency, as has been extensively discussed elsewhere, but a behavior that makes transitioning from one sleep cycle to the next an achievable goal for any child. Self-calming also acts as a buffer against too much stimulation, so that the younger infant no longer has to habituate so often or for so much of the day, and is thus less fatigued and better able to sleep at night.

Self-control and the ability to self-entertain, as they relate to sleep, are increasingly important as the child gets older. Never do they matter more than at two A.M. when the child wakes up but needs first to restrain himself from calling out to you and then to devise a means of keeping himself amused until he becomes drowsy and can go back to sleep. More nights than I'd like to count I've come home from the hospital at some crazy hour or finally decided to stop writing because the words have turned to gibberish and Albert the cat will no longer keep me company, only to find my son awake—but perfectly content on his own. When Red was eight months old he'd spend an hour running his feet along the crib slats to entertain himself as much as to calm or maintain self-control (I knew it was an hour because I couldn't get to sleep). When he was fifteen months he'd sing to himself, and ever since he's been two he gets up, turns on his light, and "reads." Recently he's added talking to his stuffed animals to his repertoire of self-organizing activities. One night last week he told me he talks to them until *they* go to sleep. The only time Red comes to our room is when he's sick or he's tired of hiding in the bathroom with the dog during a thunderstorm. When he wakes and plays by himself, he rarely makes enough noise to disturb anyone else, and the last two mornings I've found him sleeping by the pantry, having eaten half a box of cereal and then fallen back asleep again. As he gets older I'm sure he'll find other opportunities to entertain himself when I don't want to get up or be awake.

Self-calming, self-control, and the ability to self-entertain are crucial to naptime as well. In infancy, self-calming matters most, since that's what insulates the child from the overstimulation of the day and gives him a way to avoid waking up during sleep cycle transitions. During the second year and thereafter, when many children refuse to go to sleep at all in the afternoon, self-control and self-entertaining are the essentials, since some type of relaxed down time is mandatory each day, as much for the harried adult as the child. The child needs the self-control to accept that he's on his own for an hour or two, and the self-entertainment skills to keep himself happy during that time if he doesn't choose to sleep. He may use naptime to play quietly with his toys, to look through picture books, or simply to gaze out the window fantasizing. The child who can't self-entertain becomes bored so quickly that the nap becomes a parent's wishful fantasy.

Avoiding Problems

So how do you put this knowledge about sleep and sleep skills to work? While the focus of this book is toddlers and young children, in this section I am going to use younger infants as the primary example, because it's easier to explain how the neurophysiology of sleep interacts with factors in the infant's inanimate and social environment. The toddler's sleep patterns are also affected by external cues, but there are more of them because his world is more complex, and the interactions are more intricate and difficult to understand.

Nap-, Sleep-, and Bedtime Decisions— Yours and Your Child's

Going to sleep and going back to sleep are cooperative achievements, jointly realized by parents and infants working together, not independently.

Any given episode of sleep is predicated on a shared set of decisions that families make about sleep. Shared decisions feel risky since they require mutual trust. Parents must believe that the infant can communicate his needs so that they can make decisions that honor those needs, and the baby relies on the parents' being able to read his cues. The result of establishing this mutual trust is that parents get more sleep, and infants learn how to go to sleep when they need to, go back to sleep if awakened, or lie happily awake until ready to go back to sleep again. Are these decisions complicated? No. How many are there? Only four.

Decisions about going to bed and going to sleep:
1. Parents decide when the infant will go to bed or the older child will go to his room, and
2. The infant or the child decides when or, in the case of naptime, whether he will go to sleep.

Decisions about waking up and getting out of bed:
1. The child determines what he will do when he wakes up, but
2. The parents decide when they will get out of bed or, in the case of naptime, interrupt their daytime activities.

Parents can avoid many problems and quickly solve others by simply acknowledging who is really responsible for which decisions. Problems arise because parents, with good intentions, seek to accomplish what they cannot, and are reluctant to let the child do what he can: namely, go to sleep on his own and go back to sleep when he wakes up. That is the only way that parents sleep through the night.

These pragmatic decisions about sleep are influenced, for good or bad, by certain emotional realities that all parents face. In the first few weeks after a baby is born there are a number of boundaries that parents must establish, and only they can decide where to draw particular lines. Parents have a right to some time alone, as well as a responsibility to spend time together to nurture their relationship. For many adults this requires making difficult compromises about work time and career goals, and equally anguishing resolutions not to spend every available minute with their cute, fascinating new baby. Baby's demands don't disappear after infancy, however. Few couples can maintain any kind of friendship or romantic relationship if they always have a two-year-old chaperone in the evening. An even smaller number share a satisfying sexual relationship if they have a child (infant or older) sleeping in the room or they're apprehensive about a three-year-old showing up to ask for a drink or a chance to climb into bed with them. Part of raising children is keeping a healthy, happy marriage. It adds to everyone's security.

Translating the decisions you've made about boundaries into concrete terms is complicated, however, and it's easy to persuade yourself that a large transgression is only a small one or that your capitulation to it will have only a fleeting effect. For instance, last night your child climbed into your bed at three A.M. and neither of you felt motivated to take him back to his room, in part because you knew he'd put up quite a persistent fuss. So you're a little tired this morning, and although your spouse has to leave on a five-day business trip today you didn't make love last night, and you didn't have the early-morning time alone you'd counted on to discuss certain pressing matters you don't feel comfortable handling on the phone and had hoped not to delay until next week—but no one is exhausted, and your marriage isn't ruined, after just one such night. What happens, however, when it's three nights out of five, ten out of fifteen, and then three months in a row?

During the day as well as at night, a child will use his self-calming skills, his self-control, and his ability to entertain himself only when parents consistently abide by the limits they set. Therefore much of the material in this chapter about specific problems is related to the previous chapter on setting limits. The decisions you've made about the emotional time and space you need are part of setting these limits. Having listened to the experiences of many families, I know there are no hard rules about how much time a couple needs to themselves. If you and your spouse need substantial amounts of time alone, then bedtime, wake-up time, and nap time will all be hot spots of potential conflict. If your family travels a lot, waking at night will be an inevitable problem, and if you and your spouse like to go out together or individually, or you have interests which you pursue after six P.M., then it is critical that you establish successful bedtime boundaries and routines or your family life will suffer.

In our society one of the commonly if not universally accepted boundaries is that everyone sleep in his or her own room. In part this reflects the value we place on independence, but there are also good, practical reasons for this arrangement. Sometimes two people cannot sleep in the same room, but chances are no one sleeps well if there are three or more people in the same room, especially if the third person is a baby.

Another boundary concerns your availability at night. You should make it clear that two A.M. is not social time or feeding time. Rarely does the healthy fourteen-pound four-month-old really need to be fed at night, nor does he require being rocked, patted, talked to, or looked in on to be put back to sleep. Similarly, there is no reason that the two-year-old cannot get up at two A.M.—she just has to stay in her room.

Of course there are some who will feel that since the parents set these boundaries, they are necessarily unfair to the child. Anyone who says that is continuing to think of the child as a helpless dependent rather than a person who could enjoy singing himself back to sleep at two A.M. or going to get his own cereal at five A.M. The proponents of this point of view would also have you believe the child feels abandoned when you insist that he go to his room at a certain time or you refuse to get up and play at five A.M. To which I say hogwash. No eighteen-month-old child feels suddenly abandoned after a wonderful day; he just doesn't want it to end. So he cries, asks for more stories, water to drink, or whatever will work to keep you around. Just because he wants you to stay doesn't mean he feels deserted when you go back to the dining room or your bedroom—that's a self-serving adult interpretation. Most parents want to and can set emotional and practical boundaries which help make their child more self-sufficient—and that's good for every person in the family. "I wanna do it myself" is the child's fundamental credo. Honor it.

Helping Your Child Establish a Normal Sleep Pattern

The first hurdle for every family is simply to establish a normal sleep pattern for the child. Unfortunately many take months or years to successfully cross that hurdle. As everyone knows, sometimes babies seem to be confused about day and night. So what can you do to make sure your one- or two-year-old knows that nighttime means sleep time? Since children are competent, it's not all that hard to teach them as long as you take responsibility for giving—or withholding—the behavioral cues which signal a child to stay awake. What are the cues? With very few exceptions they are indications that social attention is available. Since the desire for intense social attention is such a strong motivator for the child, these social cues tend to override all other cues, sensations, and circumstances—whether it's dark or light, whether the child is fatigued or not, whether the room is familiar or strange.

What Is Day? What Is Night?

Parents want a child to sleep at the appropriate time, and conversely to be awake and alert at a time when they can play together. For a newborn, however, sunshine does not mean stay awake, nor does darkness mean go to sleep. Every child determines what is awake time by responding to parents' behavior and availability, as well as the physical environment around them and the degree of comfort they feel.

The child will be awake at the best available social time, regardless of whether that's two A.M. or two P.M. Therefore, the key to getting the baby to sleep at night is to make nighttime boring. Two A.M. becomes very unattractive to the infant if the parent keeps the room dark, does not socialize, and does nothing for the child that isn't absolutely necessary. Since your child's primary interest is in social time, any pleasurable interaction is incentive to be awake. Obviously, waking a child for any reason, *including feeding,* provides the newborn as well as the older infant with a very ambiguous set of cues.

Being socially available to your child during the day and unavailable at night, however, is not sufficient. Newborns and infants want social time, but the environment they live in may make this impossible. Too much light, noise or activity can overstimulate the baby or make him shut down (habituate). Similarly, not paying attention to his behavioral cues, so he feels either overwhelmed or ignored, will make the baby uncomfortable and consequently less social when you want him to be. If you are observant, however, your two-week-old can tell you what makes him comfortable. You don't have to rely on guesswork or instinct. Watch his face, his eyes, his body motions. In general he will like it calmer, darker, and quieter than the typical daytime environment in most homes, so television, radio, and bright sun may all need to be toned down for a few weeks. And you can bet that he wants very few transitions, especially in the afternoon, at least until he masters self-calming. Therefore, restrict the number of visitors and have them come only in the morning, and don't plan activities like shopping or car pooling in the late afternoon. The end result of making these accommodations to his preferences is an infant who is more likely to stay awake in the day and sleep at night.

Using social response and environmental regulation to orient the baby to day and night does take a few weeks. Unfortunately, parents often try to force longer blocks of sleep time by attempting to make the baby tired. This invariably boomerangs on them. When the child is fatigued no one in the family will sleep well that night. Understanding why this happens is not so difficult. Even as adults, we have all had the experience of being too tired, too angry, or too excited to go to sleep at night. *Going to sleep takes energy, so if you are extremely fatigued, it is more difficult to fall asleep.* Like you, the infant needs a modicum of energy and organization to calm down enough (by sucking on his hand for instance) to go to sleep. If he's too tired, he just flails around and fusses inconsolably.

Everyone sleeps soundly when parents put the child to bed before he gets too tired to be able to organize himself and put himself to sleep. Thankfully most children, even newborns, give timely signals to indicate when they are being pushed too far. Increasing hiccups or yawning, erratic arm or leg movements, shudders or tremors, and grunting breathing sounds are some of the signals that infants use to indicate they are fatigued. Older children will whine and fuss, start deliberately breaking the rules in order to be punished, or seem to be more hyper. Part of establishing a normal day/night rhythm is for parents to recognize the signs that indicate "I'm tired" and put the child to bed in his room, regardless of the clock time. (This is discussed in greater depth in the problem-solving section of this chapter, under "Deciding on a Bedtime," page 189.)

Parents usually fall into the trap of overtiring their child in one of two ways: They overstimulate him and cause him to go into habituation, or they try to wake him during the afternoon in order to make him go to sleep earlier in the evening or sleep longer at night. Rather than succeeding, they get a baby who fusses more, sleeps less, and may get day and night totally reversed. Matt and Emily are typical of what happens:

> When Matt was four or five months old, I thought it wouldn't bother him so much if I tried to change his sleep schedule. Since I get home from work at midnight, I wanted him to go longer than six A.M. All I accomplished by keeping him up in the afternoon was to make my husband mad. Matt was a bear to put to bed, and he still woke up at the same time. I didn't believe you when you said that would happen, and I paid the price. So did my husband and Matt.

> At five months, Emily was still getting up at three A.M. It seems there was always a good excuse. For a month I had been telling myself it was teething, but there were still no teeth. Then, convinced it was hunger, I gave her cereal. Just as you predicted, there seemed to be a slight change for a few nights, but by the end of the week it didn't matter how much cereal I gave her, she still was up at night. Then I went to waking her up in the day. Within three days, her naps had totally disintegrated and she had all but reversed day and night.

Going to Sleep and Going Back to Sleep

The most fundamental of a child's skills is going to sleep. Once this is mastered it may set the precedent not just for bedtime routines throughout childhood, but also for what happens in the middle of the night. Therefore, it's important to encourage this skill from the beginning; this requires cues, boundaries, and guidelines from you. To reiterate: the parent decides when the child goes to bed; the child decides when she goes to sleep. Ideally, the parent's decision about bedtime should be based on observations of the child. Put the baby down while she's still awake, but getting drowsy. Until you learn all the signals that indicate "I'm tired," there will be times when you don't act fast enough, and the baby falls asleep in your arms while you're feeding her or just sitting in a chair holding her. But the goal is to get her into bed awake. Don't try to coax her into sleep by feeding her, singing or talking to her, or rocking her. The infant who learns to go to sleep at night while being fed, for example, may indeed fall asleep comfortably and easily. She doesn't have to do much work, she doesn't have to develop any new skills. After six, or eight, or fourteen months of such caretaking, however, it is no wonder that her parents are angry and tired, and that she becomes helpless and scared if they try to deny her what she's used to. She wants them to get up to give her the bottle—not just once, but probably two or three times a night, about an ounce per episode, although during a normal daytime feeding she takes four to eight ounces (depending on age).

Most parents presume that satisfying her hunger is what enables the baby to go to sleep. What they do not recognize is that the infant's behavior is often unrelated to hunger. Taking one ounce, or nursing for two minutes, and then going back to sleep is a sleep mechanism, not a hunger problem. And taking more than a typical feeding may not necessarily be hunger, either. Some children continue long after they have had enough to eat, in order to use the accompanying sucking, warmth, touch, or body motion as a way to go to sleep. Eventually the child may stop nursing or taking a bottle at night, but will still expect help with sleep—from rocking, being talked to, or being held, which provide the same support or comfort she is accustomed to during feedings.

As the child gets older, the specific behaviors change, but the pattern does not. Going to bed remains a long-drawn-out affair which no one enjoys, and which is frequently fatiguing and upsetting to the child. A little water, one more story, finding the last stuffed animal—it's all no different from one ounce or two minutes of nursing. That is why I say that problems with going to sleep or going back to sleep rarely start at one or two years of age. The seeds were planted in the first months. So the same sleep disturbances can persist for years unless the parents learn how to change their patterns of behavior as well as those of the infant.

The reason for putting the child to bed while she is still awake but drowsy is that it is in this state that she can best make use of her developing self-calming skills. During the first four to eight or even twelve weeks, before the infant has perfected these self-calming techniques, there are many ways that parents can act as facilitators once they've put her to bed. If she's beginning to use vision to calm, she should have one of her favorite targets to look at and will need a night light in order to see it. As she gets older and masters self-calming, she can find a target to focus on by herself. Initially such targets are likely to be quite simple and of a nonstimulating nature—a white wall, plain bumper pads, or a low-intensity (fifteen- or twenty-five-watt) light. At this early age most babies use sucking as well as vision as a way to go to sleep. If the infant needs help, stand behind her or even lie on a mattress on the floor behind her (babies don't have to sleep in cribs) and give her your finger to suck. Staying out of her sight path, and avoiding talking, prevents this from becoming a social occasion while reinforcing the use of sucking as an activity she can practice—with your assistance as required—during the day as well as at bedtime. As the baby relaxes she'll often grab your finger, giving you a natural opportunity to transfer her own hand to her mouth. Quickly she learns to do it for herself, especially when she is encouraged to practice during the day.

Sucking is probably the most popular self-calming technique, followed by vision, but older children and even some small infants may use other techniques, perhaps maneuvering themselves into a preferred position, or wrapping their arms around their chests in a self-swaddling embrace. Older children will branch out, using multiple techniques like rocking, singing to themselves, twirling their hair, or other rhythmic behaviors involving their hands or feet. Sometimes a child discovers the ability in the most adverse of circumstances or finds the most unlikely of methods to be useful—as Robert did.

> Robert uses head banging to go to sleep at four A.M. I used to run in and stop him. But just as soon as I left the room he'd start again. One night I realized that he was singing to himself and talking while he was doing it. Seems a little weird, but I guess it's not that surprising. He was always sucking, and as a baby he loved to be rocked. They are all rhythmic behaviors.

Infants who are encouraged to manage these activities on their own are likely to be much easier and much more content than those who can't:

> I could never quite convince myself to let Michael work out how to calm himself down. At three, he's still clingy and doesn't sleep well at night. But Monika, who is only eight weeks old, goes to sleep easily because she can suck on her hand; she fusses less than Michael ever did and is much less eager to nurse except when she is hungry. The funny thing is that her sleeping pattern is almost identical to Michael's at the same age. She is up for one-half hour at exactly the same times that he was. But I don't get up to nurse her and she puts herself back to sleep.

Many adults never master going to sleep quickly, let alone going back to sleep when awakened, since they lack the ability to self-calm—unlike Monika, who quickly solved the problem of going to sleep and going back to sleep during her normal sleep cycle transitions. But even for infants it's not always easy, and they may need to practice for a number of nights, especially if their back-to-sleep technique differs from their going-to-sleep technique. It takes time to gain competence, but how quickly that happens depends in large part on the parents. You'll be tempted to intervene—pat her on the back, rearrange the covers—when you first hear your child stir at night. If you're lucky, she may go back to sleep for the rest of the night after your intervention. But that's unlikely, since your getting up is a surefire social signal to her to stay awake. True, this will make you feel needed, but the joy won't last. Rather than helping her have the satisfaction of learning how to sleep on her own, you'll be encouraging her to become dependent on your help. Sooner or later, she'll learn to think of two A.M. or four A.M. as party time, because of your availability (and you'll come to think of it as hell).

If you don't make yourself so easily available, however, you'll enjoy the same discovery that so many other parents have—that your child is a competent human being who can handle going to sleep and nighttime sleeping transitions by herself. Obviously, if parents don't feel their child is competent to do this, then they never make the decision to let her try, and she never gets the chance to prove herself, the result being no one sleeps through the night.

Sleeping Through the Night—for Parents Only

It should be clear by now, but if you opened the book to this page let me repeat: Infants, toddlers, and young children do not sleep through the night. Parents, however, *can* often sleep through the night once the baby acquires the ability to self-calm and the parents are able to recognize the behavior signals that indicate that the baby no longer needs to be fed at midnight and/or four A.M. This doesn't happen on a set timetable. A realistic expectation is that it will be two or three months before both parties learn what they need to know, the baby ceases to need multiple nighttime feedings, and a reasonably consistent, predictable daytime pattern can be established. Until then you probably won't be able to go for long blocks of time at night without getting out of bed to tend to him.

Given that there will be nighttime waking and crying during this period, the question is what can you do to minimize them? First you can act in such a way during the day that you encourage your infant to master self-calming (as discussed in Chapter 1 of this book and in even more detail in *The Self-Calmed Baby*). It is much easier on your nerves, and probably his, to practice in the daytime and not in the middle of the night.

Then there are a number of things you can do during the night as well so that you'll learn when your child is authentically in need of help and when he is just longing for company. Ultimately your aim is to become an accurate reader of your child's behavior cues.

Keep the child in his own room. Many parents have the infant sleep in their room, thinking it's easier since they won't have to walk as far when they get up. But the whole goal is *not* to get up at night. Going back to sleep is the baby's job. Most babies wake up frequently, especially from three to six A.M., and many create so much noise and ruckus that if you're in the same room you're likely to be awake every hour. Being social creatures, just as capable as anyone else at sensing wakefulness in another person, any baby worth his salt will test to see if you'll get up. Frequently the infant will start to sleep through the night (at least as far as you're concerned) as soon as you move him to another room—that is, if you do not have the monitor turned up full blast. But if you can hear every movement, every respiratory noise, every rousing in light sleep, then you will be running in to check on him and both of you will still be awake all night.

Learn to interpret your baby's noises. To someone who doesn't live with a young child the following may seem an odd question, but it's the first one most parents need to answer: Is the baby really crying? Most of the time parents go to the rescue as soon as they hear any sound. A noise that they might totally miss or voluntarily ignore during the day gets an instant response during the night. Such actions say to the child that you are more available during the night than you are during the day. That is hardly a signal that will encourage him to sleep—it will only make him try harder to get your attention.

Unless the baby is actually crying he's not giving you a clear signal (see Chapter 5 of the *The Self-Calmed Baby*). You may find that he is making noises because he is in light sleep. He may be fussing as he gets back to sleep. Older infants frequently use vocalizing as a way to self-calm, but they're not crying. Squealing, grunting, lip-smacking, sucking, chortling, groaning, fussing—none of that counts at two A.M. for the child who is not sick.

Learn to read your baby's behavior. So perhaps he is crying. Is it the cry that says he is mad because you haven't shown up fast enough to suit his pleasure? Is it the same cry that he uses to get your attention during the day? If the crying stops when he hears your footsteps in the hall, or you're greeted by a big grin as soon as you open the door, or he only cries on the nights when you are home, then you know that you've been set up. The baby is in total control, and his behavior tells you what his motives are. This is a social issue, and how badly do you want to play at two in the morning? It's time to take another look at your priorities and the types of decisions you are making.

Behavior at feedings is another indicator. For the first four to six weeks most babies do appear to need to feed at least once or twice at night (though even then some don't). If after that period you feed your child out of habit, responding before he really starts crying, you won't ever learn when feeding in the middle of the night ceases to be necessary.

What tells you it's time to change—that the baby can make it through the night without being fed? The baby's behavior will tell you, if you've been paying attention to the variations in it instead of responding reflexively to any noise or wakefulness on his part. One possible clue is body tone—does he feel different in your arms from the way he does during daytime feedings, or the way he did during night feedings two weeks ago? Another invaluable indicator is that the duration of the nighttime feeding will be different from that of a daytime feeding. If you nurse for ten minutes on each side during the day, but at two A.M. he falls asleep after six minutes on just one side, then he's using sucking as a mechanism to go back to sleep. The infant's social responsiveness will also help you determine whether a feeding is primarily to satisfy hunger or for other reasons (like getting back to sleep, or getting your attention). Babies who use night-time feedings to get back to sleep often suck without ever opening their eyes, while babies who want the social interaction can't resist stopping every fifteen seconds to flirt and see if they can rouse you out of your stupor. In each case, rather than taking his customary twenty minutes, he strings out each middle-of-the-night feeding for forty minutes or more. In short, if the feeding doesn't look and feel exactly like a hunger feeding during the day, then you don't have to get out of bed at two A.M. to feed him.

Listen to your child, not the self-proclaimed experts. Confused about what's happening, concerned that your five-month-old won't sleep through the night, you're probably listening to everybody else, not him. Grandma thinks the answer is to feed him cereal—and all that happens is that your son gets fatter. His godmother, speaking from the experience of her four children, says, "Don't worry. They all sleep when they weigh sixteen pounds." Alas, he's already crossed that threshold. Your grandmother comes for a visit, and three days of chaos ensue because she tries to wake him up from his nap, insisting that will help him sleep at night. A neighbor comes over and reassures you yet again—they grow out of it. You don't bother to ask when, for good reason. Her four-year-old has still to get to that stage.

In summary: Resting quietly through the night depends on the infant being able to self-calm and what you do to facilitate that ability. You will both be much better rested when he discovers—with your encouragement—that he can do it himself.

I have focused thus far on infants, since it is in infancy that good—or bad—patterns are established, and it's an easier time to make changes than any other. Older children, one-, two-, and three-year-olds, are the main focus of the next, problem-solving section, because they're the ones whose sleep disturbances can get serious—simply because the problems have gone on for extended periods of time and have become more deeply rooted, hence are more difficult to eradicate. The following principles, however, hold good for children of all ages and should be kept in mind as you go through the next section:

- Self-calming is the basic skill which enables children to go to sleep and go back to sleep at night. Younger infants may self-calm by sucking on their hands (or anything else available) or staring at a night light, while older children rock, talk to themselves or sing, roll back and forth, run the slats on the crib, hug themselves, or engage in a variety of other forms of rhythmic motor motions, even banging their heads at times.

- Social behavior dominates all other sleep cues. If you're available to your child for middle-of-the-night sessions, no matter what your intent, your child will conclude that this is a time to be awake, not asleep.

▪ Intentionally tiring a child by adding extra activities to the day or trying to keep her up later at night will always result in poorer sleep. If you persist in the tactic, there will only be a bigger struggle to get her calmed down enough to go to bed, which will be followed by more frequent waking episodes in the night.

▪ When it's possible, everybody will get a better night's rest if parents and children sleep in separate rooms.

▪ When a child does wake up and call out or cry at night, parents are responsible for evaluating the meaning of the behavior. Fussing isn't the same as crying in infancy, nor is complaining and whining in the three-year-old. The younger child who doesn't really nurse or finish the bottle doesn't need to be fed; the three-year-old who demands a drink but then takes only a sip isn't really thirsty. Any child, of any age, who screams and yells but is instant grins when you walk into the room doesn't feel deserted and unloved—genuine distress isn't instantly reversible.

▪ Bedtime routines must facilitate going to sleep, and that means not making bedtime into social time. The key to avoiding many different sleep problems is to put the child into bed awake each and every night or naptime, so that he gets accustomed to using his self-calming skills to get himself to sleep.

Solving Problems

Now that your child is sleeping through the night, how do you help keep this going at times of stress or disruption? Alternatively, what can you do if your child is eight months or two years (or whatever) and you didn't get off to a good start? This section will help you address the occasional problems that inevitably arise—illness, travel, dreams, and other disruptions—as well as more fundamental ones having to do with bad habits formed in the early days of your child's life which continue to affect behavior today.

In older children the sleep problem is almost always part of a larger behavioral problem as well, and solving it will require not just self-mastery skills on the child's part but limit-setting skills on yours.

To discipline a child effectively requires an understanding of the motivations behind the behavior you wish to change. Thankfully, the desire to discover and perfect new skills is rarely an issue in the middle of the night. Social attention most definitely is, however, no matter what your child says about why she has materialized by your bedside or called you to hers. Sure, the thunderstorm seems like a very good excuse—until you remember that she didn't seem scared of it earlier, and in fact tried to use her fascination with the lightning as a pretext to stay up past her normal bedtime. Or maybe she calls out for a drink, and you're sympathetic—until you remember that she is perfectly capable of going to the bathroom sink and getting one for herself. There are an infinite number of excuses, but in most cases what the child is really after is social time with you—not because there isn't enough of it at other times of the day, but because you've indicated by your own behavior that it's available on demand.

This section tells you how to deal with such behaviors (yours and hers) and foster different ones by enhancing the child's self-control and her ability to self-entertain, and by exercising your own self-control. It also helps you distinguish between behaviors that indicate a desire for more social time, which every child longs for and will do everything within her power to get, and any behaviors that really are signals of emotional problems. While most sleep behaviors tell us more about a child's wants than her needs, sometimes they can serve as indicators of more deep-seated problems. Your decision-making abilities will be much stronger if you know which is which.

Going to Bed: Fight or Fun

Once you have a day/night cycle established, and the child has learned the basics of self-calming, you may still encounter a going-to-bed problem, which is different from a sleep problem. Often it occurs at seven to nine months, although it may be as late as one year. Typically there will be a sudden eruption of rebelliousness—screaming, crying, anger—at bedtime, which will be repeated for several nights in a row, in various guises. One night you give in to the child's resistance to bedtime and she falls happily asleep on the sofa and is carried to bed. The next two nights you try to minimize her resistance by making several bedtime visits to her room to reassure her and again she soon falls peacefully asleep. By the fourth or fifth night, however, she's not going to sleep, but coming up with more and more demands—a glass of water, an orange soda, and two additional stories. When you finally put your foot down she cries harder than ever. Unless parents realize how their own decisions contribute to the waging of this battle every night, the war simply goes on. Generally it reaches a crescendo at about age two, when the child has all the necessary tools in terms of motor, language, and cognitive skills to outwit any of the parental strategies which have been transiently successful in the past. In no small part this "crisis" contributes to the not entirely deserved reputation of the terrible twos, which is why I begin the following section with the example of a two-year-old, although the seeds of the two-year-old's bedtime rebellions are planted early in life.

Deciding on a Bedtime:
Tired Time versus Clock Time

In the daily life of any two-year-old there are almost always two tough decisions to make: when to eat dinner (or perhaps whether to eat at all) and when to go to sleep at night. Parents must make an equally difficult decision—in their case about

bedtime. Ideally they decide about bedtime by judging when
the child is tired. But parents also have to juggle their own
equally legitimate needs. Are they tired? Do they require some
time alone or as a couple? Do they need more social time with
their child? The day-by-day effort to balance all of these factors
is what determines *consistency*.

Unfortunately parents often make bedtime a battle because
they are unclear about what their priorities are on a given night
and because they confuse setting a time to go to bed with telling
the child to go to sleep. Remember that one of these decisions
is yours, the other is, necessarily, the child's. Parents do have
the authority to say when it is bedtime—for the infant that
means crib time, for the older child that means stay-in-your-
room time. On the other hand, if they try to extend their authority
and override the child's autonomy by "making him go to sleep"
(an impossibility, actually), they ensure that each evening will
be a time of tears, crying, and angry confrontations. Going to
bed doesn't have to be a battle. Going to bed is threatening
only if it's "the end of the day." Children often need time alone
in their rooms before they're ready to go to sleep.

I've learned from the two-year-olds in my practice that if
they're allowed to make their own decisions about when to go
to sleep, they're willing to let you make the decision about
when bedtime should be. They'll go to their rooms and, after
a story or two and a hug and a kiss, say goodnight and let you
go. After his parents leave, however, the typical two-year-old
may get out of bed and play quietly in his room from seven-
thirty until ten o'clock—and that's fine. In fact, such behavior
is ideal. But it can only be achieved if both of you are clear
about the distinction between bedtime and sleeptime, and if
both of you acknowledge each other's area of responsibilities.

Your turf is the decision about bedtime. This can be a
difficult call. How do you recognize the signals that indicate
the child is tired enough to start winding down for sleep but
not so tired as to be unable to organize himself to get to sleep?

You certainly won't look at the clock for the signs you need. Clock time is highly inconsistent from your child's perspective because it bears no relation to how his body feels or what has happened that day. It's the consistency of being sent to bed when he's tired that you want to establish for your child—not of an arbitrary clock-determined bedtime. Your ability to read his cues will help him to do this for himself eventually.

What would you look for that determines when bedtime should be any given night? Of course this differs not only according to individual children but according to age. What follows are descriptions of typical age-related behaviors—but typical isn't universal, nor is it meant to rule out many other behaviors which may be unusual but not abnormal. Pay attention to your child's personal signals, and use my descriptions only as suggestions.

The four-week-old will show skin or lip color changes—which may be flushing in one child, paling or blotching in another. Hand or lip tremors are usually the next signals, and if you miss those, fussing and windmilling of the arms and legs. Subsequently, he'll avert his eyes and turn his head away when you play with him; he may spit up, and finally he'll start crying. At four months your child may do all of these things, although the fussing period may last longer before you see other signs. It may be difficult to recognize the sequence at times, since his ability to self-calm will help him stay better organized for a while and he'll show fewer physiologic signs like skin color changes to indicate that he's tired. At six months most infants usually have a specific cue that says, "I'm sleepy," even before they start fussing. Rubbing their eyes, pulling on an ear, yawning a couple of times in a row, are all examples of such signals, but your child may have his own. An occasional nine-month-old may spit up if you miss his other signals, but rubbing his eyes is more likely to be followed by a long period of increasingly hectic and disorganized motor activity before he starts to cry. The one-year-old will rub his eyes a couple of times and start whining, asking to be held and then immediately wanting to be put down. The fourteen-month-old simply acts out more and more.

One hopes that by the end of the first year your ability to read your child's cues and respond appropriately has helped him learn when he's tired. But his desires are not the only ones to be taken into consideration. There will be nights when you may regret that your child is already showing signs of being sleepy at eight o'clock because you have plenty of energy and were hoping to enjoy some time together, and other nights when your favorite tornado is cranked and ready to go, but you have had a difficult day that has left you drained and in need of quiet time alone. You'll have to learn to balance his needs and yours, remembering that yours do on occasion have to take priority. When they do, it helps to talk. Even a one-year-old is capable of understanding by your words and actions that mommy is too tired to play tonight.

Bedtime Routines

Once the decision about bedtime has been made, you and your child will no doubt spend some "goodnight" time together. Make sure that you use this time together to send her the right signals and set the stage for sleep. The goal of the bedtime routine is to get the child relaxed and drowsy so she can go to sleep, or to serve as a transition to quiet playtime—alone—in her room. Unfortunately this goal is often lost because the bedtime story and the goodnight chats are so enjoyed by the parents that they get extended beyond the best interests of the child. It's certainly easy to understand why this happens. Bedtime represents a unique opportunity in the daily schedule for feelings of closeness and intimacy between parent and child. This is as true for families where one or both parents are at home much of the time as it is for two-career families. Everyone is winding down from the day's activities, and for many parents this is the only uninterrupted time they have with their child—a time both look forward to every night. That's fine as long as it works. The problem arises when bedtime becomes the premier social occasion of the day.

Going to sleep has two phases: getting from awake to relaxed and drowsy, and then getting to sleep. A bedtime routine is part of the first phase. Whatever yours is, it should help your child through this phase. If your emotional need to spend time with her requires your reading so many stories to her that she's more worked up and awake than when you started, the routine has to change. This may mean having to build another social time into the day so that there isn't so much of a premium on togetherness at bedtime. Remember, social time is a child's top priority, so she'll always have a tendency to overdrive herself if you're available. Flattering, but it creates a problem for both of you.

Regardless of what your bedtime routine is, that only gets you and your child to the end of phase one. After that the child must be left on her own—free to do whatever she wishes to do in terms of sleeping or not sleeping, but not free to spend more time with you or to wander around the house. The better your child is at self-entertainment, the better equipped she will be to negotiate the transition between bedtime and sleep time. So let her read or draw. She can do whatever she wants as long as it doesn't disrupt everyone else's life. The lack of such skills, and the child's consequent insecurity about being able to be on her own for any period of time, are going to result in repeated attempts to prolong the bedtime routine—one more story, glass of water, cookie, kiss, cartoon on TV, and so on ad infinitum. And if you don't give in, there's going to be a big scene.

Is all this necessary? No. Do you really have to stay in her room until she falls asleep or check on her every few minutes? No. But how can you tell if she's protesting because she has a legitimate complaint about the quantity of time she gets with you? (After all, who among us ever really feels we've spent enough time with our child?) The child whose bedtime carryings-on are a genuine sign of emotional distress typically acts out in many other ways during the daytime as well. But your most infallible guide to what is going on with your child emotionally is the way she behaves when you respond to her bedtime weeping and wailing. If she stops the instant you walk into the room, then she is not suffering from feelings of desertion or some other emotional trauma. The immediate shutoff shows you that this is a control issue. She wasn't really in distress. Similarly, if you gave in and brought her downstairs to sit quietly on the couch beside you but she either fell asleep in ten minutes or jumped up and insisted on more playtime, then again you can be sure that the issue is control. And while the child should be given control over her own actions, to the extent that she gets to decide when to go to sleep, she shouldn't have control over yours.

Stick by your limits and refuse to let a bedtime routine become extended by pleas for one more story or one more anything else. That way your dinner won't be interrupted half a dozen times and you won't be harassed with endless screaming and yelling. Nor will you have to give up the closeness and exclusivity which makes bedtime so special.

Crying at Bedtime

Since the child on any given day is always tempted to try to finagle a little more social time, crying can be a very confusing signal for parents. What causes the crying when you say, "It's bedtime?" Did you miss a cue, meaning that you've let your child stay up too long and she's overtired, or is she crying because she really does need more social time and has a legitimate reason for saying, "I don't want to"? On days when you've been working hard or tied up with other demands—days when bedtime is at least in part determined by your justifiable desire for a little quiet time to yourself—you can't help wondering, "Am I really spending enough time with her?" Depending on your need to be needed, as well as your level of exhaustion, hence paranoia, such doubts may escalate into fears that she'll grow up to hate you or have to spend years in therapy to undo the damage you've caused her.

More times than not, however, I find that children in the preschool age group are crying at bedtime not because they need more time with their parents—or at least not at that hour of the evening—but because they are overtired. Most parents are surprised when one of my first suggestions is that they try to put the crying child down sooner, rather than later, to avoid tiring her to the point that she can't get to sleep. This kind of exhaustion occurs frequently these days when both parents work and no one gets quite enough time together. Parents are always trying to compensate—at an hour that is too late for their child.

If in addition the child has little self-control because discipline is lax, she may spend much of the limited time with her parents acting out in order to get intense attention. There is less pleasurable time together, and no matter how much attention you give, everyone feels shortchanged. Suddenly it's ten o'clock, everyone is tired, and it's time to go to bed, but the child falls apart.

Going to sleep requires enough energy for her to be able to calm herself. If she doesn't have the reserves, then she can't manage that so late in the evening. Your role as a parent requires becoming familiar with the signals that indicate the stage before that level of exhaustion. (See the section on "Deciding on a Bedtime," page 189.) If you don't get her to bed before she's gone over the edge, the child will scream and yell, won't be able to self-calm because she is agitated and overloaded, and will find it much more difficult to fall asleep. In short, any extra playtime you had together won't have been worth it.

There are daytime indicators which help you make this

judgment as well. If your child has the self-mastery skills to handle social transitions well, if she can self-entertain so that your attention isn't required every minute, and if she is able to sleep or at least rest during the day, then it's a pretty safe bet that crying at bedtime simply means that she's up too late at night and you don't need to get overly neurotic about whether she's getting enough quality time. She is getting what she needs and she's doing fine. So if your otherwise well-adjusted child cries every night from ten to eleven, for example, put her in her room earlier, say at nine or nine-thirty. She may still cry in protest, but for ten minutes, not one hour, because she can more easily get herself to sleep when she is less tired.

Bedtime Ghosts—Yours

Even when parents negotiate bedtime so that fatigue is not a factor and they let the child control when she goes to sleep, bedtime can still be a battle. In her book *The Magic Years* Seima Fraiberg coined the phrase "ghosts in the nursery"—a reference to the parents' ghosts, not the child's. Oftentimes it seems parents' actions are simply a consequence of projecting their own feelings onto their child. Stephanie's mother was a perfect example of this problem. She was tormented by the fact that Stephanie would lie awake for an hour or more each night, even though Stephanie was talking, singing to herself, looking at books, or playing with her stuffed animals. This sounded pretty good to me, and all I could think about was the number of parents who longed for a child with such excellent self-entertainment skills.

Despite all indications that Stephanie herself was perfectly content with her nightly routine, Stephanie's mother couldn't get past the feeling that her daughter stayed awake each night because she was lonely or upset about something. The mother's own memories of childhood were of solitary nights with no one to talk to. Her parents had never made much of an effort to understand her, in part "because they didn't think I could talk about my feelings, and I'm not sure they really wanted to hear them." Consequently she had given considerable opportunity and assistance to Stephanie to enable this almost four-year-old to express herself—and Stephanie was indeed quite verbal. Unfortunately, the fact that Stephanie wanted to come out of her room to play when her grandparents were staying in the house or guests remained after dinner only confirmed to her mother that Stephanie was looking for someone else to talk to—just as she had as a child.

Stephanie appeared to me to be happy, bright, and clearly affectionate toward her mother, though I had the impression she was feeling somewhat intruded upon by her mother's good intentions. She slept well once she got to sleep, and went willingly off to her naps. I thought surely her mother would be able to see she had nothing to worry about, but no matter how many office visits and phone calls we had, she persisted in her belief that Stephanie was awake out of unhappiness. This made me sad, because I thought she had really accomplished her goal: She had raised a child who felt happy and secure, in no small part because Stephanie knew she could express her feelings to her mother without fear of rejection or punishment.

After three years of this confusion the problem was escalating to the point that I felt Stephanie was withdrawing from her mother, because she actually liked having some time to herself each night. Fortunately Stephanie had a checkup just as the tension was reaching critical mass. My plan was to try to help Stephanie tell her mother that bedtime wasn't a problem, so I asked her what her favorite part of the day was. Immediately she gave me a broad grin and replied, "The end of the day when I can play by myself in my room. Mommy lets me decide when to turn out the light, and when to go to sleep. Most other kids don't get to do that." Though it was upsetting for Stephanie's mother to hear that her child actually enjoyed being

alone, she got the point and subsequently had fewer visits from
the "ghosts"—and paid fewer post-bedtime visits to her child.

I've never met the parent who didn't have at least one
such ghost, and they do tend to show up at nighttime around
sleep issues. The best ghostbuster is to watch the child's behavior.
You may be worried and concerned because of unpleasant memories of childhood, but if your child, like Stephanie, is singing
or reading after bedtime, is well rested, and shows no other
behavior signs of emotional stress during the day, then don't
let your ghosts become your child's as well.

Burning the Midnight Oil

Staying up late is a common behavior in people of all ages,
from babies to senior citizens. It's only a problem when it causes
you to be up when you normally wouldn't be. Then *you* have a
sleep problem, but the real question is, does your child? If
your child is still awake at eleven or twelve, but sleeps soundly
the rest of the night, arises bright and energetic, and is actively
engaged with you and the rest of her world, then you can relax.
I know your mother insists that your daughter needs twelve
hours a night, but Grandma's wrong. Or perhaps you fear the
reason your four-year-old sleeps so little is that he's depressed,
even though during the day he is energetic and sociable, has
plenty of friends, no discipline problems, no recurring outbursts
and no inexplicable changes in mood. Fortunately, legitimate
depression is rare in the preschool group. Neither your son nor
your daughter has a sleep problem; their total sleep needs are
simply less than you expected. But then why *are* so many children
keeping late hours?

The simplest case is the one-month-old. She's usually up
because she wants to eat. Her behavior will tell you when she's
no longer really hungry in the middle of the night (see the
section on "Sleeping Through the Night," page 182), which

will probably happen in the next few weeks. As she gets older, being up late in the evening happens most often as the result of an overly prolonged bedtime routine which isn't relaxing and doesn't provide the emotional support needed by both parent and child. Sometimes it's a struggle created by the parent trying to control when the child goes to sleep, and other times the child is trying to control her bedtime (which she would like to be as late as possible), which the parent accommodates by reading more stories, etc. What happens is that the responsibility for sleep decisions discussed earlier in this chapter are reversed, and it won't work. After the first year, such behavior is almost always accompanied by some type of acting out in the daytime and a breach of discipline. Therefore, the best move for a parent is not just to get back to a successful bedtime routine that keeps straight who's responsible for which decisions, but to get the daytime limit system back in place too.

Then there is another group who almost always, for reasons of personal temperament and body clock, fall asleep after the parents do, and this behavior can start in the first year of life. The child goes willingly to his room, but he's up until all hours singing or playing by himself. It happens at eight months; it's quite common in two- or three-year-olds. There are no discipline issues or other types of acting-out associated with this; the child simply stays up until everyone else has gone to bed and presumably gone to sleep. (After all, he doesn't realize that you're lying there wondering what is really going on and whether you should intervene and tell him to go to sleep.) Sometimes it seems as though he's just too busy reading, and other nights this seems like a rite of passage; as my son has said more than once, "I may not be as big as you are, or as grown-up . . . but I go to sleep last." These children are happy with their schedule, and you gain nothing by interfering with their right to control when they go to sleep. Don't let yourself be deterred from your commitment to honoring your child's sleep decisions by the comments—indeed, barbs—of friends and relatives who are convinced you are doing something wrong, and eager to tell you so.

Burning the midnight oil can be a problem, however, when it results in early-morning battles seven hours later as you try to get your tired and grouchy child dressed, fed, and off to day care or kindergarten. Furthermore, since the morning may be a major percentage of the very little time you have together during the day, you don't want to be angry and pushy, nor do you want to spend it with an irritable child. Unfortunately, making allowances for her in the morning, being overly so-licitous and forgiving, is part of what is creating the prob-lem.

Since this behavior is most common in the twos, threes, and older, language is a major ally. The best approach is to talk with the child about the difficulties her late-night hours are causing. Do it at a time when you're not hustling her out the door or angry because you've given in to her morning shenani-gans. Let her know that you're giving her the chance to make some different choices rather than dictating what to do, but if she doesn't make the decision to alter her nighttime routine, then you'll have to make other changes in her routine like getting her up in the morning at the time you choose. I'd mention to her that you understand that staying up late makes it hard for anyone to wake up on time, so you can sympathize with her situation, but you don't intend for it to be an excuse for fussing and whining or other departures from the usual limits. Don't attempt to coerce her into an earlier bedtime, and don't try to guilt-trip her about your getting to work late or getting a late start on your household chores. Neither tactic will have much lasting impact. Her responsibility is to go to bed at a time that enables her to fit into the routine of the household; your responsibility is to define that routine clearly.

Usually a simple statement of the problem is all it takes to correct the situation. If things aren't any different three days later, what's the next step? It's still not a good idea to try to force her to go to sleep earlier; it won't work, and all you'll get for your efforts will be a prolonged bedtime fight and continued problems in the morning. The alternative is to follow through on what you told her in phase one of this struggle: that you will have to make the decision about when she gets up. This is something you *can* make her do, unlike sleeping, which you can't. When it's time to get her out of bed, clearly state that she must get up. Moreover, she needs to understand in no uncertain terms that you don't have time to spend with her if she stays in bed until the last minute. If she's able to eat without assistance, tell her breakfast is on the table, and go on about your own business. If you aren't feeding her all meals, don't take the time to feed her since this just becomes another control game that encourages the current morning behavior pattern. If she's old enough, remind her she has to get dressed by some definite time limit that is represented by something she can see or hear, e.g., when you finish brushing your teeth or the news comes on the radio. If she doesn't do it and it's now time to leave the house, I'd expeditiously dress the three-year-old, take the four-year-old in whatever state she's in, and bring along some extra clothes she might suddenly decide to put on in the car or once she gets to nursery school. During the day don't bend rules or put up with tantrums because you know she's tired. Behavior which is unacceptable is just that. *After* she's had an appropriate time-out, take a little more time to talk with her about why she's tired, why she seems so irritable. Although you can't make her go to sleep earlier in the evening, because that's her decision, you certainly can influence her thought process and her actions in the morning. It may take a few days but she'll change.

In summary you can avoid having—or creating—problems about bedtime by remembering the following:

   You decide when the child goes in her room at night. The child decides when she will go to sleep.

- Be consistent about bedtime by making decisions based not on clock time, but on behavior cues that indicate your child's level of fatigue, and on your own needs for space and time on any given night, with the former taking precedence when possible.

- If you have a bedtime routine make sure it works to help the child get relaxed and drowsy. Don't make it an elaborate occasion for social time, which only encourages the child to stay awake.

- The child, and only the child, determines how much sleep is enough. There is no magic number of hours per night. If your two-year-old stays up until eleven and sleeps eight hours a night, rarely naps, and is still bright, spunky, and energetic, let well enough alone.

- Children who show a marked decrease in sleep time may be depressed or emotionally upset, but there will always be other behavior signs during the day if this is true. A change in sleep pattern alone doesn't necessarily indicate that the child is having trouble.

- You can't control when the child falls asleep, but you can have an impact on her behavior by setting limits on morning or waking behavior that is unacceptable or that interferes with the schedule of other family members.

Waking at Night

Once asleep, children do wake up at night for many reasons, but most of the time, if they have developed self-calming skills and self-control, they can get themselves back to sleep. In many of the cases I see, unfortunately, parents have not helped their children to acquire these skills, either because they've never heard that children have the potential to acquire them or because they're unable to place that level of trust in their own child. The first section below will give suggestions about how parents can encourage these skills in older children.

Even children who do have self-calming skills may go through periods when they wake up each night and demand your presence. For some of these children the reason has to do with breakdowns in daytime and/or nighttime discipline; for others it's a matter of temperament—they're simply more high-strung and more prone to disorganized behavior and emotional upset than their peers. Very often parents act as unwitting collaborators, their own behavior only serving to worsen the situation, by allowing these middle-of-the night episodes to evolve into premium social occasions. Though you may feel the resulting peace and quiet makes it worth your while to give in, you'll notice the pressure around your neck is a little tight from having your leash pulled. It'll just keep getting tighter if you allow a child to turn two A.M. into party time.

The second section below examines possible causes for these sporadic periods of nighttime wakefulness, and how to use both daytime and nighttime discipline to minimize them.

The third section deals with children who have strong self-calming capabilities, who customarily use them to good effect, and whose parents are equally skilled at using both day- and nighttime disciplinary techniques to reinforce good sleeping habits—but who suddenly develop problems anyway. When these children can't get back to sleep on their own, it's usually due to sickness, travel, family stress, or some other event out of the ordinary which has for the time being pushed them beyond their capacity to self-calm. All of these problems may require your attention—including the middle-of-the-night interventions which under most other circumstances I strongly discourage—but if you follow my suggestions, you can avoid setting up a pattern of behavior that you will later come to regret.

Children Who Lack Self-Calming Skills

If your experience as a parent has been chronically clouded by the absence of a good night's sleep, and your child is now three or four or five years old, then you are going to have to go back to square one to help her develop self-calming and other sleep skills, since she has clearly never mastered them—probably because she wasn't encouraged to do so. My guess is that you're having not only middle-of-the-night episodes of wakefulness but problems at bedtime too, typically consisting of an extremely prolonged bedtime routine. Since the child can't self-calm, you feed her, rock her, talk with her. Getting her to bed, or getting her back to sleep when she wakes at night, often stretches out for hours. As the child gets older and bedtime gets later, you may even resort to going to bed with her, and while one or both of you may eventually fall asleep this way the end result is such a behavioral and emotional nightmare that it's just not worth it.

After this pattern goes on for three or four months it's difficult to change; when it continues for years the whole family suffers. But the child is an innocent victim. She's only doing what she has been encouraged to do for weeks, months, or years. So you can't simply pull the plug on her and stop going to her room cold turkey. Abruptly deciding to let her cry it out would be unfair to her and emotionally trying for everyone. The crying would probably last for hours, since the child does not have the skills to be able to go back to sleep. She understandably feels abandoned when the parent suddenly deserts her after years of being constantly available.

What to Do Before the parents can stop getting up at night, they are obligated to help the child develop a way to settle down on her own; in other words, they have to foster self-calming. They'll want to rethink their bedtime routine and the way they intervene at night so that neither form of attention becomes or continues to be a social occasion that encourages the child to stay awake. Moreover, they will almost certainly look to enhance self-control by changing their discipline system. Finally, for any child over one, success occurs much faster if parents explain all these changes so that the child is aware that they're about to happen.

The easiest approach to increasing a child's ability to self-calm is to watch what she does during the day when she's upset, and with words and actions to give her appropriate recognition for techniques (which every child has in at least embryonic form) that result in successful self-calming. This learning process will take some restraint on your part, but if you see that your child is actively trying to get reorganized, then give her time to work at it, even if there's intermittent fussing or crying along the way. If you decide to intervene, try to do it in a way that helps her to succeed: you might mimic the six-month-old sucking her thumb or wave her hand in front of her face so that the power of suggestion takes over; remind the one-year-old that rocking helps or get her out of the high chair so she can do it more easily; let the fifteen-month-old hair-twirl even if her hands are covered with cereal; encourage the two-year-old to sing along with the tape or hum her favorite nursery school song; and let the three-year-old run five laps around the dining room if physical activity helps her settle down. In each instance I'd acknowledge her effort and praise her for trying to get her act back together.

For most families the work on self-calming is a three-to-five-day project. It may startle you to learn that it's so quick, but self-calming is an innate skill, and its own reinforcement. If you backslide and continue to intervene when it's not necessary, however, then the process will be longer.

Once you have fewer outbursts during the day, and your child has one or two self-calming techniques to build on, it's feasible to start to work on self-control, which you can do when the sun is shining. First of all you need to make sure her daytime schedule isn't too tiring for her (for the same reason you have to be sure to get her to bed before it's too late). Even more important, your discipline system must encourage self-control. The child who takes for granted attention on demand in the middle of the night is almost certainly a child who expects unlimited access to you during the day as well. Typically she will be accustomed to interrupting your work, your telephone conversations, your meals, or anything else that interferes with her pleasure. She doesn't accept limits because you haven't effectively imposed them. Before you'll be able to get a good night's sleep, you'll have to establish limits on her access to you, and this is much easier to do at two P.M. than at two A.M. The limits on social time have to be clear, not subject to change according to the degree of the child's protest, and you'll almost certainly need time-out as a means of enforcing those limits, as discussed in the previous two chapters. Conversely, when you say you're available, you really have to be there, not thinking about a problem at work, planning dinner, or whatever. If she doesn't get intense attention from you, your daughter will persist in waking you at two A.M. when she knows she'll be the sole focus of interest—even if the attention she gets from you then is negative.

A very useful measure of your progress in changing expectations about social availability is whether the child will take a nap—either as a period in which to sleep, or as a rest time. This says that she accepts your insistence on time to yourself, which won't happen unless she's assured that your availability during other parts of the day will meet her needs.

Once your child has had a week or two of daytime experiences to learn that the pleading, bribing, and angry speeches of the past are over, and she's now confronted with a parent who means what she says and is prepared to back it up, you can discuss with her the changes you intend to make which will affect your sleep and hers. Usually the first step is a new bedtime routine, since almost without exception that's the source of many undesirable precedents. But remember this is a joint effort. By the age of one, or certainly by eighteen months, parents find that explaining to the child what needs to change and what they're going to do solves ninety percent of the problem. Although he's listening and comprehending, the one-year-old won't have much to say, but such a conversation with a two-year-old might sound like this:

"Sally, Dad and I want to change your bedtime routine so it will be less difficult for you and for us."

"Am I going to bed in a different room?"

"No. Same bed."

"What are you talking about, Mommy?"

"Bedtime always seems like a fight. We want that to change. It seems to us that we'd all be happier if that wasn't true."

"Will you stop reading to me?"

"No. After your bath, you can choose the story that you want us to read and you can still choose what to drink to keep in your room. But once that story is done we're not going to read any more. We're going to say goodnight. You can decide whether the light stays on, and if you don't want to go to sleep right away that's okay, but we're not coming back in every few minutes to try to encourage you to go to sleep or to get you something else to drink, or to read a different book."

"Suppose I want orange."

"You can have orange if that's what you asked for, but if you told us after your bath that you wanted water, and we're done with the story, then you'll have to stick with water."

If you explain it in advance, enacting a revised bedtime routine isn't nearly the struggle you expect—especially if you've gotten the child to bed before she's gotten too exhausted to be able to calm herself down.

I'd take a similar approach in any discussion about what

you now expect to happen in the middle of the night by focusing on all the changes she's already made in her daytime behavior. Once you both see what she's been able to achieve during the day, you can express real confidence that she'll also manage going back to sleep on her own without your having to get up. Remind her about all the things she now does so well which used to be battles but aren't anymore, not the least of which is how good she's gotten at the new bedtime routine. You will get tested—are you really saying that two A.M. isn't playtime?—but for no more than one or two nights, if you've helped her gain the self-calming skills and the self-control she needs to cope with those normal, universal wake-up incidents that happen at night.

To me perhaps the most remarkable result of this step-by-step approach is that many parents never have to face the final test at all. The child's self-calming and self-control skills have improved so much that she handles the nighttime waking and goes back to sleep on her own, without any further prompting from the parents. But it does often take three or four weeks of serious work before a child who has never gotten through the night on her own has developed her self-calming and self-control capabilities to the extent that her parents can stop their middle-of-the night interventions.

Children with Only Occasional Nighttime Wakefulness

There is a second group of children whose night waking problems are not due to an inability to self-calm or to achieve self-control. They do have periods of sleeping through the night, and their daytime behavior doesn't require constant adult intervention to calm and to entertain them. They just happen to be much more intense personalities than other children—with different needs as a result. When they're happy, they're all enthusiasm. When they're upset, it looks like the world is going to end. When these babies nurse, you know it. As infants and toddlers they often have a particular cry for attention which is quite piercing, yet very controlled. If they get up from the table to run around in order to burn off energy, they do five laps, not one, and the running is clearly a self-control mechanism, it's not for attention. On the other hand, while they have more energy and are more intense than many children, they are by no means hyperactive, because they can self-calm and they do have self-control. Their natural temperament is just more of a challenge to these skills.

In comparison to children who consistently sleep without problems, the members of this group appear to be much more vulnerable to the effects of fatigue, excitement, and overstimulation, such as that caused by the holiday season or vacation travel. Similarly, any deviations from the usual limits, during the day or the night, are keenly felt by these children. When even one limit is breached, the members of this group invariably test every other limit in the system. Tantrums, acting out, and verbal abuse (from child to parent), if not stemmed by effective discipline techniques, are generally followed within two or three days by sleep disturbances. After all, once one rule has been broken, there's no reason not to think that the nighttime rules may have changed as well.

Typically, these children with erratic periods of nighttime wakefulness were able to establish an acceptable sleeping pattern as infants (sleeping or lying quietly a minimum of nine or ten hours a night), but only after a struggle. While the average three-month-old with good self-calming skills wakes and fusses for three or four minutes before resettling, these children take longer—fifteen or twenty minutes—to go back to sleep. Their sleep difficulties are exacerbated by their having greater problems not just with sleep cycle transitions but with developmental transitions as well. If handled carefully, each of these periods of change may be dealt with in a couple of weeks (a tough two weeks, admittedly), after which the child goes back to an acceptable nighttime pattern.

What to Do These children will go through some major reorganizations of their sleep system, usually at about five to seven, ten to twelve, and twenty to twenty-four months of age, and there's nothing you can do to change that. But you can prepare for it by doing everything possible to optimize and even assist their self-calming skills, so that they'll be able to deal with longer than usual periods of wakefulness at night. Ideally the child will make efforts to calm himself, and the parents will give him the time and space he needs to work at it. If, however, he doesn't seem to be succeeding on his own, and the crying or screaming get so intense that you feel you have to intervene, try to do only what's necessary to help him get reorganized so he goes back to sleep on his own. If gentle pressure on his back for a minute contains his thrashing and gets him back to head-bobbing, hair twirling, or whatever, then that's all you need to do. Picking him up, rocking him, talking, or playing will stop the crying, but it will also add social attention to the equation—and suddenly you're up every night for months.

During these periods of wakefulness it's striking how much children in this group benefit from your helping them to identify the body signals that say they're tired. While they may resist any suggestion from you that they go to sleep, they are often willing to make that decision on their own once they recognize those signals. The result, of course, is they won't get overtired. Yes, they'll still be awake at two A.M., but going back to sleep will be much less of a battle for them and much less likely to require your help. More than other children, these intense personalities depend on your scheduling wisdom to avoid busy days with multiple transitions during the late afternoon, and not to get them to bed too late.

If you're traveling, especially if you're staying in someone else's home, try to set up the sleeping spaces so that the child is less likely to disturb anyone else. You might also request that no wild gala be planned for the night you arrive. Since discipline is always a key factor in maintaining self-control, it's at even more of a premium with these children when they're on the road. So if you go visiting, prearrange some space that you can use for time-out, or you're likely to pay a bigger price than some embarrassing misbehavior.

The older many of these children get, the more prone to middle-of-the-night wakefulness they tend to be. Peer relationships, events at nursery school, weather changes, and curiosity are factors that can contribute to their being up at two A.M. Self-entertainment skills can be very helpful in enabling them to handle these episodes on their own. The two-year-old will require a night light to look at his books and the three-year-old may build Lego constructions, color, or do any of a number of other activities (as long as he stays in his room). Encouraging his self-entertainment skills during the day, and telling him how pleased you are when he uses them at night, will reinforce his abilities. There's nothing to be gained from saying, "Why don't you just go back to sleep at night, Henry?" Better to congratulate him on successfully keeping himself occupied—and quiet—during his waking periods. "Wow, I see you made a new construction when you woke up last night. I really appreciate your letting me sleep through—I needed the rest—but I hope you'll tell me about it now during breakfast."

Finally, keep in mind that these children are as intense emotionally as they are in other ways. They can be helped tremendously by parents who encourage them to verbalize their feelings, so that they're less likely to internalize them—which only causes more sleep and other behavioral problems.

Children Who Suddenly Can't Sleep at Night

Even children who go to bed without a battle and have mastered going back to sleep have occasional problems with wakefulness at night owing perhaps to illness, travel, or other brief upsets in their lives. A cold turns into an earache, or the trip to the grandparents is too exciting and exhausting. But of course parents are rarely free of anxiety about other factors that may be contributing to the sudden wakefulness of a child who is normally a good sleeper. Is it that the business trip you just completed took you away from home for too long? Or does your child sense—even though you haven't told her yet—that you and your spouse are going on a vacation without her next week? How do you decide why she's awake, and what you need to do about it?

One way is to examine your child's daytime behavior. If she is upset about something other than the events of the moment, she'll manifest her feelings in more ways than in her sleeping patterns. Preverbal children won't make eye contact and will refuse to be held. They chatter less. There are new or dramatically heightened struggles not just at bedtime, but during other routine daily transitions like going to the grocery store or getting into the car. Suddenly each transition provokes as much crying, screaming, and resistance as there was when the child was six weeks old and unable to self-calm. Many children will openly elicit attention from other adults, while turning away from you, so that you know you're being punished. In the verbal child there may be considerable talking back or swearing, an attempt to play off one parent against the other, and apparently deliberate attempts to hurt you, such as repeated demands to go live with Aunt Gail (though never, alas, at three A.M.).

Of course there is one advantage to life with even the most angry and distraught verbal child: You can describe the behavior that concerns you, and ask what is disturbing her and making her behave that way. As early as two years of age children can express feelings and possibly give you some indication of the reasons for their emotions, and any three-year-old can certainly answer the question, perhaps more fully then you'd like. It's very important to talk. I know all the psychology books say that three- and four-year-olds can't express their feelings accurately, but they're wrong. I've had three-year-old children whom I haven't seen for months talk to me about their feelings. They didn't even know me that well; it was just that they needed a receptive ear. And think of the two-year-olds who delight their parents by saying, "I love you." Children can express emotions verbally, and much earlier than many of the experts think.

Some parents say they're reluctant to ask because they're afraid that they'll create a problem by suggesting reasons or feelings for the night waking that are worse than the actual ones. Luckily no parent has that much power. Other parents are uncertain how to ask. As simply and straightforwardly as possible, is my advice. For instance, I've had the following exchanges with my son, Red, whose competency at sleeping most nights is something I and many other mortals can only aspire to.

"Red, I noticed that you've been up the last couple of nights. Are you having difficulty sleeping?"

He stopped hunting for a particular wooden block while we were building the "dog's bedroom" in the house, stared at me thoughtfully, and said "No."

"Good. I was just wondering since you usually sleep so well."

"I'm okay." And he was.

On another occasion he was dragging a little in the afternoon and grouchy.

"What do you want to do this afternoon?"

"Nothing," and he threw himself down on the rug.

"Are you tired?"

"Yes."

"Have you been sleeping okay?"

"No. The tree bothers me."

This was not exactly the answer I expected. He looked up at me, obviously puzzled that I didn't have an immediate response to this crystal-clear statement of a problem.

"I'm not sure I understand."

"I hear the tree at night."

Still in a fog, and wondering whether I was being obtuse or getting the runaround, I asked, "What kind of noise does it make?"

"It scratches."

The light still wasn't dawning on me. "Does it scratch you?"

He grinned and said, "No, stupid, the roof."

Suddenly worried that a tree limb had broken off in the thunderstorm the night before, I hustled him outside. The branch wasn't broken, but it was rubbing on the roof above his room. A quick pruning job solved that problem.

Fixing his lunch for "school" while he devoured a loaf of bread one morning, I asked, "Why is your light on in the morning? Are you getting up at night?"

"Yeah."

"What are you doing then?"

"I like to read. I want the time alone." Which made perfect sense to me since it was just after the holiday season, and for the last six days every bed and sofa had been occupied by visiting family and friends. He'd had a great time, but this was a pretty logical rebound effect.

There have been times, however, when Red has been upset about less transient issues than a tree limb or too much holiday-time stimulation, and the problem has manifested itself in sleeping alterations. One night I woke up and heard him talking to himself. This went on for more than an hour. By the end of the week it had happened two other nights. During the day he had also been much less lively, running less, wanting to spend more time inside than outside, which is distinctly unusual. One afternoon he was sitting in the chair looking at me, so I decided to plunge in:

"You've been awake quite a few nights recently talking to yourself. Is there something that we should talk about?"

"No. You don't like to."

Wondering what provoked that, I said; "I may not like the subject or exactly what you're going to say but I'm willing to talk if it will help you sleep better."

"You told me you didn't know." By then the wheels in my head were rapidly spinning, but getting nowhere. He paused: "Last week."

"I'm sorry, I don't know what you mean."

"After the meeting, you told me that you didn't know about the future and sometimes it kept you awake."

I didn't then, and I don't now. Like many three-year-olds he'd gotten interested in death—specifically mine—or what he thinks about as the future (interesting twist). The previous week he'd begun asking a long series of "why" questions, then become angry when, after the fifth or sixth "why," I proclaimed that there were to be no more speculations or questions, and that I didn't relish endless discussions of my own mortality. Now I needed to make it clear that, despite my response last week, if this was something he was genuinely upset about I would certainly be willing to discuss it with him. I don't enjoy such discussions sometimes, but he's sleeping better and looks better.

One final example of a time he came into our bedroom in the middle of the night crying. This was a time when I was glad we talked and that I stuck by my rules that he sleep in his own bed, even though I was very tempted to break them and let him sleep with me.

"What happened, Red? Why are you crying?"

"I want to be with you."

My brain finally gets up to speed. "That's flattering, but it's not time to get up yet and I need to sleep." He starts to climb in bed. "And I can't sleep with you in the same bed."

"Where's Mommy?"

"She's in Hong Kong. She'll be back in three days."

"I want her. And then you leave." My stomach twisting a little, I knew he had a point. A change in everyone's schedule had put us in this predicament.

"I'm sorry. I wish that this wasn't happening. But it's not going to be repeated."

"I don't like it. It hurts my feelings."

"We don't like it either. One of the reasons we moved up here was to spend more time together. We both miss Mommy and I'll miss you when I go away next week. But staying up all night won't make either of us feel better."

"Can I go with you?" He'd been on some trips with me, but the schedule on this one was too hectic.

"No, but there will be others when you can. Let's put you back to bed so we can both enjoy the time we have together tomorrow."

"I'm mad at you."

"I understand that. Because of how you feel there won't be any more back-to-back trips, so it's important that you've talked about it. But you still have to sleep in your bed."

"Can you carry my stuffed cat?" He'd managed to drag it upstairs. I carried it down.

He went back to bed. He was still upset, but he got back under control, calmed down, and was asleep between the time I kissed him and then paused at the door to shut out the light. We talked about the episode the next morning and again when Carol got home. And we talk about the same issue now, more than a year later, because schedule conflicts still sometimes arise and we tell him how we plan to resolve or minimize them. Part of getting him to develop self-control is for us to stick to our commitments to him, and to explain why we sometimes have to disappoint him.

Most of the time you're likely to find that it's your paranoia, not the underlying situation, which has gotten out of hand when you're confronted with a crying child at three A.M. But there is one final indicator of real trouble. The child who is genuinely distraught because he needs more attention won't go back to sleep quickly when you go to his room, or even if you take him into bed with you. If unmet emotional needs are the reason for waking at night, going back to sleep, whether you're there or not, won't be easy for him. So giving in to his demands at three A.M. won't be a solution. The solution will have to be found in the daylight hours, and it's beyond the scope of a chapter on sleep problems, because sleep isn't the real problem.

Fortunately, very few cases of sudden nighttime waking are due to underlying emotional distress. Typically they occur during or after an illness, travel, or some other disruption of the regular routine. Childhood illnesses almost always induce more waking at night. Uncertain of what's happening, concerned, and wanting to comfort the child, you get up, even if it's only briefly. If you've already been awake twice that night you may very well take the child into bed. Travel, especially if you cross multiple time zones, will also increase night waking. This can't be attributed just to strange surroundings. You don't sleep as well and neither does your child. Sometimes the actual waking isn't the problem so much as the social embarrassment. If you're in another family's house you'll feel that you have to get up to calm the child before he wakes everyone up. If everyone is sleeping in the same room, at a relative's house or in a motel, the situation is still more complicated. The child knows you are there and is much more likely to try to get you up rather than going back to sleep on his own. Or even if he doesn't do it intentionally, his efforts to entertain himself are likely to wake you and/or make you worry that he'll wake other people, especially if he's three or four years old and likes to wander. So you get up and intervene. Should you?

What to Do If your child is waking because of illness, you will of course want to go to him when he wakes and tend to any immediate physical needs. In order to prevent an acute episode from becoming a chronic problem, however, try to keep the intervention as simple as possible. Resettle the child, but don't volunteer to do a lot more unless doing more would be helpful. But if he's crying because of an earache, for example, you can't make the pain go away by suddenly showing up at his door, even though that may be momentarily distracting. If, however, he smiles when you enter the room, and is back to sleep after two minutes of rocking and sleeps for the rest of the night, then ear pain was not the likely cause of his waking. For the child who does require your attention—perhaps to be given a cough medicine or some other medication—it helps to tell him during the day why you're getting up at night. He needs to know that this isn't a sudden change in the basic rules. Otherwise you run the risk that what started as a legitimate intervention on your part will be seen as an enjoyable social occasion for the child and the demands will persist long after the symptoms are gone. Of course you will want to be sure they are gone. Any illness acute enough to continue waking your child, especially after a couple of days' worth of antibiotic or other treatment, should be discussed with, or seen by, a physician.

If your child tends to be wakeful because of the disruptions caused by travel, keep in mind that you can do advance damage control by letting the relatives know that there may be some squawking on the night of your arrival. Tell the three- or four-year-old that she'll probably wake up more often the first night or two on the trip, but remind her that she has the skills to go back to sleep on her own, and with any child of a year or more, talk to her about what she can do to help herself go back to sleep. Remember to talk ahead of time, when you're not upset or overly embarrassed because this has been going on for three days. If you add a significant negative reaction to the situation, then the behavior is less likely to go away (see Chapter 3 on temper tantrums).

Finally when you get home, talk again. If you did get

up, or the child did sleep in your bed, then make it clear that being at Grandma's is the exception. Now that you're home the same sleep limits apply that you had worked out before you left. Warn her that she may wake up more often for the first few nights after she's back, even though she's in her own bed, but affirm your belief in her ability to get herself back to sleep and assure her that the effects of travel don't last forever. Once you're home for two or three days, a child with good self-mastery skills will have readjusted.

Dreams

As a pediatrician, I was surprised by how infrequently I heard about dreams being a problem. Nary a day, in fact hardly an hour, went by that someone didn't have a question about sleep. Moreover, half the consultations with our parent help organization, Red Tae Associates, are about sleep. But dreams are rarely mentioned, perhaps because many dreams don't wake the child.

Nonetheless, children do have dreams during REM sleep. Actually there are three types of sleep disturbance. Most common are the dreams you hear about the next day: A three- or four-year-old may enliven the breakfast table with the tale of a dream he had the night before, which may or may not be related to his real world: perhaps some fight story that makes you wonder what's happening at day care, or some other more fanciful tale about space ships or alligators that seems quite remote from reality. Yet such daytime retellings seem to be infrequent—whether because these dreams rarely occur, or children don't remember them (or parents don't listen) isn't clear.

The second type of "dream" is a nightmare. Usually the child is screaming or crying, and is awake or easily rousable when the parent goes in. It may take some time to resettle the child, but she'll usually go back to sleep. The child may remember some or all of the dream. Since nightmares occur in REM sleep, they are commonly precipitated by fatigue and other factors which increase the occurrences of REM sleep. As a parent you find them disturbing not just because you're up at night and the child is scared, but because you're probably familiar enough with Freud's theories to worry about whether they represent the subconscious working out mysterious conflicts in your child's life. However, some neuropsychologists now feel that the data about brain function suggest that dreams are rooted in biochemistry, not the unconscious. The truth is, no one really knows yet what purpose, if any, dreams serve, or what causes them.

Most parents are afraid that they'll compound any problem by discussing dreams. I suggest the opposite—that talking about them, and even sharing any dreams you yourself may have had recently, will be helpful. Your child needs to know that they happen to other people as well. Fortunately, nightmares usually occur singly. If the nightmares come in clusters, however, or you think they are a manifestation of some underlying concern, especially if daytime behavior also seems troubled, then ask your child if she is worried or upset about something. Leave the questions fairly open at first. Just as she can recount the dream, she can tell you about her feelings. If that draws a blank, but you're still convinced that something is bothering her, for instance your job demands, an activity at nursery school, or a relationship, then say so and describe the behaviors that have made you so concerned about her. If your observations are on the mark or even close, she'll probably open up to you. Even if you're way off base, she may be sufficiently encouraged by your interest and empathy to talk about the real issue.

If the dreams continue, the pattern of night hysteria and crying is unabated, and the day behavior which you think is a marker of distress also persists, I'd consult a physician, therapist, or someone else with the professional training and experience to be helpful in resolving such problems. If on the other hand the nighttime crying continues but you find that she's suddenly happy and calm when you walk into the room, then what started as bad dreams has become an opportunity for a social rendezvous, which requires another type of talk at the breakfast table and the setting of some new limits. Even if dreams are an accurate index that you need to spend more time with her, don't do it at three A.M.

The third type of incident is called a night terror. The child is often more frantic with night terror than with a nightmare. Because this is only a partial waking, from deep non-REM sleep, when you go in her room she doesn't really respond. She seems to be asleep because she is. In fact, you may find it impossible to wake her up, even though she's standing up screaming. These episodes can last for thirty to sixty minutes. The nice thing is that your child has no memory of them, and wonders why you look so tired and concerned the next morning. Since she is not awake during these episodes, the worst possible move is to try to wake her up. If she moves around, you may have reason to be concerned about her hurting herself and may therefore decide to stay with her to keep her from falling or whatever; but there is no need to worry about the underlying emotional causes, because there are no known psychological correlates to single incidents of night terrors. As with nightmares, however, if night terrors begin to come in clusters, this is a cause for concern, and I would suggest talking with your pediatrician or family physician.

Early Risers

Benjamin Franklin is generally given credit for the homily "Early to bed and early to rise makes a man healthy, wealthy, and wise." Unfortunately, early to rise rarely means early to bed for most children, and early to rise usually starts grouchy and exhausted parents longing for a boarding school that accepts children who are still in diapers.

Over the years, the parents of many new patients have

come to me after suffering for months with the seemingly insoluble problem of the child who wakes in the middle of the night and decides to stay up, usually in the process waking everyone else up as well. They have tried all sorts of remedies: star charts, rewards, screaming, keeping the older child up later and dispensing with naps, and waking the infant before they themselves go to bed in the vain hope that another nursing or extra cereal will enable him to sleep through.

Many of these techniques increase family stress, while rarely alleviating the early-morning waking. Since children do wake up frequently between three and six A.M. (see Diagram 1, "Patterns of REM and Non-REM Sleep," on page 164), there is little you can do to change the actual waking time of your child, whether she's six months or four years old. As I discussed earlier in this chapter, trying to tire the child or to wake her, thereby interrupting her normal sleep rhythms, will only cause an increase in light REM sleep and a probable decrease in the ability to self-calm and maintain self-control. The end result will be the very opposite of what you want—even more frequent early-morning wakings.

While delaying the hour of waking is difficult if not impossible, changing everyone's behavior is manageable, as you'll see from the story of Allison, age eleven, whom I recently saw in the office. When I asked her how things were at home, she said they were better this year because her parents had "finally stopped trying to tell me how to sleep," and she could now get up when she pleased. After talking further with Allison alone, I asked her mother about what had happened.

You know how I've tried with Allison, but I finally understand how trying she must have found *me*. Last year the three of us talked about Allison starting to have her period soon, and rather than thinking about her as my little girl perhaps that allowed me to see her as her own person. So now she looks better and feels less tired since I stopped forcing her to do homework from seven to nine every night and let her do it first thing in the morning, as she prefers.

It's funny in a way, because she'd been giving me the message for years; it just didn't fit with what I thought was good for her. When she was a baby, she'd wake up at four-thirty and be cooing to herself. I thought she had to be fed. But even though she wouldn't take a bottle, I never quite accepted that she could be happy in there alone. When she was about a year old I tried keeping her up in the evening but that didn't help, and when she was almost two I didn't want her wandering around the house so I started to let her come to bed with us, until you suggested that she just be told to stay in her room, which she did. When she was four she was waking us up because she was hungry, and all I had to do was rearrange the kitchen cabinets so she could get her own cereal. Even then, I still thought she needed more sleep, so every time she got sick, or she was having trouble in school, or she was in a grouchy mood, I blamed it on sleep. This year was the first time that I finally admitted that she knew her own body better than I did, and her improved grades in school demonstrate that she can make this schedule work to her advantage.

As a parent it's critical not to confuse the decision the child always controls—the time she wakes up—and the decision you control—when *you* get out of bed. To make this workable you must establish limits about what she can do once she is awake, and make it clear, both by actions and words, that the child must entertain herself if she doesn't choose to go back to sleep.

The following are the keys to living with an early riser:

■ Don't try to change sleep rhythms by altering your child's bedtime or shortening her nap.

- Use the daytime to strengthen her self-control by using effective discipline (Chapter 4), so that she'll be able to live with the limits you set on her early-morning access to you. Enhance her ability to self-entertain (Chapter 1) to make it easier and more enjoyable for her to be awake on her own.

- If you have adequately poison- and accident-proofed the house, then there's no reason to make her stay in her room. She should have as many opportunities for self-sufficiency as possible. For example, the four-year-old can get her own cereal, turn on the TV, or draw in her coloring book. The more she has to do, the longer you'll sleep.

Naps

Adults who do not live with young children often cannot fathom why naps are such a big issue. It takes only one day, however, to see what a difference a nap makes to a child's behavior: The grouchy two-month-old is now all smiles and coos; the one-year-old isn't fussing anymore; the two-year-old is cooperative and talkative again; and the four-year-old actually seems to want to take care of the eighteen-month-old. While we don't understand why a one- or two-hour nap has such a magical effect on a child, that's only part of the story. The nap changes the parent's behavior as well, by giving you a much-needed breather.

Given that naps are not only desirable for children but a necessity for parents, why do they often create so much conflict? As many parents have remarked, they've heard about all the so-called benefits that come with napping, but they've never actually seen them—because their child never sleeps during the day.

And therein lies the problem: nap time should not be a sleep issue. While many children will sleep for some or all of nap time, that need not be its purpose. Nap time means time off, time alone, rest time, siesta. As at bedtime, you cannot make the child go to sleep, but you can and should make her go to her room, or put her down in her crib. As at bedtime, you need to enforce limits to protect your privacy and your need for time alone. But unlike bedtime, nap time need not lead to sleep. Most children, even by four to six months of age, can get all the benefits of a nap without sleeping. The four-month-old who plays quietly in her crib, or the twenty-four-month old who watches the birds in the feeder outside his window and talks to his stuffed animals, is afterward just as refreshed and delightful to be around as the child who chooses to go to sleep for two hours. The most important thing about nap time is that it gives you (or your child's caretaker) and your child a break in the day.

> Alyssa has always been a live wire. Up all day, party all night, like I used to be before I had two kids and I hit thirty-nine. I'd put her in her crib at two P.M., and then make it impossible for her to nap by continually checking on her, talking with her, rubbing her back—trying to make her go to sleep. It produced the same disaster as when I did it at eight P.M. I finally understand that sleeping is her job, not mine. She really can entertain herself for an hour. I can still remember reading stories under the covers with a flashlight when I was a kid and my parents insisting that I needed to go to sleep. I knew they were wrong, and I realize now that I've been wrong about her.

There are other parallels between bedtime and nap time, and one distinct difference. The parallels have to do, literally, with time. When is nap time? How long is nap time? Just as there is no normal amount of sleep time at night, there is no magic length for naps either. Just as forcing bedtime to occur at a certain hour rarely works, neither does an arbitrary decision about nap time. One day it may be one P.M., because that's when you find your fifteen-month-old whining, your two-year-old rubbing her eyes and hiding yawns, or your thirty-three-month-old stumbling and falling a lot—all clear signs that it's time for a break. You may not even have time to finish lunch, whereas the day before it wasn't until two-thirty that the telltale signs occurred. This requires that you make daily planning a flexible process, but since you wait for the child's signals it decreases the battles and it's more likely she'll sleep.

On the other hand, sometimes you can't be as flexible about nap time as you'd like to be. You may decide it's nap time because you've got other things that must be done, or you've committed yourself to spending the next part of the day working on a school project with the child's older brother. This is when self-control and self-entertainment get put to the test, since taking a nap right then may be the last thing on her agenda. If, however, you accept that sleeping may simply not be possible, the situation is more negotiable.

In short, setting a particular time for a nap every day does have the seeming advantage of taking the parent off the hook for making these decisions, but it's not ideal. Going by clock time prevents your child from learning to recognize her body's signals that she's tired. It's only when she understands these messages for herself that she'll feel sufficiently in control to identify when she needs to go to sleep, and sometimes even volunteer to do so. Fostering her recognition of these signals also helps avoid another trap—waiting too long before trying to get her to nap. Parents who ask for help with naps frequently say, "I put her down when she's fussy so I know she's tired, but she won't go to sleep." At that point she may be too tired to be able to get organized to go to sleep. On the other hand—long before she's fussy—the eye blinking, lip tremor, hand tremor, and so forth are the cues that she, as well as the parent, can learn to recognize.

The child's ability to accept your decision about the length of nap time is, like her ability to decide whether to use nap time for sleep or for resting, another test of self-control and the ability to self-entertain. No parent, either mother or father, with or without a career, is always going to be in a position to drop everything the minute a child wakes up, so it's important for the child's sake that she have the skills to play or rest quietly by herself until you tell her nap time is over. Maybe you will call out to reassure her at the first cry, but you should be able to wait a few minutes or more before going to get the fifteen-month-old, during which time she has to settle herself down and find something to do. By the time she's three, you could allow her to come out of her room alone, if you have the expectation that she'll be able to amuse herself in the living room until you get done in the office or the kitchen.

As similar as nap time and bedtime are in some respects, it's important not to forget why they differ. Nap time usually has no bedtime routine. The child has to read her own body signals, or respond to your suggestions and limits, and be able to get herself drowsy and relaxed enough either to go to sleep or to play and daydream quietly by herself for a certain interlude in each day. This isn't the easiest thing to do at night, let alone during the day when it's light out and the house is relatively noisy. So there's all the more reason to be grateful for your child's willingness to spend some quiet time alone, regardless of whether she sleeps.

Remember:

- Naps are not a sleep issue, but they are a test of self-control and the ability to self-entertain.

- Naps can be effective even if a child doesn't sleep. Nap time is to rest, to take a break, to reorganize.

- Nap time, like bedtime, varies with a parent's needs for time and space on a given day, as well as with the physical and emotional needs of the child. Trying to set a scheduled hour doesn't work for you or your child and only ensures a battle.

■ There is no arbitrary minimum time that a child must nap. The six-month-old does not have to sleep for four hours during the day nor does the three-year-old have to take a nap for two hours in the afternoon. But naps need to be a regular part of the schedule, since on any given day the caregiver and/or the child is going to need at least one break, maybe more. Just don't insist on sleep.

By the time they're two or three, many children in my practice initiate their own naps. At one year of age they get put in a crib, but two years later they have sufficient self-control and ability to self-entertain to manage for an hour or two without that kind of restriction. They know from past experience that the parent will be socially available later, so there is no sense of abandonment or need to make a crisis out of nap time.

Conclusion

In the first few years of a child's life, sleep is the ultimate test of a parent. Every child gets sick, every child travels or has visitors at holidays, every child wakes up some nights or on others has trouble going to sleep. No matter how good a parent you are, there are inevitably times when sleep is a problem. Invariably there always seem to be good reasons to go to your child's rescue. In the end, however, there are even better reasons to be a facilitator, a catalyst, so that your child gains the necessary sleep skills to sleep on her own, at the time she chooses. It's something she must learn to do for herself. So whenever you're tempted to give her just one more goodnight kiss, remember the lesson of Sleeping Beauty.

Sibling
Relationships

For most children in my practice, especially those who have had the benefit of help with their self-calming, self-control, and self-entertainment skills, the arrival of a baby brother or sister is one of the best things ever to happen to them. For the child who is continually saying, "I wanna do it myself," imagine how many opportunities the presence of a new sibling creates for her to do just that, to show how grown up she is compared to the baby. And then there are all the opportunities to help out with the baby—you'll find that many children are much more adept at understanding an infant's needs and communicating with him than you yourself are. Not to mention that within just a few months, the baby may start to adore his older sibling. You may even be jealous, since it's hard to understand why the erratic attentions of a three-year-old mean more to the baby than all your tender, loving, and self-sacrificing care.

I put this chapter at the end of the book for many reasons,

not the least of which is that since it took me such a long while to realize how true the above description of family life is (or can be) I thought readers might benefit from covering the same ground I had to travel to arrive at this perspective. It's a view far from the one I held when I started in practice. Like most pediatricians and other health care professionals, I thought of the arrival of a sibling as a traumatic process, and I often talked with expectant parents about the imminent change in their family dynamic using such accepted terms as "sibling rivalry." After all, that was what I had been taught, and what I'd seen borne out by my own experience and that of many of my friends.

After a few years, however, as more families in my practice had second or third children, I kept hearing that much of what I told parents to expect from their older children wasn't true. Contrary to expectations, the transitions often went well: outbursts were rare, disciplinary confrontations few, sleep disturbances minimal (for the child anyway—the parents on the other hand were another matter, since they had a new baby to take care of). Integrating this new addition into the family was a major adaptation, of course, but many older children responded by improving their verbal skills so they could get more attention, relying on their ability to self-entertain when attention simply wasn't available, and showing off their competence by performing quite capably at such tasks as bringing the baby a bottle, and even feeding the baby, although some of them had only just made the transition to being able to feed themselves. Moreover, many two-, three-, and four-year-old children could make better judgments than their parents about when and how to facilitate the baby's efforts to self-calm.

Though I was delighted to hear such accounts, I was continually inclined to write them off as wishful thinking, or as just the opening stages of a long process in which the problems that failed to surface early on would be revealed in the months and years to come. But some days I did wonder: Was it possible that the problems I was so busy preparing people for were not inevitable? Why was I hearing about so many unexpectedly happy outcomes to a situation I'd assumed to be universally difficult? It took a conversation with a woman new to my practice, hence unfamiliar with many of the techniques I was trying to teach, to shed some light on these questions.

I had met Mary only once before she delivered her second child. Shortly after moving to Boston, when she was about four months pregnant, she brought her three-year-old son in for a checkup. While she was with me we talked mainly about Patrick's medical history and his current health. In short, I didn't know this family very well, and since we had so much to cover in our initial visit, I had saved the discussion of my ideas about "survival skills" for the prenatal visit I like to schedule for all the expectant parents in my practice. Because both Mary and her husband traveled so much, that visit had never taken place, though they did manage to see one of the prenatal classes I gave at our local hospital. Now here she was, back in my office, completely distraught about how her family was falling apart under all the strains of trying to integrate a new baby into their lives:

> These have been some of the worst days of my life. People said it would be tough, but I had no idea what a flood of conflicting emotions there would be—the second thoughts, the wish that it could all be over as soon as possible, and the terrible anguish of knowing that it's not going to end right away, that the worst is yet to come. Talk about being torn apart. Any choice I make always seems to turn out wrong, no matter how right it sounded when I thought about it. Somebody in the room is always crying, and as often as not it's me.

We were of course talking about what it felt like to come home with a new baby and still try to do right by a three-year-old who is accustomed to being the center of his mother's universe. The baby is making the difficult transition to the extra-uterine world; the older sibling with every possible justification is feeling angry and rejected; and the mother has discovered that she can't be all things to both of them at once.

In one fashion or another I had heard other mothers say this, and to some extent I expected it. What made me really pay attention was what she said next:

> It's ironic, but I knew this was going to happen after I saw the session you did with the baby in your prenatal class. When you got him to respond to you with twenty couples looking on, it was just magical. And when you went on to talk about how much babies were capable of, if we as parents acted as facilitators, I vowed right then that I would do things very differently with the new one than I had with Patrick. Which made me feel so sorry for Patrick that I decided I had to somehow make things up to him as soon as possible, since there wouldn't be nearly as much opportunity for me to be with him after the baby was born.
>
> I spent every minute of extra time I had with him, went easy on the discipline, bought him lots of fancy toys, and tried to sell him on the idea that the baby would be a wonderful addition to his life. I was trying to build up an unlimited line of credit with him so that he wouldn't mind it so much when I had to spend time with the baby instead of him. But that seems to have backfired, because the contrast between then and now is even sharper than it would have been if I hadn't doted so much on him in the last few months.

What she was telling me made perfect sense—that by giving Patrick extra attention before the baby was born, she had of course made things even worse for him after. This wasn't news. What was a revelation was the idea that the prenatal class had been a missed opportunity. I now realized that my prenatal classes had to concern themselves not only with the unborn, but with the siblings of the unborn, or else, in families where the older children didn't have the abilities to self-calm, self-control, and self-entertain, there was going to be hell to pay. Patrick was a virtual textbook example of the kind of sibling rivalry that can result when a child who doesn't have these skills must confront the challenge of a new baby in the family. So I talked to Mary about how there was no need to give up on Patrick. Just because he hadn't developed those skills yet didn't mean he couldn't start now. Indeed, once we put that process in motion, reinstated his previous limits, and, with the help of neighbors whose children were my patients, provided him with an extended family he and his parents could rely upon to take some of the pressure off them, life improved dramatically.

The most interesting part of this whole experience for me was that it finally enabled me to understand why so many of the children who'd been in my practice for a while were having so few problems with the arrival of a new baby in their family: the survival skills that stood them in such good stead in other areas of life were precisely the skills that would help them to meet this challenge successfully too.

Rivalry: Competitive Challenge or Blood Feud

Every two-year-old wants to do it herself. I can think of no better stimulus for success than the arrival of a sibling. Over and over again you hear parents talk about how much fun the older child has helping with the baby or teaching a younger sibling how to do something. Likewise, parents are always pleased and frequently amazed to see how hard the second struggles to keep up with the first—often walking at an earlier age, talking sooner and more fluently, and even toilet training earlier in an obvious attempt to catch up with big sister. Sibling relationships can be ideal settings in which to observe the concept of mutual gain at work.

Why then do we constantly talk of rivalries—a word which suggests unfriendliness or hostility? According to the dictionary "rivalry" can mean competition or a blood feud. Because of the experience with Patrick, I recognized that traditional pediatric advice about bending discipline or giving gifts tipped the balance in a precarious situation toward blood feud.

Actually, the hostility can begin long before the new baby is delivered, even before conception. Parents offer many positive reasons for deciding to have another child, but if any of the following are the prime motive then trouble often ensues:

"I want to do it better this time."
"I know I'll have more fun with this baby."
"Surely this one will have a better personality."
"It will really please Grandma if we have a daughter."
"Dad wants a son after three daughters."
"I need a little girl to be like me."
"Maybe a child will save our marriage."
"My son needs to be more independent, and having a baby will help him stop clinging to me."

Since pediatric prenatal interviews occur after, not before conception, there is rarely the chance to help such parents understand their motivations. It's not really a child they want, but a remedy for feelings of need and inadequacy, which is unrealistic (and unfair) to expect a baby to provide. The needier the parent, the greater the investment in the new baby, a recognition the older child invariably comes to long before delivery.

At least two other factors often compound this problem, both related to the type of parenting that society has tended to extol. Mothers have been encouraged, indeed obliged, to be available on a full-time basis to their child. So what happens to the child—and her mother—while the mother awaits the birth of a new baby? Decreased energy and the need for more personal time are typical consequences of the physical and psychological changes of pregnancy. Even the most self-demanding mom has to say no to much that has up until now been taken for granted by the older child. Unless parents build up the child's self-control and ability to self-entertain in the ways I'll discuss below, the older sibling's sense of being abandoned and displaced by another increases with each day of the pregnancy. And eventually this sense of displacement is all the more exaggerated in homes where the mother has tried to prolong the exclusivity of the mother-child relationship, at precisely the time when she knows it is soon to end. Traditionally we've counseled mothers to try to make special time for the sibling-to-be during the pregnancy. Many pediatricians urge parents to take the child out of day care or reduce the number of half days per week in nursery school so she'll have more time at home with mom before the baby comes. Somehow this is expected to cement the mother-child relationship and make it easier for the older child to accept the new baby when he finally arrives.

But as Mary discovered, both logic and the widespread existence of sibling hostilities prove that it doesn't work that way. Rather than trying to perpetuate an exclusivity which is about to be broken, parents would do better to encourage the survival skills that promote the child's opportunities for independence and autonomy, and to create an ever expanding social world in which those skills can be used. That way the child's self-esteem is enhanced at just the time she is most going to need it. She's then in a much better position to view her role as big sister in a positive light, which can set the stage for a relationship at least as valuable and sustaining as that between parent and child. After all, the sibling-sibling relationship lasts much longer—what a shame if it's not all that it can be. Which is why I devote the latter part of this chapter to what the parents in my practice have taught me about how to ensure that the inevitable rivalries between their children result in mutual growth opportunities, not blood feuds.

Preparation for a New Baby

Having a baby is a major transition for everyone in the family. No matter how good your child is at self-calming, self-control, or self-entertainment, commencing a new relationship is demanding, and this one especially requires preparation. So what can you do to make this nine-month gestation as much of a growth period for your older child as it is for the unborn fetus?

Timing the Pregnancy

Because of infertility, age, or other medical problems, many people do not have the luxury of planning exactly when to have another child. For them, any pregnancy that goes to term must be considered a blessing. Modern medicine, however, has provided most couples with the opportunity to plan the timing of their children's births. And if you have that luxury, you might want to consider the following when thinking about how best to space them.

Much has been written about the correct age span between children, emphasizing separation issues and other factors such as weaning, walking ability, toilet training, and even the capacity for abstract reasoning—all of which *are* relevant for those concerned about how best to perpetuate the exclusive and heavily dependent parent-child relationship that a new baby of necessity ends. From the child's perspective, however, none of these is likely to matter as much as the ability to express himself in language.

If the child can speak, then he can tell his parents what

he is thinking and feeling, just as the adults can communicate with him. With the preverbal child, it is hard to know whether he is upset because of something related to the new sibling, your choice of dinner entrees, or the fact that he temporarily can't locate his favorite toy. Since you'll have your hands full with learning about the new baby, once the older child's crying starts it's helpful to be able to determine whether this is a real crisis of the kind that might require you to stop a nursing, or a minor problem that can be dealt with later.

Furthermore, once a child talks, parents need only respond to verbal messages, not temper tantrums or other shows of power (see Chapter 3). Now I realize that young children tend to over-state things, saying "I hate you" instead of "I'm mad at you for spending so much time with the baby" or "I'm disappointed that you didn't buy me ice cream." But if you listen, and offer a few appropriate synonyms, instead of the more absolute declara-tions in which two- and three-year-olds typically express them-selves, they can become quite precise at expressing their feelings, wants, needs, desires, and opinions. The ability to get those feelings out into the open, to ventilate them, has a cleansing effect for all concerned—most especially the child. So waiting at least two years from one delivery to the next is advisable if you want to give your child the advantage of being able to express feelings which might otherwise fester or come out in ways difficult to interpret and unpleasant to be around.

Discussing the Pregnancy

Long before the baby arrives, parents can start setting the stage for the change. Many parents, anticipating that the new arrival will be a traumatic blow, attempt to hide the pregnancy until the changes in Mom's body become undeniable. If the baby is discussed at all, it's often in terms of what a good companion he'll be for the older child—with no acknowledgment that there will be many months before that can happen. Out of concern for the child, parents may neglect to explain anything about the changes that will take place in the mother during pregnancy, so that her increasing exhaustion, frequent doctor visits, and eventual trip to the hospital will all seem much more alarming to the child than if they had been discussed in advance. Families who practice this kind of denial try to pretend that nothing will change, but all children perceive, even at the beginning of a pregnancy, that something monumental is about to happen. As we all know from our own experience trying to make sense out of some ill-defined change that everybody is busy denying is much more anxiety-provoking than knowing the truth.

Many parents start out on this path of nondisclosure inadvertently. Because of the fear of miscarriage or the need to wait for the results of a chromosome analysis, an AFP, or other tests from an amniocentesis, they wait until the middle of a pregnancy to tell the child anything. To them it's a reasonable precaution, often defended by a statement like "I didn't want to disappoint her if we ended up losing the baby" or "I didn't want to have her get caught up in our concerns." That's admirable. Most children, however, are so perceptive that they know something is up even if they're not told. They notice that their parents act different, they may be aware of the mysterious change in their mother's appearance, they overhear conversations that sound alarming, they wonder why mom is suddenly going to the doctor so often and why there are so many abrupt silences when they walk into a room. More than one four-year-old has asked me, "Is Mommy sick?" or, "What's wrong with my parents? Living with them seems different these days." That's because it is, and regardless of whether or not the parents have said anything about the pregnancy, the child senses the change in the air.

This policy of rationing information has another major liability. Three and four years of age is a time when parents are often trying to decide when a child can be held accountable for telling the truth, and at office visits they invariably ask what should they do to quelch early incidents of fibbing or lying. This can be much more treacherous to negotiate when the child perceives that the parent has been hiding something from her for months. The parents' credibility is hurt and the child's anxiety increases further because she asks herself, "Why didn't they tell me?" She knows that when she keeps silent or doesn't tell the truth, it's because she has something bad to hide.

It's important, then, to answer questions truthfully as they arise. As adults we often find inquiries about the whys and hows of babies embarrassing because of the sexual connotations, but the child asks out of curiosity, with no lascivious intent. That's not to say the questions don't take you aback, but if you do not tell the truth, the child will go elsewhere for the information, usually coming up with a distorted and often horrifying version of the facts. So my advice is, when your child asks, "Where did the baby in your tummy come from," tell her. A simple explanation about eggs from mommy combining with sperm from daddy will usually suffice. During discussions with older children and adolescents, I have been amazed at the number of times the lack of forthrightness about a pregnancy made an indelible impression that undermined the credibility of the parents and tainted feelings about sexuality for a long time thereafter.

No less important are conversations concerning the child's anxieties about how things are going to change after the baby comes. Again I feel that honesty is the best policy, since children have built-in lie detectors. When I was visiting one day I overheard the following conversation between a mother at the end of the second trimester and her five-year-old daughter. It shows what talking can accomplish:

"What will you and I do when the baby comes?" Laurie was busy at the moment slicing apples for a pie.

"Just about everything we do now," Elaine said, "and lots of other things as well because the baby will need both of us to help care for her. And I'll need your help."

"Oh."

There was a long pause, with Laurie sort of digging at an apple. "You don't seem to be comfortable with that."

"Not quite. If we have more to do, how do we get the time to make pies? And when I start kindergarten I won't be here as much, so how am I supposed to help?"

"Quite a challenge, isn't it? The important part is to keep talking—or neither one of us will be able to know what the other wants. We can—"

"But how does the baby help with pie?" Laurie interrupted.

"The baby will watch, or hopefully sometimes will nap so that we'll be better able to work together."

"And if she cries?"

"Then one of us will have to go see what's wrong. So maybe you go find out and I finish the crust."

"If I don't want to?"

"Then I probably will, but I hope you'll enjoy becoming expert at all the things you can do with the baby, and I know that you'll enjoy discovering what a wonderful feeling it is when the baby smiles at you. And if you don't want to help with the baby, then I'll have so much to do that we'll have even less time to do things together."

"What if we just let the baby cry?"

"Well, that's pretty noisy, and it's not fair if she can't help herself. So for a while it's probably going to feel like the baby is running everybody's life."

"Not mine. Maybe yours."

"That's the whole point. I am going to be a lot busier, so there are going to be times when you feel ignored or you get impatient. That's why you have books and puzzles. That's why we taught you how to use the tape deck and the VCR. I still want to make pies with you, but there are other times when I'll need to rest or take care of the baby and you'll be happier if you entertain yourself for a while. Otherwise you may end up crying or screaming and I'll have to send you to your room."

"Like the other day when I wouldn't keep the seat belt on in the car?"

"Yes, exactly."

"That wasn't worth it."

"I'm delighted you feel that way."

By leveling with her daughter, Elaine made Laurie feel like a full-fledged member of the family with choices to make about how involved she wanted to get with caring for the baby, as well as limits to accept.

Time Sharing

Pregnancy is a tumultuous time—involving much more than the physical growth of the fetus. The expectant parents may need to use this time to resolve problems in their relationship, and with their own and each other's parents. Those problems are beyond my scope, but what many couples have come back to thank me for is the help I gave them in preparing their older child or children for the birth of a baby. For this relationship too is going to come under new pressures and be seen in a new light, and it too probably needs to undergo some changes in anticipation of the big event.

Hence the advice to spend more time with children as the pregnancy advances so that "They'll adjust easier when the baby comes" or "They'll know you really care and won't feel so abandoned when you have to spend time with the baby." Ah, would that it were true. But, as Patrick's mother put it, you can't build up a credit line with the older child while waiting for the baby. And even Laurie can see that there will be less time for her and a different relationship with Elaine after the baby is born. Only self-control and the ability to entertain herself can minimize for the child the effect of the upcoming changes, and those skills won't develop as a result of pampering.

One thing you can do to prepare a child for the kind of time-sharing that's going to be the rule after the new baby comes is to start taking time for yourself before the delivery—time during which the older child will be developing skills that will stand her in good stead when you're too busy to give her attention. You, or the caregiver if you're not at home, can insist on three or four thirty- or forty-minute periods a day when you take time off. As a self-discipline builder for the child as well as a personal break for you, these periods can be very useful. Elaine takes her breaks in the rocking chair she likes to sit in for nursing. At first, however, she had some difficulty convincing Laurie that she was serious about having time to herself each day:

> "Laurie, I'm going to sit down in my rocking chair and read for a while. You can do whatever you like but I want you to let me rest. Do you need a drink or anything else from me before I take my break?" Laurie shook her head no.
>
> Over the course of fifteen minutes Laurie's noise and activity level slowly rises. "I want to play."
>
> "I'm not doing that now, and if you don't let me rest, you'll have to spend the rest of the time in your room."
>
> Laurie shuffles out, head down, and Elaine has a moment of wondering why she's engaging in this exercise—it all seems so abstract—until she recalls the horrific scenes she went through with Steve when Laurie was born. Steve, who was three at the time, would be screaming and clawing at her leg, yelling for her to pick him up, while Laurie chimed in with cries of hunger. Those memories provide more than enough incentive. Elaine lets the book drop in her lap and nods off.

Moments later she snaps to. "Mommy, read to me. I don't remember this word." Elaine feels trapped. She's been encouraging Laurie to read, so how can she withdraw her support now? "My time to rest isn't done and you've interrupted again. I'm glad you're trying to read the book, but you have to wait and learn to give me a break. You need to go to your room until I'm ready, since you can't leave me alone."

Tears streaming, protruding lower lip quivering, Laurie howls. "I don't want to."

"If I have to take you, then you'll be in there longer." Laurie moves slowly toward the door—getting there more by osmosis than by walking. "Hurry up. Stalling will only get you more time."

"But I want a drink."

Since all these delaying tactics indicate that the vocabulary question was more of a social ploy than a real interest in reading, Elaine feels she's off the hook, and she reminds herself again of how miserable all of them will be if she doesn't create some workable limits on her availability now. With that in mind, she sets a timer for thirty minutes, heads to her bedroom, and commits herself to a nap.

Elaine got better at reminding Laurie which books she liked, finding out which toys needed to be retrieved from the playroom in the cellar before she took her rest, and making sure there was a tape already loaded in the cassette machine. And it did pay off. Soon Laurie was able to manage enough time on her own to allow Elaine a couple of breaks each day. This is not being self-indulgent; it's being realistic. A baby does demand attention, and no matter how hard you try as a parent your day is only just so long. If you don't make building your child's ability to entertain herself a priority during the pregnancy, everyone pays a big price later on.

For similar reasons, discipline becomes another area to reassess. As one mother put it a few years ago, "Saying no on the regular things made no when the baby came much easier, for both of us." Therefore the rules need to be firmly in place before the baby comes. If instead you ease up on the rules, out of guilt and the hope that your older child will feel so well loved by the time of the birth that she won't feel threatened by the baby, you're asking for trouble. The limits you'll have to place on your time when you're dealing with the baby will make his sibling angry and resentful. Suddenly you have a new favorite— the baby—and all the extra time and attention you lavished on his sister before he arrived will only make the new situation look all the worse. Of course this problem is compounded when parents make the last few weeks before the delivery a time of special outings and frequent gifts.

When I first met Kyle, she was trying to prepare her nineteen-month-old daughter, Bari, for the arrival of a new baby— a difficult endeavor, since every time she talked to her about the baby, Bari would point at herself, say *"Me* baby," and start to cry.

Not surprisingly, Kyle was hollow-eyed with fatigue, because Bari woke repeatedly during the night, as she had ever since a colicky infancy, and Kyle always went to her when she heard her cries. Almost nothing makes a parent feel more helpless and unloved than colic, and it was my theory that that rocky beginning to their relationship had increased Kyle's need to feel needed, so that she was eager to respond to any demands that Bari made.

Kyle, a psychiatric social worker, was quick to grasp the truth of what I said, but very apprehensive about how Bari would react to the new guidelines I suggested to handle sleep problems. Both her obstetrician and her husband, however, were so concerned about her current state of exhaustion that she knew she had to make a change. A week later, she was astonished: "I was anticipating a battle that would last months. But on Friday morning Don and I told Bari about the new rules and said we would start using them Sunday night. Do you know she barely protested? She cried the first couple of nights, but after about twenty minutes, when she realized I really wasn't going to come, she quieted down and hasn't cried since. It's like a miracle."

I had wanted to tackle the sleep problems first, because no one was going to be able to make other changes until they'd all gotten some rest. Now that those problems were resolved, and there were only six weeks left until the baby arrived, I felt some urgency about moving forward.

I thought Bari's time at day care should be increased, in preparation for the time when Kyle would be busy with the baby during much of the day. As expected, Kyle protested: "But even with just two days a week she cries whenever I try to leave her at day care. Yesterday it took half a dozen attempts and forty minutes before I was able to leave. It hurt so much to walk away."

"Did you ask the teacher how long it took her to calm down after you finally left?"

Long silence. Finally, in a barely audible voice, came the reply: "Well, apparently she was fine in thirty seconds."

Kyle got the point. She added another half day to Bari's day-care schedule, and the following week she had to admit that Bari seemed happy enough. There were still scenes at separation time, but Kyle was getting better at cutting them short and she followed through on my suggestion that she let Bari herself make a decision about whether to spend more time at day care. Impossible with a child just over a year and a half? Not at all. Bari said no at first, but the following week Kyle had an afternoon doctor's appointment so Bari had to stay until two o'clock. When she came to pick her up, Bari didn't want to leave. In fact she cried even harder when Kyle tried to take her away than she used to cry when Kyle tried to leave her. In an effort to calm her down, Kyle offered to let her stay late the next day:

"We have to leave now because Grandma's coming over to visit you. But tomorrow you can stay until lunch, like you always do, or you can stay late if you want to."

She wasn't sure if Bari understood, but the next day she asked her in the car: "How long do you want to stay at day care today? Lunch or late?" Bari said, "Late," and from then on that became their routine. Each day Kyle would ask, "Lunch or late?" and Bari would choose. Reveling in her newfound independence, Bari soon was spending five five-hour days a week at day care—and even asking to go on weekends, when it was closed. It was hard for Kyle to see her baby girl becoming so self-sufficient. On the other hand, she had to admit that Bari seemed much happier now than when she had wanted Kyle by her side every moment.

One other dividend: "Lunch or late?" allowed Kyle to see that Bari was capable of making many other choices as well, about what food to eat, what clothes to wear, and so on. Suddenly she saw her as a little person, not a baby, which was great fun. She started to recognize that there were compensations for letting go emotionally—and that both she and Bari were the beneficiaries.

Bari's growing enjoyment of day care showed Kyle how much pleasure her daughter could get from an enlarged social circle. Once she stopped thinking that by encouraging these other social outlets she was trying to escape her own responsibilities, she became more willing to see Bari develop relationships outside her immediate family. Kyle's sister and two of her close friends had all offered to take Bari on outings but been refused. Fortunately, the offers were still good, and soon Bari was off to the zoo, the park, the swimming pool, and other places Kyle no longer had time or energy to take her to herself. As a result, Bari made several adult friends, and became more gregarious and much more fun to be around. Relieved to see that Bari was thriving, Kyle also began to reestablish a social life by going out with her husband one night a week. She decided to think of it as a last fling before several months of being housebound once the baby arrived.

There was one other major change that I wanted to see Kyle make. I thought it important that Bari understand, before her little brother arrived, that sometimes Mommy couldn't drop everything she was doing to play with her. With only three weeks to go before her due date, I suggested that on weekend days, and any days when Bari came home at lunchtime or didn't go to day care at all, Kyle was to take a forty-five-minute break for herself during which Bari had to stay in her room and play quietly in her playpen. This period was not to be during Bari's nap time, because I wanted her to get used to the idea that sometimes she had to play by herself, and it wasn't to be anything like time-out, which they had just started using in the last month. The playpen was to be well stocked with dolls and toys and books and stuffed animals—whatever Bari wanted. We seemed to be getting nowhere in our discussion of this problem on the night we held the last of our scheduled meetings, two weeks before the baby was due—"It's so hard to put her in another room when I know she wants me with her," Kyle kept telling me—when her husband, Don, finally spoke up.

"It's interesting that she functions so well on her own at day care," he remarked, "but seems so needy at home. I wonder if she's like that only because we're encouraging her to be. Last night was my night to care for her, but I told Bari that I felt sick in the tummy, like she did last week, so I needed to lie down on the couch and rest. That seemed to get through, and she tiptoed around and whispered to her doll about how Daddy was sick. She did okay for a little while and then she started to fool with the compact disc player. I told her that was off limits, and she would have to go to time-out if she did it again. She started to stomp her feet and yell while reaching for the CD again. So I put her in the crib for ten minutes. She screamed the whole time, but when I got her out she did fine for the next hour. She twice sort of checked in—but didn't really make an effort to get me to play. When I got up I told her how proud it made me feel to have a little girl who was so nice to her sick old dad, and she just beamed."

Kyle couldn't believe her ears. "Well, if Don can do it, I guess I can too."

"Of course you can," I reassured her, and soon the forty-five-minute breaks were routine too. When I checked in with Kyle a couple of months after her son was born, Bari was a joy to her—and to herself. She loved being the grownup sister to a new baby, had a whirlwind social schedule of her own, and was as excited about being reunited with her mother at the end of each day-care day as she was eager to leave her in the mornings—finally the perfect balance. Although Kyle still had twinges of sorrow at seeing her daughter growing up so fast, she was grateful she had allowed the inevitable separating to occur, since she shuddered to think what she would have done with two totally dependent babies on her hands!

Anticipating Problems

As the third trimester begins, there are some other practical matters to tie up. If you're going to move the older sibling out of her present room, or change the sleeping arrangement in some other way, then do it now. Waiting till the last minute only heightens the anxiety and the distress of the transition, given everything else that goes on as you wait for the big event. Similarily, changing from a crib to a bed may be asking for trouble, or worse. Once you put the child in a bed, she's free to wander when she wakes up at night and may be tempted to do so, especially when she hears you up with the baby. You can imagine what will ensue. So if the older child isn't actively climbing out of the crib, don't choose this time to put her in a bed.

Use these final months of waiting to consolidate your relations with the members of an extended family who, it is hoped, will be playing a big part in helping you with the logistics of life after a baby. If you have to car pool, or whatever, arrange the trade-off now. You may not feel like it, but it's easier to do some extra driving in the second and third trimester in expectation of the benefits you'll enjoy later. Just think how hard it's going to be driving around with a screaming six-week-old who can't self-calm. Moreover, you might try to make some dates for the older child(ren) for soon after the baby is born. It provides them something to look forward to and gives you the expectation of a break. If you're due in April it may seem like you're a little bit ahead of yourself trying to arrange these dates in January, but be warned that people's schedules get booked early. If you're there first, they're more likely to keep their commitment to you, *and the child.*

Finally, there is the issue of hospital tours. Innumerable three- and four-year-olds have told me in so many words that tours are a waste of time, especially if done too far in advance. And it's not just the timing. Usually the intent of these tours is to try to make physical familiarity with the maternity ward somehow compensate for the emotional turmoil that surrounds the delivery and the postpartum events. Moreover, the tour has to compensate for the anxieties that merely being in a hospital will create in the child. Given the size and impersonal design of big hospitals, and the fact that any three-year-old can tell you this is a place where people go to get sick or die, the tour has a lot to accomplish. It's not going to make everything okay.

I think the tour can serve a definite purpose, but your primary goal should be an understanding of the events to come and how they will affect your family, rather than physical familiarity with the hospital. When you see a mother walking slowly, painfully down the hall don't ignore the sight—tell your child generally what delivery is like and specifically how you're probably going to feel. You may not even be able to get out of bed for a few days afterward. It's fine to point out the playroom or whatever else may be attractive about the hospital from the child's point of view, but use this opportunity, which isn't as emotionally loaded as the postpartum period, to discuss more serious things with her as well. She needs to know that she's not going to be shut out of what is obviously a momentous event, and to feel that you respect and trust her enough to allow her to participate in the big events of her family's life. To further strengthen this bond I'd discuss what she's likely to feel after the birth. You'd be wise to acknowledge that she may not want to come to the hospital at all. While telling her that you'll enjoy seeing her, and you hope she'll come, let her know ahead of time that you want her to feel comfortable about a visit and that your interest is in her feelings as well as your own. Saying you really care about her but making her come to the hospital without giving her a choice is a mixed message.

The Last Few Days

For almost everyone, the last days before the due date are filled with expectation, and usually tension. Whether it's your first child or not, there is always the threat of pain, even death. Everyone is jumpy. Not that you can't attempt to cover it up, but only in part. A few extra smiles, or gifts, won't trick your child into complacency, whether he's eighteen months or five years old.

Certainly no one wants to burden the child, and there's always the argument that he can't understand what you're really afraid of, so why tell him anything? Why? Quite simply because your behavior, even if you're a professional actress, is going to reflect your feelings. Your child may not like your behavior or your mood when you're pregnant, but when you talk to him about it, at the very least he knows that he's not the reason you're off your stride and not your usual self.

Your feelings aren't the only ones that will need discussion. As a reflection of the anxiety in the household, aggression often increases. Just as you find yourself on a short fuse, your child too may kick, throw more tantrums, and act out more, sometimes even justifying his behavior. One particularly ingenious twenty-three-month-old, whose mother had often shown him the baby kicking her stomach, asked: "If the baby can kick you, why can't I?"

Parents are reluctant to use discipline at this time, out of guilt over the emotional trauma they expect the new baby to cause the child, or remorse for an earlier blowup which got out of hand. The best way to defuse the emotions which lead to aggression—yours and his—is to talk. On the other hand, don't put ideas in his head by saying, "I bet you wish there wasn't a baby in my stomach," when he punches you. Even if he does say he's angry, acknowledge the feeling and let him tell you what he's angry about. It's not likely to be the baby. The anger or the punch means, "I'm upset because you've been withdrawn, preoccupied, and perhaps infatuated with somebody/something else for the last nine months. You don't tell me anything and you stop talking as soon as I walk in the room, and I feel confused and left out and frightened because I don't know why everything is changing around me"—or at least that's a much more likely translation than the ones that adults sometimes put in the mouths of their children. It is of course normal for an expectant mother to go through a number of emotional changes during the pregnancy, many of which peak in the last week or so as she actually gets ready to deliver. If you haven't explained what is happening, the child's aggression may also peak then, and this mutual emotional turmoil is a less than ideal jumping-off point for the transition ahead. So try talking things through. You'll be astonished at how much your child understands.

Helpful Hints on What to Do in Preparation for the New Baby

- Answer questions truthfully and fully.

- Don't try to hide the pregnancy. If the child has no context in which to understand your changed behavior, it's alienating and confusing.

- By the middle of the third trimester work toward a daytime schedule that lets you have a minimum of three forty-five-minute periods of time to yourself. You'll need them for baby care and should pave the way for them now. If you aren't home all day, make sure your care provider works with you to reach this goal.

- Get serious about discipline, if you haven't already. When the baby comes you'll have even less time for tantrums, acting out, and long arguments.

- Create an extended family, of children and adults, who offer positive relationships for the child. You may be deprived of the illusion and the gratification of an exclusive relationship, but by choosing to be pregnant you've elected to end that anyway. You owe it to your child to do it in a way that isn't emotionally traumatizing for her.

- Don't expect hospital tours to do the impossible: they can't and won't make the emotional transactions easier if you haven't done the necessary preparation work during the pregnancy.

Greeting the New Baby

Hospital Days

Please don't think that the emotional well-being of your child is an adequate excuse for a home delivery. I've been asked about that with alarming frequency in the last few years. Home delivery may be more attractive to you for many reasons, but it's not so for your child. If something goes wrong, and it does all too often (even once is too often), the effects on the person you were supposedly making it easy for can be devastating. Some of the most anguishing moments I've spent as a doctor were trying to explain a life-threatening emergency delivery to a sobbing, confused, frightened child who's been unexpectedly dragged off to a hospital in the middle of the night. I fully acknowledge that hospitals have faults, and if you can walk out of your own free will and under your own power hours after a delivery, that's your choice. But if something goes wrong during a home delivery, it can be a nightmare that never goes away.

Of course, the other end of the spectrum from those who bring the delivery home are the parents who sneak away under cover of night. Having continued so long with this charade of telling the older child nothing will really change, they can't face the moment of truth. If labor comes on in the night, this is one of those rare emergencies where I'd wake the child. Even if you've made arrangements for someone to come immediately and stay there until morning when the child wakes up, explain what is going to happen before you leave for the hospital, and tell him who will be taking care of him while you're gone. Don't leave it to the person who is there to account for where you are and why you left. If, however, there is no one available when you go into labor, explain the situation when you wake the child. Even if he's old enough to be left alone for a few hours, you should never take the chance that he might wake up and find you gone. Once he's awake, give him a choice about whether or not to accompany you to the hospital.

Now that you've delivered, the next obvious question is: When should your child come to see you—and the baby? If you delivered at two-thirty-seven A.M., and the initial high is wearing off by the end of the day when your child gets out of kindergarten, getting a good night's sleep could be a better option than trying to act peppy and excited while you can hardly keep your eyelids open. If you're recovering from a C-section or a major laceration repair, the first twenty-four hours may find your body and mind unwilling to do what your emotions might desire. Your condition, however, isn't the only consideration. If the baby isn't doing well and you're worried, trying to detach and pay attention to anyone else is very hard. If your head is really in the nursery, then your child will sense that and not be overjoyed to see you. If you can talk and share what your concerns are, just as you did during the last week of pregnancy while waiting for the delivery, then maybe a visit will work for everyone.

But that's assuming the older child wants to come. Hospital tours notwithstanding, he may not, especially if he's already upset about Mommy being away. It may be particularly important to him at this time to be allowed to make a choice, even (perhaps especially) one that makes a statement about his independence from you. Or maybe he's just enjoying the extra attention he's getting from whoever is taking care of him. Whatever his reasons, and despite your wish to reassure him and yourself of your unchanged feelings for one another, it may happen that he says, "No, I don't want to go to the hospital." I'd respect that wish. More than likely it will change by the next morning. And if it doesn't, that's okay too. Disappointing, of course, but you'll get over it quickly—whereas his resentment if he's forced may linger. Too often, parents just won't take no for an answer. So they bribe or force the child to make the hospital visit, and when he does, something like the following exchange occurs:

"Come give me a hug. I miss you and I still love you."

"I don't want to be here."

"We wanted you to see your brother—he's so cute I'm sure you'll like him. Here, look at this picture."

"He looks all blue at the edges and his nose is funny."

"Oh, honey, that was taken right after the delivery.

Your father took that picture because we were so happy that he was born. Most people think babies are cute. I know you'll get to like him."

"No I won't. I don't want him to come home with us."

"I know you're angry now, but you'll love him in no time."

"I will not!"

You may suffocate your child with love and understanding, but you won't change his mind or his feelings, and you shouldn't try. Part of respecting him is respecting his feelings, even if you don't like them. If a child does agree to pay a visit, however, that doesn't mean he'll be happy once he's actually in the hospital. And again, it's a mistake to read too much into his behavior or expect him to share your feelings about the blessed event. To him the blessing may seem far from obvious. "What's in it for me?" is a fair enough question—and the answer may be months in coming.

Making hospital rounds one day, I visited Malinda, who was on her second postrecovery day. She barely responded to my greeting.

"You look like you've been crying," I remarked when I drew nearer. With a bit of coaxing, the story came out. Her son Jeff had been in to see her that morning. But when he was there none of her elaborate fantasies about what this visit would be like came true; everything had gone wrong. Jeff wouldn't sit beside Malinda on the bed; he left the room when his baby sister arrived, saying he wanted to go to the playroom, "not look at some dumb baby," and came back only when his father promised him that the baby was gone. Not an auspicious beginning.

Trying to ingratiate themselves (and her) with Jeff, they asked him for help naming the baby. But when he suggested "Alfred," his mother reported, "Ron and I both laughed, which wasn't the thing to do. 'See, you don't care what I think,' he said, and to stop the crying I got Ron to run down to the gift shop and buy him the truck he'd been asking for ever since he saw it during the hospital tour two months ago."

"And did that help?" I asked, knowing the answer in advance, since bribes never do help.

"All he said when he opened it was, 'I'd rather have the crane that kid in the playroom has.'"

Not surprisingly, Malinda and Ron were both upset by the whole episode, Ron because he thought they had raised a brat, Malinda because she felt so hurt that Jeff didn't share their joy in the baby or even seem particularly interested in seeing his mother. "I was actually glad to see him go. I cried then because I was afraid that this is just a taste of what's going to happen once we get home."

That same day I paid a visit to Helen, whose four-year-old daughter Adrianna was just leaving after meeting her brother Will for the first time. Since everyone was all smiles as Adrianna sailed out the door, dragging her father behind her while insisting, "I wanna go now!" I was curious to know what the visit had been like. Interestingly enough, it had in many ways been similar to Malinda and Jeff's encounter—Adrianna had been reluctant to come to the hospital, perhaps because she herself had spent some weeks there after a bout with meningitis and still had nightmares about it; she had shown very little interest in her mother, and less in Will, distracting herself from his presence by sitting in the corner of the room working on her coloring book; and on leaving had remarked that he was fat, "so he'll never be in ballet like me." But Helen seemed perfectly cheerful, glad that the work she and Adrianna had done on self-entertainment was already paying off—which was how she interpreted Adrianna's choosing to sit quietly doing her drawings while Will was being nursed. She got a kick out of her daughter's pride in her own ballet skills, and she appreciated Adrianna's being willing to come to the hospital at all, even though she had been so eager to leave. "Perhaps I miss the ego massage of

her rushing in the room screaming, 'Mommy, Mommy!' or clinging to me when it's time to go, but on balance I'd rather have
it this way. I don't feel I have to buy her love with a gift, and
she knows I'm not mad at her. I know it'll take a little while
before she's comfortable with all these changes, but I think
she's pretty terrific about them even now."

This is a difficult time—one huge transition soon to be
followed by another. How your child behaves is a test of your
preparation, during and even before the pregnancy. Parents feel,
and rightly so, that their child's reaction tells them whether
they get a good or a bad grade on those months of work. If
your child has enough self-control and ability to self-entertain
to get through the two or three days while you're in the hospital
without major scenes or tantrums then you should feel satisfied,
regardless of whether he shows any interest in the new baby.
There is every reason to anticipate that he'll be able to deal
with your divided interests and affections when you bring the
baby home.

Homeward Bound

And what kind of event should the trip home be? Logistics
may not leave you many options. If possible, however, just as
with visiting the hospital, try to give the older child a choice
about whether to participate. Maybe he'd prefer to use those
last few hours to extend the great time he's been having with
the person who took care of him while you were gone, or maybe
he'd prefer to go to nursery school as usual. In that case, rather
than feeling affronted, you should be proud of doing such a
good job with the prenatal preparation that he's thriving even
in your absence. He's happy in activities outside the home, in
relationships with people who are part of the extended family
you worked so hard to create for him.

If he does decide to accompany you home from the hospital,

the ride may be his first indication of what life is going to be like now that the baby, about whom he's heard so much, is finally here. Starting with the seating. Unless you're planning to be relegated to the back seat for a long time, it's generally better for the mother to ride in the front and the sibling in back with the baby. Such an arrangement indicates that you trust the older child and it makes a statement about your interest and your role in the family, while helping to prevent the polarization that sometimes happens in the first few weeks when sides get taken, as in "Dad and me versus Mom and the baby."

Before you even get in the car, definitely take all the time you want, as long as the child is receptive, for hugs, kisses, and a chat about how delighted you are to be going home so the two of you won't be separated any longer. Even if the baby cries, keep your attention focused on the older child—put dad or the nurse to work for a few minutes. But on the way home don't miss the opportunity to make sure that coming home really will be enjoyable. You can use the ride to prepare the child for what he can expect once you get home. Perhaps you're still not physically recovered from childbirth, and want to warn him about your need for naps and a slower than usual pace. You may also want to discuss discipline. Almost inevitably, no matter who took care of the child while his mother was in the hospital, some of the rules will have slipped. As I discussed in the chapter on discipline, this reprieve, whether granted by grandma or dad or a babysitter, can result in an avalanche of unacceptable or provocative behavior—which has nothing to do with the baby at all. A little talk on the way home can be an immense help in paving the way for a restoration of the former system of doing things. An acknowledgment of the change— "I hear Aunt Sally is taking you out for ice cream three times a day"—followed by a statement of your intentions—"but now it's back to our old routine of ice cream only on weekend nights, and no more bedtime at eleven o'clock every night either"—is a good start. Nobody need be made to feel guilty about what took place when you were gone; the caregiver no doubt felt sorry for the child or was trying extra hard to be liked. Just make sure that you don't pay the price.

Finally, there's the question of which person should be the one to actually carry the baby in to the house. Like many such issues, I think this one has been given way too much symbolic weight. The child whose parents used the prenatal period to build self-sufficiency probably couldn't care less who brings the baby in, and why should he? It's really a token event. But if you're convinced this matters, and are determined to do it right, then you should use the moment to carry a message about who the baby's primary caregivers will be. If Dad and a babysitter/nanny are going to have a big role, then one of them can carry the baby in. If, on the other hand, the mother is the primary caregiver, no older sibling is going to be reassured by having Mom not bring the baby over the threshold. Delaying the severing of their exclusive relationship by a few more minutes, as mother and child walk in the house hand in hand leaving somebody else to bring the baby, will only increase the older child's eventual feelings of being deceived and abandoned. The exclusivity of their relationship should have ended before the pregnancy did; maintaining the artifice even longer serves no one's interest.

To Hospital and Home Again: Reminders

- Let the child decide if and when he wants to come visit the hospital.

- If the child comes, don't force yourself or the baby on him. If he's independent enough to want to play with other children or entertain himself, you should be proud, not hurt.

- Just because a child doesn't jump all over you doesn't mean he isn't interested in seeing you.

■ Gifts are a bribe which never settle emotional issues. If you didn't do the prep work, don't expect to buy your way out now. It might work for a night, but not forever.

■ Try to ensure that the caregivers at home are maintaining your limits and sticking to the child's typical routine. It will make the return to normal much easier.

■ Sit in the front seat going home. The baby can manage in the back seat. Don't worry too much about who carries the baby into the house. It's of little concern to the three-year-old in the long view.

At Home: Getting Off to the Right Start

No matter how relieved you are to get out of the hospital, the next few weeks at home are a big challenge. Many women recognize this and long for the good old days when the insurance companies didn't boot you out of the hospital in two days or less—lots of people need an extra day, or more, to get ready. And it's understandable. A new baby, a new relationship—it's a lot to handle when your body is still weak and possibly in pain. Those who get through this period with the least amount of trauma are the families who accept—and even ask for—help.

Let's start with the adults. If friends are coming to visit, and ask what they can do for you, see if they'll do something practical that can also be an adventure for your older child—like go to the grocery store or perhaps fix lunch. Since it's easier on the new baby, morning visits are preferable to other times of day. Perhaps they'll do a car pool substitution for you and pick up the kids at nursery school—which also serves the purpose of making the older child feel connected to someone in the extended family. Such connections are to be encouraged, now more than ever. People will of course want to see the baby, but I'd remind them that they'll have more fun with your three-year-old.

One of the ways to show your confidence in the older child is to give him as much to do as possible. While he may do it clumsily, it's rare that a three- or four-year-old can't bottle-feed an infant. He's also capable of carrying clean laundry into the rooms where it belongs and even putting it in the right drawers, fetching various items for you when your hands are full or you're too tired to move, and so forth. Opportunities abound for the older child to prove over and over again how competent he is, and they should be met with a warm, glowing response.

His most amazing display of competence, however, is likely to be in the area of helping the baby to self-calm. If he himself is good at all the survival skills, then the older child can become an invaluable ally to you and a truly unique source of help for the baby. Far from engaging in a rivalry with her, he will from the very beginning be involved in a mentor relationship that will be a wonderful boon to both parties—and to you. You'll have the advantage of receiving advice from a real expert on self-calming. When he says, "Wait, Mommy, finish the story, because the baby's looking for her thumb," then you can afford to wait, because he's probably right (even if his self-interest is involved). Children who know self-calming can also shift the baby around until she finds a comfortable position, help her learn to suck, and guide her toward visual targets she can use to self-calm. Moreover, while there will occasionally be less than altruistic motives at work, it's often the sibling who first identifies the cry that says, "Put me down, I'm tired and I can't take any more."

While you may feel tempted to compensate the child for his help, or to try to make up to him for this intrusion in his life, it's better not to give in to these feelings. For example, don't bend on rules. He'll probably test you to see how much he can get away with in this time of obvious transition and change; but you'll be doing him no favor by being lenient. Feeling sorry for him will only produce a rising tidal wave of trouble. So when he comes out of his room at three A.M. because he hears you up with the baby, as he surely will, explain to him that he's still required to stay in his room at night. You appreciate his offer to help, but at this hour the only thing you want is for everyone, including him, to get back to sleep as fast as possible. And no, you're not playing favorites by getting up with the baby. For the first months she *has* to eat in the middle of the night, and still doesn't know how to self-calm and get back to sleep (unlike "You-Know-Who"), so you have to get up with her—as you did with him when he was her age.

Just as there should be no bending on the usual rules, there should be no special gifts to the older child at this time. Gifts make him think that you're trying to buy him off; and he can only conclude that the new baby is the reason you think you owe him something. Don't set that thought process in motion. When people bring baby gifts, explain to him that they are presents for you, not the baby, as indeed they are. If people ask what to bring the older child, explain that the best present they could possibly give him right now is time and attention. Rather than an expensive fire truck or electronic toy, which is basically used as a bribe so that he won't notice that all the adults are focused on the new baby, not him, what a treat it would be to go to the zoo—or even on the most ordinary of errands—in the company of somebody who has specially requested his presence! Now, that's a real gift. And unlike material gifts, which only fuel feelings of rivalry between children, it does not suggest to him that his and his sister's comparative worth is henceforth to be measured in booty.

In general your major priority during these first weeks is to get back to normal. Not only do you need to enforce the usual limits and minimize the giving of gifts, but you should establish a regular schedule as soon as possible too. Keeping the older child home from school or day care, whether it's because you think he'll be happier if he can spend more time with you or because you think it'll be easier on you, is likely to have disastrous results. The older child needs to continue to have a life of his own outside the home. The excitement of spending time with other people is your best insurance against his feeling that you're an emotional traitor, the baby a rival. Furthermore, given the unpredictable demands the baby is likely to make, as well as your exhaustion because of the inevitable sleepless nights, you're probably not going to be very good company for him anyway. If you nod off while reading him a story, but snap instantly awake as soon as the baby cries, your bright, observant, intelligent older child will draw one conclusion: you care more about the baby. You have the energy for her, but not for him. Encouraging him to continue his outside activities not only provides other outlets at a time when you're less available, but also indicates that you don't think this is such a big change that his life has to be altered or limited. The less dramatic the transition, the less threatening it will be. And the more time you have to yourself without a small child to tend to whenever the baby is quiet, the more rested you'll be.

Speaking of rest, there is probably no time in your parental existence when naps are more mandatory or essential. Sleep is imperative in order to maintain your perspective and your stamina. Of all the suggestions I've made to postpartum mothers, this one is by far the one most appreciated. If you don't rest, and your older child can't slow down, then you have the delightful combination of a fussy, grouchy parent trying to cope with a frazzled, erratic toddler and an overstimulated, inconsolable baby in the early evening. If nothing else, you may get a new understanding of what really causes postpartum depression and how child abuse could occur.

Reminders for Getting Off
to the Right Start

- Limits and discipline remain intact—no special dispensations.

- Encourage the sibling to help out in any way possible—from bottle feeding to laundry sorting to helping the baby master self-calming.

- Stick to the old rules about bedtime, night waking, and naps for the older child. It's more important than ever to maintain an acceptable day/night schedule.

- Maintain the schedule and commitments that have created an extended family for the older child. The stronger these relationships, the easier the emotional transition of adjusting to the new member of the family.

- No special gifts for the older child. Bribes are not in order.

Life as a Sibling

The friendship that can develop between siblings is utterly astonishing to those of us taught—both in school and by our own experience—that rivalry is inevitable. Often we are so blinded by our own prejudices that we don't understand the evidence to the contrary. But there's plenty of it.

A Special Relationship

One of the most puzzling aspects of my fellowship work involved a phenomenon that Dr. Jenny Lewis, another fellow, and I observed during the course of our research but couldn't explain at the time. We were testing the social responses of babies during their first three months by using the Brazelton Newborn Assessment Scale. There were two groups of babies: firstborns and those with siblings one to three years of age. One of our hypotheses was that the babies with older siblings would have different social responses, hence different scores on the Brazelton exam. They were different—but in a way that we never anticipated. By about eight weeks, when evidence of improved responsiveness became visible, we noticed that the babies were significantly more responsive to their siblings than to either their mothers or us. Although we thought this was interesting, we had no idea what to make of it. It didn't fit into the existing understanding of a baby's social impulses (what could be more important or enticing to a baby than the mother-child relationship?) and was actively contrary to the prevailing ideas about sibling rivalry. I never would have understood what was happening without the insights of the parents in the practice, who came in with wonderful stories of the blossoming friendship between their children, where I had expected conflict and misery.

Siblings have to grow into their relationship with each other over time, just as parents and children do. When a baby is born, neither you nor your older child or children has a relationship with the baby. No one really falls in love with the baby right away. True, you feel elated; you have a sense of accomplishment, and a set of expectations and fantasies at the completion of delivery which you may falsely be labeling as love. It just isn't so, though you certainly have much to celebrate, and should indeed break out that bottle of champagne. The baby's sibling, however, has little to celebrate—yet. It's ridiculous to give the three-year-old blue or pink lollipops to take to day care, and inappropriate to suggest that she come kiss and hug the day-old baby, unless she offers to. Both are attempts to project your feelings onto the child, and both are likely to be resented. But how can you promote the development of a relationship that has the possibility of enduring long beyond the parent-child relationship, and for many people is just as crucial to the quality of their lives? In my observation, during the first few years there are five basic stages the older sibling goes through as she gets to know the new baby in her life. Being able to recognize them should help you in your efforts to guide her through the process. Following is a brief description of the stages:

The lull. During this first phase, a combination of intense curiosity about the baby, and an equally intense desire to ingratiate herself with her parents, who are obviously consumed by the new baby in their midst, may make the child unusually agreeable and pliable. It feels like the calm before the storm, and often it is.

It's time for a change. The initial phase gives way to a period of boredom. As the child sees the parents' earlier postdelivery glow and enthusiasm wear off, her own fascination with the baby and with the new responsibilities she has (fetching diapers, bottle-feeding the baby, and so on) is liable to wane. After all, the baby rarely gives much predictable or sustained positive response to anyone, and if the sibling gets really animated or excited, the baby cries, spits up, or tunes out by habituating. The parents, however, seem stuck. They don't want to move on. Over and over, children ask me, "Why isn't Mommy bored?" or "When is she going back to work?" Self-control and the ability to self-entertain are at a premium at this stage, since the baby's initial entertainment value as a novelty has dwindled, and the baby's responsiveness is probably too subtle to be enjoyed by a small child. Moreover, the parents remain as consumed as ever with changing diapers and feeding the baby.

Rapprochement. Just when there may seem to be no hope, an almost magical event occurs. As Dr. Lewis and I saw, a special ability to communicate and relate begins to develop between the older sibling and the baby. For instance, at the five P.M. arsenic hour, the sibling may be the only person in the family who can get a smile or facilitate self-calming in the otherwise disconsolate seven-week-old. Suddenly the baby is attractive and the sibling feels special for what she alone can do. That doesn't mean that there aren't conflicts, but a new basis for a relationship has been established. Over the next few months it becomes possible to play with the baby, with or without a parent involved. This is a very exciting development.

Hey, this is my world. Having negotiated the necessity of sharing parental time and attention, the older sibling faces another challenge—a literal invasion of space. As the baby learns to crawl, and then to walk, nothing is safe from him. Furthermore, with the acquisition of language and a rapidly growing understanding of the social rules, the toddler can now engage in all kinds of gamesmanship. Not only is the older child continually provoked, but she's often made to look like the bad guy. This is a tricky period, but bearable if parents handle it right.

Mentor and Competitor. Once everyone is mobile and talking, there's increased opportunity for the older child to continue the teaching role that may have begun with self-calming and continued through the period when the baby was learning basic motor skills. Not only can the older child help the younger gain increased prowess at new skills, but those very skills will challenge the older child to stay ahead. Teasing and provocation by the younger sibling may spur the older one to acquire new language skills; her increasingly complex feelings may be the catalyst for acquiring a larger, more expressive vocabulary (including some expressions you don't want to hear, alas); and the necessity to stay one jump ahead without resorting to brute force may even result in tactical thinking on the part of the older sibling.

The desire for intense attention and the drive to master new skills are as always the prime motivations for each child during this period. Self-control and the ability to self-entertain will help the older child channel these drives in such a way that the inevitable competition between her and her sibling produces an enduring friendship rather than a hostile rivalry. Self-calming will be crucial in the younger child.

The Lull

If you've done the prep work, then the first week or two after the baby comes home may seem like a just reward. There may be an occasional clinging episode, but your older child seems to adapt remarkably well. Many parents have told me, "It seems too good to be true," and in a way it is. Much of the good behavior can be attributed to curiosity: After waiting all of this time, sensing everyone else's expectations, and having a few of her own, even an eighteen-month-old will be curious, to say nothing of the three-year-old. And then there's the politics of the situation. Any child can sense the parents' involvement with the baby, and will be inclined to play along if doing so generates an intense positive response.

Don't push an emotional agenda at this time. "Do you love the baby?" is an unwise thing to say to any two- or three-year-old. She may indeed be fond of the baby, but on a relative scale she's probably more curious. If she says yes she knows she's not telling the truth. If she says no she knows she'll probably spend the rest of the day as an emotional outcast, a bad girl for not giving the correct answer. So the answer to your question becomes difficult for her to calculate. Though you should of course continue to reward positive actions with lots of positive attention, which means expressing pleasure at anything she does for the baby, she shouldn't be required to have positive feelings as well. Feelings can't be forced; they will develop with time. Give her that time.

You can usually get through these first weeks relatively painlessly, at least in terms of the older sibling's response. If you're careful to give her lots of positive attention for positive acts, and to enforce consistent limits as you try to get your household back to normal, things should go smoothly. The one event which is most likely to change all of this is a visit from someone bearing gifts. Presents for the older sibling convey two messages: a bribe and a warning. She knows people are trying to buy her off, though she may not immediately be sure why, and she senses that something dire is going to happen, though she's not sure what. It doesn't make any difference who brings the presents. Even if they're from grandparents, they're not okay. And toys don't really help children entertain themselves. Any child has more than enough resources without another toy. As I said before, time spent with the child is a worthy gift—a toy is not.

It's Time for a Change

After the initial honeymoon, which typically lasts two to four weeks, the glow is quick to wear off. The child's curiosity has been satisfied, she discovers that no matter how good she is there are limits to the amount of attention her parents can give her, and nobody is much fun. After all, at this stage the baby is likely to cringe, cry, or shut down to block off the typically noisy, energetic approach of a toddler, and her parents are tired and grouchy from being up at night with the baby and are making new demands on her, like "no running around while the baby is sleeping." The baby is so needy that the sibling feels she's constantly being put on hold—indefinitely. It's always "the baby has to be fed, the baby's crying, the baby needs to be changed, the baby . . . the baby. . . ."

Of course the parents also feel trapped by all these demands. And though they have their fantasies about the future to keep them going, when their older child, who is sustained by no such rosy visions, says, "I want to throw the baby out in the trash," this is likely to strike a resonant chord within them. In fact, children often say these things because they sense that that is how their parents are feeling too.

Although it's hard for parents to hear those words—particularly if they express their own hidden desires—it's important for the child to be able to feel free to say them. This is one of those times when the ability to use words really counts. If your child can verbalize her very understandable disappointment at having her game with you interrupted by a crying, hungry baby, there will be much less of a tendency for her to strike out— either physically or through tantrums and other extreme forms of acting out. Even the child who has good self-control and self-entertainment skills is going to have a lot of resentment to get off her chest at this time, when demands on her are great and rewards all but nil. You'll see it expressed in many ways that you don't like and must not allow to continue—aggressive behavior toward yourself or the pets (if the dog suddenly starts cringing at the two-year-old's approach, you know), attempts to regress to babyhood in order to compete more directly with the infant, and so forth. But verbal aggression, as in "I hate the baby" and, even harder to hear, "I hate you," is to be welcomed (or at least accepted) because it is a valid outlet for feelings that need to be vented. It's also to be respected, rather than immediately denied. The following conversation between a mother and her thirty-nine-month-old daughter, a big, bouncy girl with a two-month-old baby brother, is typical of the kind of pressure well-meaning parents inflict on their children:

> "I hate you. You never spend time with me anymore."
> "Now dear, I know you don't really hate me."
> "Yes I do."
> "Well, that's okay, I still love you."
> "No you don't. You only love Timmy. I hate him."
> "Don't talk like that. Daddy and I both love you very much and soon you're going to love your brother. It's just that babies take a lot of time and effort at this

stage. But you know we'll always love you, and I know you love us too."

"I don't, I don't—I really, really, *really* hate you."

As you can see, this child has the words to express what she feels, but she's not getting anywhere, since she's being stifled with understanding and affection. A much better approach is not only to encourage the expression of these feelings but also to admit to your child that there is merit to her argument. Remember, more often than not, she's only saying what you yourself are feeling. Sure, I'd encourage her to say she's mad rather than that she hates you, but I'd also discuss the activities that are causing the negative emotions.

Joan, whose nearly four-year-old son Henry is of the "Let's throw the baby in the trash" school of thought, knows that his feelings are natural, but she is not comfortable hearing them. However, she's trying hard to allow Henry to vent them, since she knows they'll come out in worse ways if he can't express them in words:

"Can Ben come over after school today?" Henry asked one particularly awful morning when Joan was functioning on about two hours of sleep.

"Normally I'd say fine, but I'm very tired today and I think that the two of you running around would be too much for me and Amanda."

Henry uses his fork to poke holes in his toast while he considers his next words. "Didn't you sleep, Mommy?"

"Amanda still needs to eat every three hours, so I have to get up a lot in the middle of the night. Which reminds me. I heard you wake up last night when I was with Amanda, and I want to thank you for not getting up. It's a big help to me to know that you can take care of yourself. As soon as Amanda doesn't need to eat so often, I'm going to stop going into her room whenever she cries and then we'll all get more sleep."

Henry's bearing shifted. "We'd all get more sleep if we

didn't have Amanda. Let's put her on the bus or the subway this afternoon." Slight calculated pause. "I'm sure someone will take care of her, she's such a cute baby," this last said in the high-pitched, singsong tone of voice that many adults use with babies and that Henry had obviously appropriated from some of Amanda's visitors.

"Oh, Henry, we can't do that," Joan said, then, managing a laugh, added: "But I have to admit I can see why you'd want to."

"Maybe if she was a boy." Henry had requested a baby brother because he thought a boy would be more fun to play with.

"Even if Amanda was a boy I'd still be tired. I'll feel better this afternoon."

"You said that yesterday." Score another point for Henry.

"Yes, but Amanda had an unusually bad day. I don't think she liked going to the pediatrician."

"Did she get a shot?" The famous grin returned for the first time that morning.

"No."

"She should have"—said with a little more venom than Joan was expecting.

"What's the matter, Henry?"

"You don't love me anymore. This afternoon Amanda will have another bad day and I'll never get to have Ben over and you won't have any time to play with me and . . ."

"Henry, that's not true. . . ." What could she say to reassure him? After all, Henry was right. She didn't have as much time for him as she used to, and denying this was so wasn't going to make him feel better. "Henry, this will change in a little while, but for now I have to give extra time to Amanda because she can't do anything for herself. Sometimes I don't feel very happy about it either. She's not much fun yet, the way you are, and sometimes it gets really boring."

"But why does Amanda always have to come first?"

"Because she's just a baby. This won't last. You know how you twirl your hair when you're upset and it helps to calm you down?"

Henry looked startled, since he was doing just that as his mother spoke. "Yeah."

"Well, when we try to get Amanda to suck her hand, that's the same thing. If you'll help me with that some more, she'll be able to calm herself down a lot of the time and then I won't need to run to her as soon as she cries the way I do now. Since you know all about self-calming, you'll be great at teaching her if you want to take time to do that."

Conversations like this don't magically bring problems to an end, but they do defuse potentially explosive situations and reassure the child. Which doesn't mean he won't need reassuring again a little while later. When Henry came home from school that afternoon Joan had to spend an hour with Amanda, feeding and quieting her down. By the time she finished, Henry was feeling very sorry for himself and asked her if he could be a baby again. Joan was about to say something along the lines of "Don't be silly, you're a big boy" when it occurred to her to reason this one out with him: "Well," she said thoughtfully, "if that happens I'll have to feed you every three hours, and you'll have to wear a diaper and I'll get to choose what you're going to wear and dress you, since you won't be able to do that for yourself." Henry's smile was rapidly fading. Each point she mentioned was something on which he prided himself. "And you can't talk on the telephone when Daddy calls. And you can't run the electric train set. And . . ."

Henry interrupted: "Okay, Mom. I understand. But don't get another baby soon, okay?"

"Word of honor!"

The desire to return to babyhood gets expressed in many ways—sometimes quite explicitly in words, as with Henry, sometimes with a request to be breast-fed, sometimes by regressing to very babyish behavior. Parents are often tempted to give in—"What difference will it make if we indulge him just this once?"—but as with all such temporizing rationalizations, one breach in the usual limits can lead to a deluge of problem behaviors and repeated instances of testing. This is not what the parents of a new baby need; nor will it be helpful to the child. Nurture that "I wanna do it myself" spirit, as Joan did with Henry, even if it seems to have disappeared. Reminding the child of his many wonderful accomplishments, and making him your ally in helping to teach the baby, will do wonders to bolster his ego and to reawaken that spirit, even if it's gone momentarily dormant.

Aggression at this time is as normal—and as much to be discouraged—as regression, especially for the child who is not yet verbal. I indicated above some ways to be supportive to the child who is struggling to put his feelings into words, but younger children are necessarily limited in their means of expression. Usually the aggression is indirect—it's not aimed at the baby, but at a stuffed animal or a pet, or, in the case of tantrums and other extreme forms of acting out, at you. You'll have to work with the child at finding acceptable ways to blow off steam. Tantrums, hitting, biting, and kicking of creatures animal or human, breaking things—these are all clearly unacceptable; to give in on the limits regarding them is a big mistake. It's also a mistake to allow them to evoke a *big* response, since, as discussed in the chapter on tantrums, that's precisely what the child wants, even if the response is negative. Time-out, imposed quickly, calmly, and with minimal discussion, will soon put an end to these behaviors.

If the child does express aggression directly—that is, by making any sort of physical move against the baby—you've had a severe breakdown of limits in your household, or, worse still, have never imposed them. Now's the time. You'll want to read the chapters on setting limits and on tantrums immediately, to learn about time-out, and you'll probably be in need of the chapter on sleep problems as well. But don't make the mistake of thinking, as you read them, that they apply only to normal situations and will have to be adjusted to the needs of a family in major transition. Families with newborn infants and older children who are acting out need to follow the advice in these chapters all the more closely. If your child hits the baby, for example, you're no doubt thinking that this is evidence of some profound underlying emotional problem. You couldn't dream of just sending him to time-out. No, you think it would be better to talk his feelings out with him. So, you sit down (probably after first yelling hysterically at him) and have a serious talk with him about how you understand his feelings and you'll always love him but he's not allowed to hit the baby. Bingo! He's scored twice in a row, having first roused you to hysteria, then gotten plenty of loving concern from you.

Any sort of aggression must always be met with an immediate exile to time-out. "If you ever hurt the baby, or anybody else, you'll have to go to time-out, starting now" is all the conversation that you need to have. The serious talk can come afterward, when everyone has cooled off. This goes for verbal as well as nonverbal children, for children who can't talk can often understand virtually everything that is said to them. Try them. You'll be amazed.

During this difficult time, you'll be very glad if you encouraged other relationships for your child during your pregnancy. The older child has every reason to be unhappy now, and if she has resources beyond her immediate family, she'll have a much better time. As one mother said, "Thank God for day care"—not so much because it gave her a break, important as that might be, but rather for the social outlet it offered her daughter, which is so valuable in helping any child maintain her emotional equilibrium.

Rapprochement

"Mommy, Mommy, she did it and I helped her." Billy was shouting loud enough to tell the neighborhood, and predictably

Melissa started to cry again. Mary Pat turned as he came stampeding into the kitchen, about to reprimand him, but he beat her to it. "Oops, I made too much noise. Guess we'll try it again," and off he scampered.

"Billy, don't—" but he was gone. He had for a few moments gotten Melissa to quiet down, and he obviously thought that he could do it again. Mary Pat certainly hoped so. It was one of those days when Melissa wouldn't eat, and nothing seemed to console her. When all else had failed, Mary Pat put Melissa in her crib, tried to help her to find her hand, and left her there, but the crying had continued. So when Billy said he wanted to try to stop the crying she had been willing, if skeptical. Amazingly enough, it seemed to have worked. Now he was in there trying to do it again. After a few minutes she decided she'd better check on him. She had been impressed with Billy's general helpfulness, but she was still anxious about letting a child not even three years old be alone with a baby.

When she got to the door she saw Billy standing by the crib talking to the baby: "Come on, Melissa, try it." She couldn't tell if he was trying to get her to suck his hand or her own. He was speaking very softly, standing still and off to the side of the crib so he wasn't confronting her face to face. Well, he'd certainly listened to what she'd said when he asked her what would help Melissa stop crying. Maybe he'd succeed.

Mary Pat went back to the den and lost herself in her thoughts until a tapping on her arm caused her head to snap up. Grinning like a beaver, Billy whispered, at a barely discernible volume, "Listen, Ma, no noise. She took her hand and I think she's gone to sleep now."

"That's fabulous. I couldn't get her to settle down. Maybe you should take over for the rest of the day."

"No way." The decibels were going up.

"Sssh. Don't ruin all your hard work. I was only kidding."

That incident was only the start. Over the next few weeks Billy actually got to like his sister, even though a month earlier he'd been trying to give her away to the neighbors. Moreover, he was as proficient as either of his parents at discerning the meaning of her cries. Even more remarkable to Mary Pat and Russ, at times like the late afternoon or upon awakening from a nap, when she was very unresponsive to them Billy could actually get her to smile and giggle. In fact, she responded to him so positively that Mary Pat, like hundreds of other mothers I know, said she felt "simultaneously grateful and jealous."

Though I've been curious about what enables the two- or three-year-old to cue in to the baby so adeptly, none of my young consultants have really explained the mechanics to me. What's clear is that some mutually enjoyable process is occurring which enhances self-esteem in the older child and gives the younger child a confederate already capable of a combination interpreter/mentor/advocate role.

In the case of Jane and her two daughters, Marie changed from being overly aggressive with her baby sister, Emily, in the first weeks to being wonderfully sensitive and tuned in shortly thereafter. As Jane said during the three-month checkup, "I'm humbled to admit that sometimes Marie seems to be able to tell me what it is Emily needs when I've run out of options. Like the other day. It was about three o'clock. Emily wouldn't nap. She was fussy. I tried to feed her and it wasn't working out. I had put on a tape that helps me relax because I had thought it might help Emily. So I was startled when Marie came up and said to stop the music. At first I was reluctant, then I tried it. Sure made a difference."

"Yeah, and I even figured out about her nap time." Three-and-a-half-year-old Marie, sitting next to her mother, was beaming at the compliment. She had been holding Emily's hand—occasionally giving it a twist, I thought. Perhaps I was looking for things, but even the most loving of sibling relationships in these early years betray occasional signs of ambivalence.

"It's true, twice now I've thought that Emily wouldn't be able to go to sleep, but Marie has said yes. Both times we were reading a story, so I figured there was a healthy dose of

self-interest at work, but she was right. We kept reading and
Emily did settle down."

The opportunity to parent and be grown-up makes any
child's day. It's much more gratifying than acting like a baby.
Children see that they really can do this remarkable thing themselves, in circumstances that sometimes defeat even their parents.
From then on, the relationship with the younger sibling, while
not always a bed of roses or total tranquillity, will be a constant
source of interest, and often of excitement and pleasure. The
child has a new arena in which to try her rapidly developing
skills, and many inventive ways to garner significant attention
from the adults around her. Reveling in newfound feelings of
competence, the child may also take this opportunity to make
developmental leaps which had previously been resisted. I know
many a child, for example, who's suddenly decided it's time to
be toilet trained. Not having to wear diapers is a wonderful
way of being able to distinguish oneself from a baby.

All children with infant siblings like to point out the contrast
between their own skills and the baby's. This can lead not just
to toilet training but to many other welcome changes as well.
Previously whiny, clingy children may suddenly get on the school
bus without a scene. Fussy eaters take great relish in being
able to eat grown-up food while the baby is stuck with some
mush that looks much less appetizing. The child who'd been
content to ride in a baby car seat because he didn't want to
have to be strapped in with a seat belt now objects to being
treated like the baby and demands the seat belt.

There's always the potential for regression rather than progression. With encouragement, and perhaps even a bit of goad-
ing—"You don't want to act like the baby, do you?"—the regres-
sive tendency can be limited. Being a baby again may look
good to a child who's feeling momentarily displaced. But if
parents emphasize what the child can do, and make it clear
that the old expectations about limits and self-control and self-
entertainment still apply, enormous spurts of growth can occur

at this time. The pride the child feels because of his skill with the baby and the baby's attraction to him, on top of the feelings of competence he has when he contrasts himself with the baby, may be just the catalysts necessary to set these new developments in motion.

Sometimes, in fact, the child's sense of self-confidence and pride becomes so inflated that a kind of "king of the hill" attitude sets in and causes a sudden discipline problem. Just as everything seems to be falling into place—the baby beginning to adore the sibling, the sibling reveling in his newfound status as object of worship—the older child starts acting out in a variety of ways. It's very hard to tell how much of the behavior in such circumstances is ego trip, how much just normal testing, how much an expression of underlying resentment. Parents need to be very observant at this time, so that they can interpret what are often subtle signals. Stacey, Elizabeth and Molly's mother, describes how they play together:

> Elizabeth can be playing with Molly wonderfully, but then suddenly things change. She'll tell Molly "I love you" three times, and then hit her over the head. Molly just looks up at Lizzie and grins, because she adores her so. And what a great situation for Elizabeth—anything she wants to do is okay with her baby sister. I'm sure she hurts Molly sometimes, but all Molly ever does is grin at her.

From the adult point of view, this does look like aggression. And at first Stacey punished it as such, sending Elizabeth to time-out and speaking very sternly to her. But Elizabeth was so indignant, becoming even more rebellious after time-out than before, that Stacey felt she might have misjudged the situation. After all, if Molly was still smiling after being clunked on the head, perhaps this meant the intention was basically friendly. So Stacey then tried to judge each incident on its own merits. If she was in any doubt, she would talk to Lizzie about what was going on, telling her that she saw the bang on the head and wondered why she did it—was it an affectionate tap, or did she mean to hurt Molly? The ultimate arbiter was Molly herself. As Stacey told Lizzie, "As long as Molly keeps smiling, this can be just a topic of conversation for us. The minute Molly starts crying, it's a different matter altogether. So play things on the safe side and make sure you don't ever hurt her. If you do, there's no excuses, no warning, no second chances—you go straight to time-out."

Since Molly had good self-calming skills and Lizzie was terrific at entertaining her and knowing just how far she could push her before things would get out of control, relations between the two sisters, like those between many siblings at this stage, remained very happy for a while. The middle of Molly's first year was a delightful time for everyone. Molly remained smitten with her older sister, and Lizzie's self-esteem, as well as her social standing with her peers, rose daily, with each recounting of her active involvement in caring for Molly.

Hey, This Is My World

In most families, even if instances of physical aggression don't occur, the mutual cordiality of the rapprochement period eventually starts to wane, especially as the younger child becomes more of an equal competitor. For example, as Molly grew increasingly mobile and talkative, Elizabeth, wasn't able to maintain so much control, and soon the ambivalence that Stacey was worried about had changed to hostility. "I can't blame Elizabeth for being mad at her. Molly's always into her things," Stacey said, "but it's primarily because she worships her so." Perhaps. But Elizabeth is no longer the only one capable of a complex agenda.

At times like this, the older child may need help from her parents so that she doesn't lash out at the younger one in order to protect her own turf. For example, when Molly sits down in the middle of the puzzle Elizabeth is doing, or interrupts her while she's drawing or reading a book, Elizabeth needs to be able to retreat to a place Molly can't get to—whether it's her own room or some other area her parents have blocked off for her use only. This shows respect for Elizabeth's integrity and gives Molly one of her first inklings of the meaning of limits.

Many other changes have to be made to respond to this new, more contentious stage of the sibling relationship. To minimize turf wars, Stacey told Elizabeth she could choose four toys as her personal possessions, with the others all having to be shared. "Elizabeth seems to be doing better since we gave her some separate space," Stacey explains, "but the personal property idea was a little trickier, since every day for a week she changed her mind about which four toys were going to be hers, making it impossible for Molly—or anyone else—to keep track." Once it was clear to Elizabeth that she had to choose four and stick to them, however, things calmed down. Not that that was the end of the issue. Soon Elizabeth was using the toys to torment Molly. She'd offer them to her sister, which would get her all excited—"like eating the forbidden fruit"—and then she'd take them away, squealing "My toy, my toy." A few episodes of time-out and a number of conversations helped clarify those rules, but it's an ongoing process, obviously, and the rules will change as the players do (and they're changing fast).

If anything, Molly is changing even faster than Elizabeth. No longer just an innocent victim, Molly can now do a lot more than simply crawl around. She's become a very wily and sophisticated social player—in short an instigator. But it took Stacey a while to catch on.

"There were days when Molly would come howling into the kitchen three or four times, screaming 'Hit me, hit me,' and I'd end up sending Lizzie to her room over her protests that Molly had started it. It just never occurred to me that Molly *intentionally* started it, until one day a certain smug look on her face when Lizzie was being sent to her room made me suspicious.

"Not long after that I was watching them, unseen, in the

hall outside Lizzie's room when suddenly, out of the blue, for no reason at all, Molly started screaming at Elizabeth. She was already yelling, 'Hit me, hit me,' when she noticed me standing in the doorway. She stood a moment, big tears already rolling from her eyes and her lower lip sticking out like a little shelf, then ran over to hug my leg. There was no doubt in my mind whatsoever that she knew what she was doing and was terribly embarrassed at having been caught. Once I was on the alert, I saw two more incidents that same week in which Molly was the bad guy."

As Stacey and I agreed, it's impossible for a parent to keep such close watch over two (or more) young children that questions of blame can be resolved with total accuracy. So now whenever there's a blowup between Lizzie and Molly, unless Stacey was there and knows what happened, both girls get sent to time-out—which has cut down on the scenes very considerably. This change in the rules has made it difficult for either child to win the game—which used to consist of vying for victim status, since the victim was the one who got all the attention. Every time Molly would come running to Stacey, for example, she would have the satisfaction not only of seeing her sister punished but of receiving lots of sympathy and snuggling, often followed by a story or a game. More than ample reward for her efforts.

Time-out solves another problem, too. Even when neither child can hope to be named the victim (hence the winner) in the latest battle for what Stacey has called the "lightweight title fight for championship of the house," both children may find the process of vying for the title reward enough. They scream and fight, and then Stacey comes in to adjudicate, and there may follow as much as twenty minutes' worth of conversation about who did what and why the other one is a liar and a bully. In other words, both children have her undivided, intense attention as their reward, regardless of the outcome. From their point of view, what could be better?

My advice to all parents in such circumstances is: Don't

play into the game. Even if only one child was the actual inflictor of bodily harm, send both (or all) parties into time-out, where they can calm down and reestablish self-control.

Better still, take a preventive approach: The next time you hear trouble brewing, issue a brief warning. Keep it low key, but make sure they understand that if you have to intervene again, all participants, regardless of who's actually to blame, are going to time-out. Since this is probably a technique quite new to them, you'll have to back it up a few times. But eventually, when the reality of absolute zero sets in, it will work. There will be less fighting and more creative problem-solving.

Don't forget, though, that the opposite of absolute zero—maximum recognition—is the best way to encourage and perpetuate the resulting positive behaviors. Don't just sit back and enjoy the hours of peaceful activity taking place on what used to be the family battleground. If the warriors have beat their swords into plowshares, thank them for it. Tell them how much you appreciate their effort to settle their difficulties themselves, and, by planning a special activity as a reward, demonstrate that the time you used to spend mediating their battles can now be used for much more enjoyable things.

Mentor and Competitor

Once both (or all) children are walking and talking, there are inevitable struggles like the ones I've been describing. But also all the more opportunity exists for a new kind of rivalry, in which both children end up being winners. While the older child may continue in the role of mentor, protector, and confidant, the younger one is likely to become more and more of a challenge to him. The relationship that results as the younger child comes into his own need not be negative. It can offer an opportunity for both children to learn more about their own strengths, and discover ways of compensating for their weaknesses.

Adam, for example, is two and a half years older than brother Jonah, but only a pound or two heavier. Jonah used his size and strength to intimidate his older brother, but was adept, as their mother, Lola, put it, "at hiding his maneuvers under a cloak of friendliness." So he'd come running up to Adam when Adam got off the kindergarten bus, ostensibly all happy to see him, and bang into him so hard that it would knock him over. This was, of course, very embarrassing to Adam since all his schoolmates could see what was happening, but it was hard to discipline Jonah, who was genuinely happy to see Adam, and it didn't seem right to tell a three-year-old to be careful of his five-year-old brother. Lola also realized that talking to Jonah was only exacerbating the problem, since the more attention he got for the behavior, the more determined he was to pursue it. He simply disguised it ever more cunningly. Finally Lola told Adam he had to figure out his own solution. Though he looked dubious, Lola assured him that she knew he would rise to the occasion.

"Well, the next day, here comes Jonah hustling across the lawn to greet Adam, and just as he gets there Adam steps aside and Jonah falls flat on his face. A couple of kids who get off at the same stop applauded, and Jonah could hardly look up he was so embarrassed." Now Adam feels much better about himself, and Jonah has a new respect for his brother. Unfortunately a child may experience embarassment in order to learn the lesson that being a bully ultimately results in no gain at all. As time goes on both Adam and Jonah will find words more valuable than actions. But this doesn't always happen between siblings three and five years old respectively.

Kids can be amazingly resourceful when challenged. In the case of Jessica and Annie, physical strength isn't an issue, but social skills are. Five-year-old Jessica is what her mother calls "one of those good souls who's never had a manipulative thought in her life," whereas two-year-old Annie is a real schemer. Having gotten into trouble on numerous occasions because of

Annie's persuasiveness, Jessica is now learning a measure of caution and skepticism.

"She now knows better than to go along with all of Annie's plots," says their mother, "so they don't paint in the bedroom anymore because she got into trouble when Jessica somehow convinced Annie to smear finger paint on the wall. And there are certain books she won't read with Annie around because she doesn't want the pages ripped. And she's stopped building constructions out of sofa pillows with Annie because she now realizes that Annie never helps when cleanup time comes around."

The overall result is that Jessica has become much more savvy dealing with peer pressures. "She came home from the children's center yesterday and announced very proudly that she had not participated in an episode in which her best friend along with two others in the class had chased one of the other kids with 'shooters.' Courtesy of the caution she's had to learn to use in dealing with her pushy and crafty younger sister, she's learning how to say no, which she was never able to do before. We were thinking of holding her back from kindergarten for another year because until recently she was so easily maneuvered by her peer group that we were worried about her. But with Annie at her heels, she's catching on very fast."

Of course the challenge is two ways, and usually it's the older sibling who's in the dominant position—in terms of both physical and verbal skills. So you may be tempted to try to equalize the situation. Don't. Not only does this open the opportunity for the type of manipulation that Molly became adept at, but such parental intervention tends to short-circuit the competition which the younger sibling requires to come into his own. Remember that rescue efforts always carry the underlying message: "You need to be rescued."

"I spent the first year or so worrying about Jared and how he'd cope with two brothers four and five years older than he is, to say nothing of his adolescent sister," Sally recounted. "But that turned out to be a total waste of psychic energy."

Once Sally realized that her interventions were only undermining Jared, she stopped trying to coerce his brothers into including him. "Since he's at a physical disadvantage he couldn't get involved in most of their games, but forcing them to play with him only made the older boys angry because they didn't enjoy it, and it certainly didn't help Jared find a way to use his talents."

Howard nodded in agreement. "I remember all those afternoons when everyone got frustrated trying to play basketball. His brothers never wanted to include him, and since he was embarrassed by his inability to compete, Jared would call them names or hit them, which just got him sent to his room. Of course there was nothing I could do to make him bigger, and I thought we were in for a replay when football season came and everyone thought Jared was too small. Jared taunted his brothers: 'You're afraid I'll beat you.' And he did. He's quick, so punt returns became his specialty. He insisted that everyone call him 'Rocket.' Since hardly anyone could catch him, the other kids would choose him for their team, sometimes even before his brothers, who make great linemen and blockers. Everyone got a new sense of appreciation for each other's talents, so they learned to work together and insisted on playing together—employing a secret set of blocking signals which made Jared even more dangerous."

"I identify with him in a different way since he's small like me," Sally said. "I feel responsible that he's so tiny. He still sheds an occasional tear that he'll never be as big as his father or his brothers, but he never lets physical size get him down like I did. If he can't reach something he tells one of his brothers, 'You're not tall enough,' or 'You're really just as short as I am since you can't reach the cookies either.' He always gets what he wants.

"In fact he's given us a few pointers in dealing with Hillary. The other afternoon she wouldn't read him a story, but then Hillary tends to ignore everybody these days. Shortly afterward the phone rang. Jared feels very important answering all the calls, and he always beats everyone to the phone. So he loudly announces, 'Hillary, it's Steven calling,' when he knew very well it was her other boyfriend, Tom. Hillary grabs the phone and says, 'Oh Steve, I've been waiting all day for you to call.' Did she blush when she realized it was Tom. In the last week Hillary has been very compliant with Jared's requests, and Jared on his part has gotten quite adept at screening her calls for her. You can see a whole new alliance building."

Jared obviously knows how to get help and assistance, and because of what he's learned by having to compete with his siblings, he now knows how to make the most of his abilities. Despite his disadvantages of age and size, each new situation helps prepare him for what lies ahead in life. But this happens because Sally and Howard have chosen not to allow the sibling relationship to become a conflict over parental attention. This always results in hostility and there's never enough gain for the effort. By emphasizing the survival skills Howard and Sally have aided each of their four children in gaining a sense of self-sufficiency and competency which makes the sibling relationship no less a competition, but not a blood feud. This comes at no expense of parental love given or child love incurred, and it's a foundation that helps each sibling throughout life while forming a relationship which is as valuable as the parent-child relationship and much longer lasting. Despite their earlier concerns, Howard and Sally can see that Jared gives new meaning to the proud motto of childhood: I wanna do it myself. He's got the world by the tail. In fact he has a new saying: "I want the whole of it." And he'll get it.

Conclusion

"I want the whole of it" is clearly a beginning. Jared looks ahead with the expectation that he will find a way. He's not going to be better than everybody else, but he'll be satisfied. The sibling competition helps him, providing perfect opportunities to fine-tune his strategies. That's mutual gain—what families should be all about. When Jared succeeds, his brothers realize new stature as teachers and leaders; his sister becomes more of a friend and less isolated within the family. His parents, by acting as facilitators, feel they're making a positive contribution, finding greater enjoyment in life and sharing more genuine affection with all their children. Having set clear limits which are consistently enforced, just as Peter and Marcie did with Jackie, Howard and Sally have allowed each child the latitude to discover where his or her abilities to self-calm, establish self-control, and build self-entertainment can lead in life. In actions and words they recognize that each individual is different—what makes being a parent part joy, part intrigue.

And what if your child is two or three years old—is it all over? By no means. Harvey and Pam would never tell you that after the week he spent with Carrie; and Linda learned much more about self-calming, self-control, and self-entertainment as Nell, her second child, began to walk. Each day as a pediatrician, and as a parent, I continue to be surprised and enthralled. Like me, and countless others, you'll be amazed to discover how rewarding family life can be when parents recognize each child's competence and build on that.

What we all want for our children is for them to have the gratification of doing it themselves while they get the whole of it. Since parent and child share the same goal, the means can be found. In the world they're growing up in, as never before, reaching that goal requires the survival skills: self-calming, self-control, and the ability to self-entertain. When parents are allies and facilitators, immediate objectives, and then new ones beyond, are reached with minimal conflict because children do love those people who help them to succeed rather than those who simply do for them. They all remind us "I wanna do it myself"—and they mean it. Listen, watch, take part, and cherish the time while you have it. There's no better experience in life.

Index

■ ■ ■ ■ ■ ■ ■ ■

RED TAE ASSOCIATES

Red Tae is a non-profit organization I started three years ago to help parents and their children solve problems with colic, sleep, discipline, feeding/eating, sibling relationships, school readiness, and adjusting to school. Parents from Europe, Asia, Central America, Canada, and all fifty states have called for assistance. Hopefully this book will provide the answers you need, otherwise please call me at:

1-800-422-6661